DI006082

3rd Culprit

CLEWSEY'S CLICHÉS

HAVE A CARE, CONSTABLE, IT MAY BE A CLUE.

3rd Culprit

An Annual of Crime Stories

edited by

LIZA CODY, MICHAEL Z LEWIN & PETER LOVESEY

St. Martin's Press
New York

'Too Many Crooks' © Donald E Westlake 1992
'Trumpets for Max Jericho' © Robert Brack 1993
'Cold and Deep' © Frances Fyfield 1992
'The Birdman of Bow Street' © Joan Lock 1984
'Give us a Clue' © Joan Lock 1993
'Good Investments' © Celia Dale 1980
'A Needle for the Devil' © Ruth Rendell 1980
All other contributions © individual authors 1994

ISBN 0-312-11736-1

First published in Great Britain by Chatto & Windus Ltd.

First U.S. Edition: January 1995
10   9   8   7   6   5   4   3   2   1

❦❦❦ CONTENTS

The Annual Anthology of the
Crime Writers' Association

A Needle for the Devil

RUTH RENDELL

The devil finds work for idle hands to do, as Mrs Gibson used to say to her daughter, and Alice had found that in her case the devil (or her own mysterious inner compulsions) led her to violence. As a child she would strike people who annoyed her and when she was fourteen she attacked her sister with a knife, though no harm was done. But if her hands itched to injure, they were also gifted hands and as she was taught to occupy them with handicrafts, the impulse to violence grew less. Or was sublimated, as she learned to say when she began training to be a nurse.

Only her mother had opposed Alice's choice of a career. Perhaps it was only her mother who understood her. But her objections were overruled by Alice's father, by Alice's headmistress, by the school careers officer, and by Alice herself. And certainly Alice did well. There were no unfortunate incidents of the kind Mrs Gibson had feared.

Naturally, in her new life, she had had to abandon her handicrafts. One cannot keep a loom or a potter's wheel in one's room in the nurses' residence. And there were many occasions when Alice would come off duty worn out, not so much from lifting patients, making beds, and running to and fro, as from the exercise of an iron self-control. The impulse to hit, slap, or otherwise manhandle a patient who had angered her had to be constantly suppressed.

Then the girl who shared her room came back from two days off duty wearing a knee-length white wool coat.

'I love your coat,' said Alice. 'It's gorgeous. It must have cost the earth.'

'I made it,' said Pamela.

'You *made* it? You mean you knitted it?'

'It wasn't very difficult and it only took three weeks.'

Alice had never thought of knitting. To Alice, knitting was something one's grandmother did or one's aunt or pregnant women making layettes. But if Pamela could make that coat, which neither savoured of aunts nor was layette-like, she was very sure she could. And it might solve that problem of hers which had lately become so pressing that she was afraid she might have to leave without finishing her training.

Knitting has the advantage over sewing or weaving in that it requires basically only a ball of wool and a pair of needles. It can be done in one's lunch break, in a train, during night duty. It calms the nerves, occupies the hands, provides therapy – and supplies a wardrobe. Alice began knitting with enthusiasm and found that, because of the way it can be taken up at any free moment, it answered her purpose better than any of her other crafts had.

She progressed in her chosen career, became a staff nurse, a sister, and by the time she was thirty had full charge of the men's medical ward in St Gregory's Hospital for Officers. It was there, some three years later, that she first set eyes on Rupert Clarigate who had been brought in after suffering a mild heart attack.

Rupert Clarigate was fifty-two at the time of his coronary. He was a bachelor who had retired from the army two years before with the rank of Lieutenant-Colonel and had since been living very comfortably – too comfortably perhaps – on his handsome pension. Had he smoked less and walked more, eaten less lavishly of roast pheasant at his club and drunk less special old Napoleon brandy afterwards, he might not, according to his doctor, have been seized one Saturday night by a fierce pain down his left arm and up his left side and found himself a moment later lying on the floor, fighting for breath.

His doctor was one of those who believe that a coronary patient should never be left unattended for the first days after an attack. Hence, St Gregory's and Sister Gibson. On his first morning he awoke to look into the sea-blue eyes of a slim young woman in a trim uniform and with her blonde hair half covered by a starched white coif.

'Good morning, Colonel Clarigate,' said Alice. 'My goodness, but aren't you looking better this morning! It just shows what a good night's sleep can do.'

Alice said this sort of thing to all her new patients but Rupert, who had never been in a hospital before and had in fact been riotously healthy all his life till now, thought it was specially designed for him and that her tone was exceptionally sweet. He did not hear her, five minutes later, telling one of her students who had dropped a kidney dish that she was not only hopelessly unfitted to be a nurse but mentally retarded as well, because this diatribe was delivered in the cleansing department off the ward known as the sluice. He thought Alice must have a delightful disposition, always cheerful, always encouraging, endlessly patient, as well as being the sort of girl who looked as if she knew how to have a good time.

'Who's the lucky chap that's taking you out tonight, Sister?' Rupert said as Alice put her head round the door before going off duty. 'I envy him, I don't mind telling you.'

'No chap, Colonel,' said Alice. 'I'm going to have a quiet evening doing my knitting in front of the TV.'

Those statements were quite true. There was no chap. There had been in days gone by – several, in fact, including one whom Alice would probably have married had she not once slapped his face (and thereby dislodged a filling from a molar) for teasing her. But she had been very young then and without her prop and resort. Since those days she had put her career before a possible husband and had become so used to the overtures and the flirtatious remarks of patients that she hardly took in what they said and scarcely thought of them as men.

Rupert Clarigate, however, was different. He was one of the handsomest men she had ever seen and he had such a wonderful head of hair. For although his face was still youthful and unlined, his hair was snow-white – white and thick and ever so slightly wavy; and since he had left the army it had been allowed to grow just long enough to cover the tops of his ears. It was the first thing Alice had noticed about him. She had always felt a peculiar antipathy to baldness, and though accustomed to the most repulsive sights and to washing a wound or cleaning an abscess without a flicker of distaste, it was still as much as she could do to wash a man's bald pate or comb the hair that surrounded it. Rupert Clarigate looked as if he would never be bald, for not even a coin-sized bare spot showed amid the lush snowy mass.

Besides that, she liked his hearty jovial manner, the public-school accent, the Sandhurst voice. The slightly lecherous admiration in his eyes, kept well under control, excited her. By the end of the first week of his stay she was in love, or would have said she was in love, having no criterion to judge by.

As for Colonel Clarigate, he had always intended to get married one day. A long-standing affair with another officer's wife had kept him single till he was thirty-five, and after that was over he felt too set in his ways to embark on matrimony. Too selfish, the other officer's wife said. And it was true that Rupert could see no point in having a wife when he didn't want to stay in evenings, had no desire for children, disliked the idea of sharing his income, and in any case had his officer's servant to wait on him and clean his quarters.

But he would marry one day – when he retired. Now retirement had come and he was living in the big inconvenient old house his parents had left him. There was no one to keep it clean. He ate rich food in expensive restaurants because there was no one at home to cook for him and he told himself he smoked too much because he was lonely. In fact, he had had his heart attack because he had no wife. Why should not pretty, efficient, kindly Sister Gibson be his wife?

Why not retire from nursing? thought Alice. Why should she not marry Colonel Clarigate and have a home of her own instead of a two-room flat that went with the job? Besides, she was in love with him and he had such beautiful thick hair. He must be in love with Sister Gibson, thought Rupert, otherwise he would surely not feel so uneasy about her in the evenings when he was certain she must be out with some chap. This, he knew from his experience with the other officer's wife, was jealousy and a proof of love.

He left the hospital after three weeks and went to convalesce in the country. From there he wrote to Alice nearly every day. When he came home again he took her to the theatre to see a slapstick sexy comedy at which they both laughed very much, and then to the cinema to see a reissue of *Carry On, Nurse* which had them equally convulsed. On their third evening out together they became engaged.

'People may say it was sudden,' said Alice, 'but I feel we know each other through and through. After all there's no more intimate situation, is there, than that of nurse and patient?'

'I can think of one,' said Rupert with a wink, and they both fell to laughing.

His fifty-third birthday occurred about a month after their engagement and Alice knitted him a pullover. It was rust-red, bordered at the welt and on the neckline with fine stripes of cream and dark green, and it suited him well, for Rupert, in spite of his high living, had never become fat. Alice insisted on looking after him. She took him out for sensible walks and gently discouraged him from smoking.

The Clarigate house was not to her taste, so he set about selling it and buying another. The prospect of furnishing a new house which was in a seaside resort on the south coast – they could live anywhere they chose, Rupert said, there was no need to stay in London – filled Alice with excited anticipation, especially as Rupert was giving her a free hand with his savings.

The marriage took place in May, three months after their first meeting.

It was a quiet wedding, followed by a small luncheon party. Mrs Gibson, now a widow, was present and so was Alice's sister and that friend Pamela who had introduced her to the charms of knitting, and Pamela's husband Guy, a freelance writer and author of mystery novels. On Rupert's side were a cousin and his former commanding officer and Dr Nicholson, that conscientious medical man who had been responsible for sending him to St Gregory's. The newly married couple left at three to catch the plane that was to take them to Barbados for their honeymoon.

Alice had never before been away on a holiday without taking her knitting with her. In Palma de Mallorca she had knitted a Fair Isle cap and gloves for her niece, in Innsbrück she had begun an Aran for her brother-in-law, and in the Isles of Greece she had finished a slipover for herself. But some instinct as to the rightness or suitability of certain actions told her that one does not take knitting on one's honeymoon, and indeed she found there would scarcely have been the opportunity to knit. One can hardly knit on a beach and they were mostly on the beach when they were not dining and dancing, for Rupert had been right when he assessed his wife as a girl who knew how to have a good time.

Alice would have danced harder, eaten more heartily and stayed up even later were it not for her prudent care of her husband's health. While Rupert, vigorous and virile as he was, might in some ways seem as young as she, there was no getting away from the fact that he had had one coronary and might have another. She was glad to see that he had given up smoking and if, towards the end of their stay, she noticed an edge to his temper, she put this down to the heat.

Furnishing the new house took up all her time once they returned. There were carpets to choose and order, plumbing and heating and electrical engineers to call, upholsterers and curtain-makers to be urged on. Alice worked briskly, refusing to allow Rupert to help, but taking him out each evening with her for a therapeutic stroll along the seafront. He looked fitter than he had in all the five months she had known him and he could run upstairs now without shortness of breath.

It was on the morning after the day when the new carpets were fitted, after Alice had rearranged and polished the furniture, that she felt she could at last begin to relax. Rupert had gone to Dr Nicholson's for his monthly check-up. She set out for the shopping centre to buy herself some wool. On the previous evening, while they were out for their walk, Rupert had pointed out a man leaning over the sea wall who was wearing just the kind of sleeveless pullover he would fancy for himself. Alice had said nothing but had smiled and squeezed his arm.

During the years that had passed since Pamela walked in wearing that white coat, Alice had become an expert at her craft. She knew all there was to know about it. She understood the finer points of grafting, of invisible casting off, of the weaving in of contrasts. She knew every kind of yarn available from top heavyweight natural wool to two-ply cotton, and exactly which needles to use with each. Without reference to charts she could tell you that an English size-fourteen needle is equivalent to the European two-millimetre and the American double 0. She could with ease adapt a pattern to a different size or, if necessary, work without a pattern at all. Once she had seen a jumper or cardigan she could copy it and turn out a precisely identical garment.

And besides all this, the whole area of knitting was an emotive one to her. She could not help regarding it as having been a life-saver and therefore it had become far more to her than some other woman's embroidery or crochet work.

So it was natural that on entering a wool shop she should have a sensation of sick excitement as well as experiencing the deep pleasure felt, for example, by a scholar going into a library.

Woolcraft Limited she quickly judged a good shop of its kind and she spent a happy half-hour inside before finally choosing a pattern for a sleeveless pullover and six twenty-five-gram balls of a fine saxe-blue wool and acrylic mixture.

There was no opportunity to begin knitting that day. Rupert must have his lunch and then there would be an afternoon's gardening for both of them and in the evening they were going to a dinner-dance in the Pump Room. But on the following afternoon, while Rupert was down the garden trimming the privet hedge, Alice drew out her first ball of blue wool and began.

On moving into the house, she had appropriated the large bottom drawer of a chest in their living-room for her knitting materials. In it were all her many leftover balls of wool and ends of wool from a multiplicity of garments made over the years, her gauge, her tape measure, her bodkins for sewing up and her sewing-up skeins and, ranged in front, all her pairs of needles, a pair of every possible size and each pair in its long plastic envelope. Alice had selected a pair of number fourteens, the very finest size, for beginning on the welt of Rupert's pullover.

As she cast on the required number of 150 stitches and felt the familiar thin metal pins against her hands and the soft, faintly fluffy yarn slip rhythmically between her fingers, a great calm descended on Alice. It was like coming home after a long absence. It was like having a cigarette (she supposed) or a drink after a month's abstention. It was wonderful. It seemed to set the seal on her happiness. Here she was married, with a charming husband whom she loved, very well off, living in the home of her dreams, and now she was settled in her new life, once more taking up the hobby that afforded her so much pleasure.

She had knitted about half an inch, for the work was slow with such fine materials, when she heard Rupert come in from the garden and rinse his hands under the kitchen tap. Presently he walked into the room where she was. He stood a yard or two in from the doorway and stared at her.

'What are you doing, sweetie?'

'Knitting,' said Alice, smiling at him.

Rupert came and sat opposite her. He was fascinated. He knew there was such a thing as hand-knitting, or that there used to be, for he seemed to remember his mother mentioning it about forty years before, but he had never actually seen it being done. Alice's fingers flicked up and down, making precisely the same movement about a hundred times a minute. And they seemed to move independently of the rest of her, of her body which was gracefully relaxed, of her eyes which occasionally met his, and of her mind too, he suspected, which might be wandering off anywhere.

'I didn't know you knitted,' he said after a while.

'Darling! Where do you think your red sweater came from? I told you I made it.'

Rupert had not given much thought to the provenance of the red sweater. 'I suppose I thought you must have done it on a machine.'

Alice laughed heartily at this. She continued to knit. Rupert read the evening paper which had just been delivered. After a time he said, 'Can I talk to you while you're doing that?'

He sounded so like a little boy whose mother cannot be bothered with him that Alice's heart was touched. 'Darling, of course you can. Talk away! I'm a practised knitter, you know. I can not only talk while I'm knitting, I can read, watch television – my goodness, I could knit in the dark!' And she fixed her eyes on him, smiling tenderly, while her fingers jerked up and down like pistons.

But Rupert didn't talk. He hardly said a word until they were out for their evening walk, and next day when she again took up the blue pullover she was once more conscious of his stare. After a while he lit a cigarette, his first for several weeks. Without a word he left the room and when she went into the kitchen to prepare their evening meal she found him sitting at the table, reading one of his favourite war memoirs.

It was not until Alice had had four sessions of work on the pullover and had completed six inches of the back, having changed by now to the slightly coarser needle, number twelve and made of red plastic, that Rupert made any further reference to her occupation.

'You know, sweetie,' he said, 'there's absolutely no reason why we shouldn't buy our clothes ready-made. We're not poor. I hope I haven't given you the impression that I'm a tight-fisted sort of chap. Any time you want the money to buy yourself a blouse or a dress or whatever that is, you've only to say the word.'

'This isn't for me, Rupert, it's for you. You said you wanted a pullover like the one we saw on that man on the seafront.'

'Did I? I suppose I must have if you say so, but I don't recall it. Anyway, I can pop down to the men's outfitters and buy one if I feel inclined, can't I, eh? There's no need for you to wear yourself out making something I can buy in ten minutes.'

'But I *like* knitting, darling. I love it. And I think home-knitted garments are much nicer than bought ones.'

'Must make your fingers ache, I should think,' said Rupert. 'Talk about wearing one's fingers to the bone. I know the meaning of that phrase all right now, eh?'

'Don't be so silly,' snapped Alice. 'Of course it doesn't make my fingers ache, I enjoy it. And I think it's a great pity you've started smoking again.'

Rupert smoked five cigarettes that day and ten the next and the day after that Pamela and Guy came to stay for a fortnight's holiday.

Rupert thought, and Alice agreed with him, that if you lived by the sea it was positively your duty to invite close friends for their summer holidays. Besides, Guy and Pamela, who hadn't a large income, had two children at expensive boarding-schools and probably would otherwise have had no holiday at all. They arrived, while their children were away camping, for the middle two weeks of August.

Pamela had not knitted a row since her daughter was two but she liked to watch Alice at work. She said she found it soothing. And when she looked inside the knitting drawer in the chest and saw the leftover hanks of yarn in such delectable shades – pinks and lilacs and subtle greens and honey yellows and chocolate browns – she said it made her feel she must take it up again, for clothes cost so much and it would be a great saving.

Guy was not one of those writers who never speak of their work. He was always entertaining on the subject of the intricate and complex detective stories he yearly produced and would weave plots out of all kinds of common household incidents or create them from things he observed while they were out for a drive. Alice enjoyed hearing him evolve new murder methods and he played up to her with more and more ingenious and bizarre devices.

'Now take warfarin,' he would say. 'They use it to kill rats. It inhibits the clotting of the blood, so that when the rats fight among themselves and receive even a small wound they bleed to death. I understand they give it to human beings too.'

'That's right,' said Alice, the nurse. 'It stops clots forming in people who've had a thrombosis.'

'If I were going to use that method in a book I'd have the murderer give his victim warfarin plus a strong sedative. Then a small cut, say to the wrist – '

Another time he was much intrigued by a book of Alice's on plants inadvisable for use in winemaking. Most illuminating for the thriller-writer, he said.

'It says here that the skunk cabbage, whatever that may be, contains irritant crystals of calcium oxalate. If you eat the stuff, the inside of your mouth swells up and you die because you can't breathe. Now your average pathologist might notice the swellings but I'd be willing to bet you anything he'd never suppose them the result of eating *lysichiton symplocarpus*. There's another undetectable murder method for you.'

Alice was excited by his ingenuity and Pamela was used to it. Only Rupert, who had perhaps been nearer actual death than any of them, grew squeamish and was not sorry when the two weeks came to an end and Guy and Pamela were gone. Alice too felt a certain relief. It troubled her that her latent sadism, which she recognised for what it was, should be titillated by Guy's inventions. With thankfulness she returned to the gentle placebo of her knitting and took up the blue pullover again, all eight inches of it.

Rupert lit a cigarette.

'I say, I've been thinking, why don't I buy you a knitting machine?'

'I don't want a knitting machine, darling,' said Alice.

'Had a look at one actually while I was out with old Guy one day. A bit pricey but I don't mind that, sweetie, if it makes you happy.'

'I said I don't want a knitting machine. The point is that I like knitting by hand. I've already told you, it's my hobby, it's a great interest of mine. Why do I want a big cumbersome machine that takes up space and makes a noise when I've got my own two hands?'

He was silent. He watched her fingers working.

'As a matter of fact, it's the noise I don't like,' he said.

'What noise?' said Alice, exasperated.

'That everlasting click-click-click.'

'Oh, nonsense! You can't possibly hear anything right across the room.'

'I can.'

'You'll get used to it,' said Alice.

But Rupert did not get used to it, and the next time Alice began her knitting he said, 'It's not just the clicking, sweetie, it's the sight of your hands jerking about mechanically all the time. To be perfectly honest with you, it gets on my nerves.'

'Don't look, then.'

'I can't help it. There's an awful sort of fascination that draws my eyes.'

Alice was beginning to feel nervous herself. A good deal of her pleasure was spoiled by those staring eyes and the knowledge of his dislike of what she did. It began to affect the texture of her work, making her take uneven stitches. She went on rather more slowly and after half an hour she let the nine-inch-long piece of blue fabric and the needles fall into her lap.

'Let's go out to dinner,' said Rupert eagerly. 'We'll go and have a couple of drinks down on the front, and then we'll drive over to the Queen's for dinner.'

'If you like,' said Alice.

'And, sweetie, give up that silly old knitting, eh? For my sake? You wouldn't think twice about doing a little thing like that for me, would you?'

A little thing, he called it. Alice thought of it not twice but many times. She hardly thought of anything else and she lay awake for a large part of the night. But next day she did no knitting and she laid away what she had done in the drawer. Rupert was her husband, and marriage, as she had often heard people say, was a matter of give and take. This she would give to him, remembering all he had given her.

She missed her knitting bitterly. Those years of doing an active job, literally on her feet all day, and those leisure times during which her hands had always been occupied, had unfitted her for reading or listening to music or watching television. With idle hands, it was hard for her to keep still. Incessantly she fidgeted. And when Rupert, who had not once mentioned the sacrifice she had made for him, did at last refer to her knitting, she had an only just controllable urge to hit him.

They were passing, on an evening walk, that men's outfitters of which he had spoken when he first saw the beginnings of the ill-fated pullover, and there in the window was a heavyweight wool sweater in creamy white, with an intricate Fair Isle pattern in red and grey on it.

'Bet you couldn't do that, eh, sweetie? It takes a machine to make a garment like that. I call that a grand job.'

Alice longed to slap his face. She not make that? Why, give her half a chance and she could make it in a week and turn out a far more beautiful piece of work than that object in the window! But her heart yearned after it, for all that. How easily, when she had been allowed to knit, could she have copied it! How marvellously would it have occupied her, working out those checks and chevrons on squared paper, weaving in the various threads with the yarn so skilfully hooked round three fingers! She turned away. Was she never to be allowed to knit again? Must she wait until Rupert died before she could take up her needles?

It began to seem to Alice a monstrous cruelty, this thing which her husband had done to her.

Why had she been so stupid as to marry someone she had known only three months? She thought she would enjoy punching him with her fists, pummelling his head, until he cried to her to stop and begged her to knit all she liked.

The change Rupert had noticed in his wife he did not attribute to the loss of her hobby. He had forgotten about her knitting. He thought she had become irritable and nervous because she was anxious about his smoking – after all, none knew better than she that he shouldn't smoke

– and he made a determined effort, his second since his marriage, to give it up.

After five days of total abstention it seemed to him as if every fibre of his body cried out for, yearned for, put out straining anguished stalks for, a cigarette. It was worst of all in the pub on the seafront where the atmosphere was laden with cigarette smoke, and there, while Alice was sitting at their table, he surreptitiously bought a pack of twenty at the bar.

Back home, he took one out and lit it. His need for nicotine was so great that he had forgotten everything else. He had even forgotten Alice was sitting opposite him.

He took a wonderful long inhalation, the kind that makes the room rock and waves roar in one's head, a cool, aromatic, heady, glorious draw.

The next thing he knew the cigarette had been pulled out of his mouth and hurled into the fireplace and Alice was belabouring him with her fists while stamping on the remaining nineteen cigarettes in the pack.

'You mean, selfish, cruel beast! You can keep on with your filthy evil-smelling addiction that makes me so sick to my stomach – you can keep that up, killing yourself, while I'm not allowed to do my poor, harmless, useful work. You selfish insensitive pig!'

It was their first quarrel and it went on for hours. Next morning Rupert went into town and bought a hundred cigarettes and Alice locked herself in her bedroom and knitted. They were reconciled after two or three days. Rupert promised to undergo hypnosis for his smoking. Nothing was said at the time about Alice's knitting, but soon afterwards she explained quite calmly and rationally to Rupert that she needed to knit for her 'nerves' and would have to devote specific times to it, such as an hour every evening during which she would go and sit in their little-used dining-room.

Rupert said he would miss her. He hadn't got married for his wife to be in one room and he in another. But all right, he hadn't much option, he supposed, so long as it was only an hour.

It began as an hour. Alice found she didn't miss Rupert's company. It seemed to her that they had said to each other all they had to say and all they ever would have. If there had been any excitement in her marriage, there was none left now. Knitting itself was more interesting, though when this garment was completed she would make no more for Rupert. Let him go to the men's outfitters if that was what he wanted. She thought she might make herself a burgundy wool suit. And as she envisaged it, longing to begin, the allotted hour lengthened into an hour and a half, into two.

She had almost completed the back of the pullover after two and a half hours of concentrated work, when Rupert burst into the room, a cigarette in his mouth and his breath smelling of whisky. He snatched the knitting out of her hands, pulled it off the red plastic needles and snapped each needle in half.

Alice screamed at him and seized his collar and began shaking him, but Rupert tore the pattern across and unravelled stitches as fast as he could go. Alice struck him repeatedly across the face. He dodged and hit her such a blow that she fell to the floor, and then he pulled out every one of those two or three hundred rows of knitting until all that remained was a loose and tangled pile of crinkled blue yarn.

Three days later she told him she wanted a divorce. Rupert said she couldn't want one as much as he did. In that case, said Alice, perhaps he would like to pack his things and leave the house as soon as possible.

'Me? Leave this house? You must be joking.'

'Indeed I'm not joking. That's what a decent man would do.'

'What, just walk out of a house I bought with my inheritance from my parents? Walk out on the furniture you bought with my life savings? You're not only a hysterical bitch, you're out of your mind. *You* can go. I'll pay you maintenance – the law forces me to do that, though it'll be the minimum I can get away with, I promise you.'

'And you call yourself an officer and a gentleman!' said Alice. 'What am I supposed to do? Go back to nursing? Go back to a poky flat? I'd rather die. Certainly I'm staying in this house.'

They argued about it bitterly day after day. Rupert's need overcame the hypnosis and he chain-smoked. Alice was now afraid to knit in his presence, for he was physically stronger than she, even if she had had the heart to start the blue pullover once again. And whom would she give it to? She would not get out of the house, *her* house which Rupert had given her and for which, in exchange, she had given him the most important thing she had.

'I gave up my knitting for you!' she screamed at him, 'and you can't even give me a house and a few sticks of furniture.'

'You're mad,' said Rupert. 'You ought to be locked up.'

Alice rushed at him and smacked his face. He caught her hands and threw her into a chair and slammed out of the room. He went down to the pub on the seafront and had two double whiskies and smoked half a pack of cigarettes. When he got back, Alice was in bed in the spare room. Just as he refused to leave the house, so Rupert had refused to get out of his own bedroom. He took two of Dr Nicholson's sleeping tablets and went to bed.

In the morning Alice went into the room where Rupert was and washed his scalp and combed his beautiful thick white hair. She changed the pillowcases, wiped a spot off Rupert's pyjama jacket, and then she phoned Dr Nicholson to say Rupert was dead. He must have passed away in his sleep. She had awakened to find him dead beside her.

'His heart, of course,' said Dr Nicholson, and because Alice had been a nurse, 'a massive myocardial infarction.'

She nodded. 'I suppose I should have expected it.'

'Well, in these cases – '

'You never know, do you? I must be grateful for the few happy months we had together.'

Dr Nicholson signed the death certificate. There was no question of an autopsy. Pamela and Guy came to the cremation and took Alice back home with them for four weeks. When Alice left to return to the house that was now entirely hers, they promised to take her at her word and come to stay once again in the summer. Alice was very comfortably off, for by no means all Rupert's savings had been spent on the furniture, his life insurance had been considerable, and there was his army pension, reduced but still generous.

It was an amazingly young-looking Alice, her hair rinsed primrose, her figure the trimmest it had been in ten years, who met Guy and Pamela at the station. She was driving a new white Lancia coupé and wearing a smart knitted suit in a subtle shade of burgundy.

'I love your suit,' said Pamela.

'I made it.'

'I really must take up knitting again. I used to be so good at it, didn't I? And think of the money one saves.'

On the following evening, a Sunday, after they had spent most of the day on the beach, Pamela again reverted to the subject of knitting and said her fingers itched to start on something straight away. Alice looked thoughtful. Then she opened the bottom drawer of the chest and took out the saxe-blue wool.

'You could have this if you like, and this pattern. You could make it for Guy.'

Pamela took the pattern which had apparently been torn in half and mended with sticking tape. She looked at the hanks of wool.

'Has some of it been used?'

'I didn't like what I'd done, so I undid it. The wool's been washed and carded to get the crinkles out.'

'If you're thinking of making that for me,' said Guy, 'I'm all for it. Splendid idea.'

'All right. Why not? Very fine needles it takes, doesn't it? Have you got a pair of fourteens, Alice?'

A shadow passed across Alice's face. She hesitated. Then she picked up the plastic envelopes one by one, but desultorily, until Pamela, fired now with enthusiasm, dropped on her knees beside her and began hunting through the drawer.

'Here we are. Number fourteen, two millimetres, US double 0 . . . There's only one needle here, Alice.'

'Sorry about that, it must be lost.' Alice took the single needle from her almost roughly and made as if to close the drawer.

'No, wait a minute, it's bound to be loose in there somewhere.'

'I'm sure it isn't, it's lost. You won't have time to start tonight, anyway.'

Guy said, 'I don't see how you could lose one knitting needle.'

'In a train,' said Pamela, peering into each needle packet. 'It could fall down the side of the seat and before you could get it out you'd be at your station.'

'Alice never goes in trains.'

'I suppose you could use it to unblock a drainpipe?'

'You'd use a big fat one for that. Now if this situation happened in one of my books I'd have it that the needle was a murder weapon. Inserted into the scalp of a person who was, say, drugged or drunk, it would penetrate the covering of the brain and the brain itself, causing a subdural haemorrhage. You'd have to sharpen the point a bit, file it maybe, and then of course you'd throw it away afterwards. Hence, you see, only one number fourteen needle in the drawer.'

'And immediately they examined the body they'd find out,' said his wife.

'Well, you know, I don't think they would. Did you know that almost all men over middle age have enough signs of coronary disease for a pathologist, unless he was exceptionally thorough, to assume that as the cause of death? Of course your victim would have to have a good head of hair to cover up the mark of entry.'

'For heaven's sake, let's change the subject,' said Pamela closing the drawer, for she had noticed that Alice, perhaps because of that tactless reference to coronaries, had gone very white and that the hands which held the wool were trembling.

But Alice managed a smile. 'We'll buy you a pair of number fourteens tomorrow,' she said, 'and perhaps I'll start on something new as well. My mother always used to say that the devil finds work for idle hands to do.'

The Hampstead Vegetable Heist

MAT COWARD

'So, you're going to use a zucchini, right?'

'Zucchini, yah. Basically I'm thinking, they can't do you for using a weapon, or going equipped, or whatever, if all you've got in your pocket is a vegetable, see?'

Toby lifted his Pernod-and-Perrier to his lips and kissed it. Then he put it down again. I picked up my pint of bitter, stuffed half of it down my throat, and slapped the glass back on the table. I've got nothing against people who don't drink, but what I can't stand is someone who doesn't drink properly. I mean, why go to a pub if you're not thirsty?

'A zucchini,' I said, 'that's what, a courgette?'

'OK, right, a courgette, yah. Sorry, I should've said. I spent a lot of time in the States before, and they call them zucchini over there. A courgette, that's right.'

'And, let me get this straight: this is because of your mortgage?'

'Please, please, don't even say that word! I mean, we're not talking *mortgage* here, we're talking *mega*-mortgage. This isn't just a *mortgage*, yah? This is The Mortgage That Ate The West.'

I don't know what we're supposed to call these types now – these people who used to be yuppies. I mean, they're certainly not Young and Upwardly Mobile Professionals any more, not since the crash, and the property collapse, and the never-ending recession. 'Rapsids,' perhaps:

Rapidly Sinking Idiots who thought their luck would last for ever.

Toby's luck had run out later than some, and heavier than most. I think this was because, even by yuppie standards, he wasn't all that bright. I don't care how solid the property market looks, or how much the bank pays its Vice-Presidents (Securities); no one with a fully functioning brain takes on a half-a-million-pound mortgage at age twenty-seven.

Anyone who does, if you ask me, *deserves* to lose his home fourteen months later.

'Why are you telling me this, Toby? Not that it isn't very interesting and everything, but if you want to stick up a betting shop with an American marrow, just go ahead and do it. I'll read about it in the local paper when you get sent down. What do you want from me, the name of a bent greengrocer?'

'I don't know,' Toby pouted. 'Some sympathy for the devil, maybe? A word of encouragement?'

He had to be kidding. Not that I disliked Toby Reynolds, the yuppie who fell to earth. In fact, as an example of his breed, he wasn't too bad. Word in the pub was, he'd even been heard to crack a joke once or twice – after he was laid off, obviously, not before.

But I first knew this place in the seventies, when Margaret Thatcher was just a crazy woman on the TV, there were no mobile phones or personal organisers, people didn't drink bottled French water in pubs, and estate agents didn't have swimming pools, or personalised licence plates on their Jaguars, until they were too old to enjoy them. I won't pretend they were great days, but at least the area had a bit of tone back then.

Look at a map, and it'll tell you that Hampstead is a suburb of north London. But maps can lie. Hampstead, as any local will tell you, usually unprompted, is a village. True, London is only a few minutes away by tube, but in spirit it's on a different planet.

To succeed in the area known to jealous outsiders by its postal code, you only had to be one thing: a character. Same as any English village, right? You could be rich (more millionaires per square inch than anywhere else in the country), or you could be poor (plenty of bedsits, full of Marxist students, gay runaways, and Irish poet-bricklayers). You could be a pop star, a librarian or a Zoroastrian priest. Just as long as you were interesting to know. That's the sort of place it is.

Or used to be, before the mid-eighties, when all the yups moved in, with their lookalike designer suits, and their coloured spectacle frames, and their one-track conversation – deals, deals, deals. And now, if the mysterious revolutions of the money markets were forcing them out again, I wasn't going to complain. Cheer maybe, declare a public holiday, but not complain.

'Well, Toby, me old son, I wish you all the luck. And if you get banged up, I'll send you a postcard of the Heath, to remind you of happier days.' I stood up. A few of the serious darts players had arrived, and I was eager to get into the game.

'Yah, sure, mate. But just wait a second. There's more. I know how I can make certain I get away with the robbery, and at the same time pin it on Danny Royal.' He smiled, smugly. 'Why don't I buy you a drink, yah, while I run it by you?' I looked at him more closely. Yeah, now I came to think of it . . .

I sat down. I can play darts any night. A chance to frame Danny Royal only comes along once in a lifetime.

I won't bore you with what there was between me and Danny, except to say that it went back about a dozen years, and it involved a knife, a broken arm, a deposit on a studio flat that wasn't actually for rent, an innocent country boy, and a guy who got thrown out of the north London mafia for being too much of a scumbag.

Danny was definitely Old Hampstead – an interesting character, you had to give him that – but if I could hurt him by helping one of the despised yuppie invaders, then I didn't have to think twice about whose side I was on.

Besides, a man has a right to pay his mortgage, doesn't he?

Thus, on the morning of the Great Hampstead Bookie Blag, Toby and

I met in a tarted-up coffee shop, just across the High Street from the betting shop. The place used to be a pub, but yuppies don't use beer, so now it sold pseudo-American Danish pastries, and pseudo-European coffee. I was maliciously pleased to notice, at ten in the morning, that it was virtually empty.

As Toby sat down next to me, I spoke to him out of the side of my mouth: 'You got da piece, Bugsy?'

'Oh yah, sure,' said my accomplice, loud as you like. 'The zucchini's right here in this brown paper bag. You got yours?'

'Don't wave it all around, stupid,' I screamed, very quietly.

'Why? It's only a vegetable. You can't be arrested for waving a vegetable around a café.'

'It's a fruit, not a vegetable.'

'Right. Sure.' He looked puzzled. 'That make a different in law?'

'No difference at all. I just don't want my face associated with your face – or your fruit, or your brown paper bag – in the memory of any lurking witness. All right?'

'All right, yah. Sorry, mate. I wasn't thinking.' He thought for a moment; I could see his ears turning pink. 'You recognised me straight away.'

'I was expecting you. Don't worry about that, you look just like him. His own mistress'd be fooled.'

It was true. Of course, Toby was a good bit younger than Danny, but then Danny's body was as crooked as his character – it lied about his age. The false moustache looked fine (plenty of actors in Hampstead; and, actors being the sort of people they are, you can always find one that owes you a favour). The clothes were spot-on: camelhair overcoat, smart denim shirt and leather tie, expensive black jeans. He'd do.

Then he really surprised me. 'Listen . . .' he said, and paused to gulp some cold coffee. 'Do you have any, y'know, moral qualms about any of this? Um, basically,' he added. I goggled, boggled, and burbled a bit. *Morals?* Wow, this poor lad hadn't just lost his yuppie job, he'd lost his entire yuppie code. His orientation was shot all to buggery.

'You mean the stick-up? Or the frame-up?'

'Well, y'know, like, both I suppose. I mean, this isn't really my sort of scene, right? I used to be in banking.'

'Exactly,' I said. 'So whatever you do today can't be half as wicked as what you've been doing for the past ten years. Now get up. It's time to go.' He got up, put on his dark glasses, and began walking towards the door. 'Hey, Toby,' I called after him.

'Yah?' He looked back expectantly, like a dog about to get a tickle on the tummy for luck.

'You forgot your bloody courgette!'

Moral qualms? Sure, I had qualms, a little squeamishness, but nothing I couldn't handle. The bookie's would be insured, there wasn't really a gun, so no one could get hurt, and as for Danny Royal . . . if law and order was a real thing, not just a phantom they conjure up at election time, he'd have been in solitary confinement since the age of six. Justice delayed is justice just the same.

Danny's office was located, very conveniently, above an off-licence, a few doors down from the betting shop which my confederate, Toby, was about to rob with a zucchini in a paper bag. Quite why a villain needs an office, instead of, say, a low dive or a murky alley, I couldn't imagine.

But, hey – this is Hampstead. Hampstead smiles on style.

'Good morning, Danny. How's tricks?'

Danny was alone, as we'd been sure he would be so early – even so, I was relieved. We'd known he'd be in the office; he always was on weekday mornings, just like a regular businessman. He didn't look surprised to see me, which irritated me somewhat.

'What you doing here, boy?' He was concentrating on his paperwork now, he wasn't looking at me. He'd looked at me once already, and he didn't see any need to look at me again.

'I'm here to bring you a little gift, something I thought you'd like. Here, Danny – catch!' I chucked the paper bag at his head. A zucchini doesn't weigh much, but it makes you feel awfully silly if it bounces off your head when you're not expecting it.

The only man in the world that I really hated sprang out of his swivel chair, and screamed, 'What's your game, boy? Just exactly what is occurring, you grubby little – '

He was going to call me something rude, I knew he was, and that's something that my mother particularly warned me about when I first moved to the big city. So I hit him, quite hard, on the right eye. I shouldn't have, of course, it wasn't in the script, but there comes a time in a man's life when improvisation is the only show in town. Know what I mean?

I was just wondering what was going to happen next, and thinking it probably wouldn't be anything particularly funny, and watching Danny Royal sprawl across his desk, howling, when the office door opened, and a tough-looking kid of about eighteen walked in.

I froze, like a string bean alone in a catering-size deep freeze. I knew this kid: he worked on a stall in the community market. More to the point, he knew me.

'So what was all that about?' the barrow boy asked me, as I hustled him out of the street door. 'I was just coming up to pay my rent to the King Rat. Did you floor him?'

'Er – yeah. Listen, Nigel, it's very important that nobody finds out about this, you understand? Absolutely nobody. Not about the fight, not even that I was there. OK? You with me, Nigel?' I was pretty sure he hadn't seen the zucchini in the bag, which had rolled under Royal's desk, but I didn't want anybody who could place me in the office, when the cops started asking questions. So I gave Nigel a brief but tastefully dramatised version of my long-standing grudge against his landlord.

'Don't worry, mate, anyone who thumps that piece of filth is OK with me. You have any idea what rent he charges me and my girl for one room and a shared lav? It's disgusting, I'm telling you, it's diabolical!'

We parted in the street, with a heartfelt handshake. As I had hoped, Nigel was thoroughly outraged on my behalf. I'd not only silenced a potentially hostile witness, I'd made a friend for life.

I ran to the phone booth at the top of the hill, jabbed out three nines on the dial, and told the police that the man who'd just robbed a bookmaker's in Hampstead High Street, armed with a suspicious bulge in a paper bag, was a certain Danny Royal, known criminal. I'd heard him planning it in the pub the night before. No I wasn't willing to give my name, he'd kill me if he knew I'd grassed him up. Just get there quickly. They wouldn't recover the money – that was with his accomplice – but I was sure he wouldn't have ditched the weapon yet. His address? Yeah, as a matter of fact, I did know his address . . .

Toby Reynolds, ex-banker, ex-yuppie, one-time stick-up merchant, is currently serving three years in Ford Open Prison. It's true what they say: the rich never do hard time. Not even when they're not rich any more. He got away from the bookie's with five thousand quid: enough to keep a chap like him in comfort for, ooh, at least three months . . . if he hadn't blown a good thousand of it in one night's champagne-quaffing with his old pals from the City. At a wine bar right here in Hampstead. Right on his own doorstep.

And if he hadn't, when deeply in his cups, snatched a courgette (sorry, *zucchini*) from a passing waiter's tray and proceeded to point it around the room, shouting 'Bang! Bang! Give us all the dosh!', while standing on a table. I said he wasn't very bright, didn't I?

I still think he might have got away with it if the frame-up had worked out better. It wasn't a great plan, but the cops were hot to nail Danny Royal, and would have found a way of stitching him up somehow.

But when they got to his office they found him unconscious, covered in blood, and badly in need of emergency treatment. By the time he was fit to answer questions, he had more lawyers hanging off him than IV drips, and all the police had was an anonymous tip-off, a six-inch fruit, and a brown paper bag. Not much of a lunch, even, and as evidence it didn't amount to – well, to a hill of beans.

Royal must have known it was Nigel the barrow boy who injured him so thoroughly. Nigel who, disgusted by my tale of treachery, and by his own experiences with the King Rat, and figuring me (correctly) for the largely non-violent type, had decided to do us all a favour. He'd gone back up to the office as soon as I was out of sight, and given Danny a very, very deep massage.

Royal must know, but I don't think there's much he can do about it. Times are changing. Danny still has his friends, but Nigel comes from a big, close West Indian family, well endowed with big, close brothers, uncles and cousins. And an even bigger, closer grandmother. I think he's safe. As safe as any of us are these days.

I think I'm safe as well. Toby the yup may not be very clever, and he may not be my kind of people, but he knows about keeping his gob shut. And, given the incredibly stupid nature of the offence, the cops weren't exactly looking to round up a gang of criminal masterminds.

Toby will be out before long, and I'm going to try and get him a job. Maybe in one of the local boozers. After all, he's one of us now, kind of.

I see Nigel in this pub or that, about three or four times a week. The first dozen or so occasions, he would give me a conspiratorial wink and send over a drink with his compliments. That got embarrassing after a time, so now, when our paths cross, I try to get *my* conspiratorial wink and complimentary pint in first.

Well, why not? Like I always say, Hampstead is a village. This is how people behave in villages.

Mr Idd

HRF KEATING

Mr Idd came into my life one summer evening in 1986. It was in the West End of London. Just as dusk was falling, as I remember. Of course, Mr Idd was not his real name. How should I know what a total stranger called himself? But, as you will see, 'Mr Idd' was a good label to attach to him, and I bestowed it unconsciously the moment I became fully aware of him. The moment he did that extraordinary thing. The first of many.

Freud may be somewhat discredited nowadays. But all the same his great simplification of the human psyche into workaday Ego, sternly controlling Superego and anarchic, pleasure-first Idd still seems to me a model that helps to explain our often wonderfully strange goings-on. And my own extraordinary experiences with the man I at once at that first encounter named Mr Idd surely bear this out.

Not that what happened that evening was, in itself, utterly extraordinary. You might with reason even have described it as no more than a piece of spontaneous fun. But by the standards of anything like normal behaviour in the sober daylight heart of a great city it was certainly more than a little eccentric.

What happened was this. I was walking down Regent Street, never tremendously crowded at that hour, on my way from my office, where I had been working late, to the theatre. Mr Idd must have been almost beside me going in the same direction. Not that I had any idea at the time who it was who for the past several minutes must have been seeing the same odd spectacle a little way ahead as myself, a man dressed, heaven knows why, from head to foot as a parody of the great detective, Sherlock Holmes. Deerstalker hat, Inverness cape, and even, just visible when he chanced to turn his head, curved pipe in mouth. Altogether an eye-catching sight, if a ridiculous one. The fellow was not exactly hurrying, sneaking looks round all the time in fact, as if secretly hoping to catch passers-by in glances of approbation. And I remember thinking how it would pay him out if I were to overtake him, turn and sharply greet him face to face as Holmes.

It was Mr Idd who did just exactly that. He marched briskly forward until he had just gone past the fellow, and then, turning abruptly, he confronted him with the immortal words Irene Adler called out in the story, 'A Scandal in Bohemia'.

'Good-night, Mr Sherlock Holmes.'

It was a highly comical moment. The Holmes lookalike, though he evidently had been seeking admiration or at least covert recognition, was absolutely put out to have his get-up acknowledged in this blatant fashion.

He stopped in his tracks. His mouth opened, and the famous drooping pipe fell with a little clatter to the pavement. He even produced some sort of a sound, though what he was trying to say, if he even knew himself, came out as no more than a choked gurgle.

I stood there looking, and by the time the Holmes figure had recovered his wits, scrabbled up the pipe and stalked furiously away Mr Idd had vanished.

I might perhaps never have thought of the incident again, comical though it had been – inwardly I giggled over it long after the curtain had gone up at the theatre – except that within a week there was Mr Idd once more. Again it was in the West End, though I suppose it is not really very surprising to encounter there more than once any one of the many people who have occasion to be in what is after all quite a small area, a mere square mile or so.

What Mr Idd did this time, however, was a whole step further removed from normal conduct. Once again, it seemed, we had been walking along side by side, almost together. This time, though, it was in the morning, and we were going down St James's Street towards Pall Mall where I was to lunch at one of the clubs. Ahead of us, in much the same way as the Holmes doppelgänger had been a week earlier, there was striding a more-than-typical businessman. Black jacket, striped trousers, rolled-to-needle-thinness umbrella and, crowning the whole, a particularly well brushed bowler hat worn aggressively tilted forward. He was carrying himself very upright, and even from behind he looked infuriatingly self-confident.

For a little I watched hm making his way along nine or ten yards in front of me, swinging slightly that rolled umbrella, and I wondered whether anything would knock him off his perch.

Mr Idd showed me what would. From somewhere close to me he quickened his pace, caught up with the stiffly correct figure ahead and simply reached over and lifted the bowler off his head. For a few swift paces he marched onwards carrying his trophy. Then, placing it with immense care on the roof of a car parked beside the pavement, he strode off.

I had not recovered from my astonishment – nor had the abruptly deflated businessman – before Mr Idd had disappeared. But now he was firmly established in my mind, name and all, and I felt certain that, somewhere, at some time, I was going to see him again.

Several months passed, however, before he manifested himself. But then it was in an altogether more disconcerting way.

It was not, this time, in that part of London where because so many places of business and entertainment are concentrated you are not surprised to see almost anyone you know. It was actually in the pleasant, mildly prosperous inner suburb where I live myself.

A few discreet yards off its bustling High Street there is a shop – no, establishment is the right word – that offers to the trendy, and well-padded, a variety of luxury bathroom fittings. Its window is usually made over as a mock-up of the sort of bathroom its clientele is expected to have. There is often a long, deep tub with taps that at least look as if they are gold plated. Beside it, artfully scattered on the tiled flooring, there will be an assortment of toilet preparations bearing exotic names. Sometimes the window is given over to a whole collection, tub, basin, toilet and bidet, all decorated in the same prettified pattern, little multicoloured flowers or perhaps a ceramic spread of bright green ferns.

To tell the truth, the whole place gets under my skin. I would never think of replacing the plain white tub and basin in my own flat with any of its products. 'Pretentious' is the word that comes to my mind each time I pass by. Yet I must admit that, if I do not exactly linger in front of its wide plate-glass window, I do almost always glance in. If only to see how far they have gone this time in the way of up-to-the-minute fancy décor.

But imagine my feelings one day, having thought as I had turned the corner that the exhibits had been renewed, when there in the window, in full view of anybody in the street, was Mr Idd. He had marched up to the toilet bowl of the display – its smart wooden seat, I saw, was painted to look like marble – and, turning now, he dropped his trousers and sat.

Can he really be going to -

But before he did, if that was his intention, two of the shop's staff came pushing through the narrow entrance at the rear of the window area, seized him, one by either arm, and hauled him to his feet. I foresaw then, in a moment of chill realisation which swept away the inward laughter bubbling through me, the arrival of the police. Mr Idd would be given in charge. There would be a court appearance. Perhaps detention as being of unsound mind.

None of that happened. Mr Idd simply reached down, hauled up his trousers and, with what might be thought of as superhuman strength, flung the two staff members aside and strode out. Disappeared.

Soon I even began to wonder if the incident had happened at all.

But the thought of it left my mind awash with conflicting feelings. On the one hand I could not help admiring Mr Idd for his daring. Yet doing what he had threatened to do – would he really have gone as far as the ultimate defilement, I asked myself – was something more than unsettling to think about. Mr Idd, I decided, was not a person I wanted ever to encounter again.

And I had a disquieting feeling that somehow I had not seen the last of him. By any means.

Yet it was, again, several weeks before he materialised once more. This time it was not even in London. I was, as it happened, up in Birmingham for a meeting. It had ended sooner than I had expected, and I found myself at a loose end in that unfamiliar city, waiting till it was time for my train back. I was wandering about, unable to make up my mind whether to go for a drink I did not particularly want or to find the Art Museum and spend a few minutes there – too few, no doubt, to be worth while – or simply to stroll about absorbing the atmosphere, such as it was.

Then I saw him.

He was, of course, immediately recognisable although, as I said, it had been weeks since I had had sight of him trousers down in that bathrooms shop window and months since I had been a hapless witness of those two more innocent West End incidents. This time, instead of apparently walking along somewhere just behind or beside me, I became aware of him a short distance ahead. I was making my way aimlessly along a greasy narrow pavement bordering a wide sweep of comparatively deserted roadway. I have no idea what the short street is called, or even exactly where in Birmingham it is, except that it cannot be far from the centre. It links two much busier streets and traffic along it is sparse, although the vehicles that use it go at a fair speed.

I had taken in the presence of Mr Idd just after I had noticed a blind man standing waiting to cross at the pavement's edge, waving his white stick in a manner that struck me as more than a little peremptory. With that sharpness of hearing the blind develop, he must have detected approaching footsteps above the unending grumble of the nearby traffic because he turned and directly requested – no, demanded – assistance.

And in answer Mr Idd did an altogether extraordinary thing. Even a terrible thing. Instead of taking the man's arm and, after looking to left and right, seeing him across the wide roadway, or instead even of ignoring the brusque request – I remember, just, thinking how some disabled people seem to feel they have almost seigneurial rights over others – he simply stopped just behind the fellow and snarled at him.

'Don't be so damned helpless. If you want to cross, cross.'

Whether he then gave him, in fact, a little push, or whether the blind man was so startled that he unthinkingly set off without listening for any oncoming vehicle I have never been able to decide. But set off he did. Unhesitatingly, out on to the wide expanse of tarmac.

I stood where I was.

Was a car going to come zooming round and be unable to avoid the sudden, unexpected figure making his way over to the far side, white stick waving like the pointer of an out-of-kilter metronome? If anything came round the bend, it was almost certainly not going to have time to take avoiding action.

My heart was, as they say, in my mouth. And yet, I must admit, at the same time I experienced a tiny, subterranean whickering of pure excitement. Much as if I was watching some dangerous sporting event on television, and knew it was all right to seem callous because if anything too appalling happened it would be edited out. But the excitement was still there, despite the blind man's wavering progress being no TV recording.

In fact, the car that did come speeding round did not actually touch him. It must have skimmed his coat-tails, though, before it whirled on, horn furiously hooting.

So no real harm done. But there I was, left with the horrible suspicion – or more than suspicion, somehow a certain knowledge – that the next time I encountered Mr Idd what he would do would be yet more unthinkable.

I came to dread the day. It became an obsession with me. I knew – though I was aware, too, that rationally I could not know – that sooner or later I would see Mr Idd at work again. And that, when I did, something a whole stage worse than the incident with the blind man was going to take place.

Before long I could scarcely think of anything else. The least circumstance would cause that irrational fear to bubble to the surface of my mind – the sight of a blind person's white stick, an advertisement making use of the Sherlock Holmes deerstalker and curved pipe image, each and every time I happened to see a bowler hat on some smart City gent. Anything remotely connected with Mr Idd would set my fears spiralling upwards.

My work began to suffer, quite seriously. I would be busy reading the journals it was my task to keep abreast of, and by chance come across a single word that would trigger me off – *pipe, umbrella, bath*. Even one of my colleagues saying 'Good-night' as we left in the evening would connect in a single jagged instant with the impish desire I had once had to confront that comical man in Regent Street, and I would hear again the words 'Good-night, Mr Sherlock Holmes' which Mr Idd had, as it were, pronounced to him for me.

Soon I even found I could no longer bear to set foot in any part of Regent Street. I would go almost any distance to reach a destination I could have got to in ten minutes by the direct route. It was not that I feared seeing Mr Idd there where I had seen him before; it was that anywhere in the whole street might cause me just to think about him. To wonder in dread when he would make his reappearance.

Worst of all, perhaps, I developed an aversion to using the lavatory. A phobia. Each time I needed to go to it I would see in my mind's eye Mr Idd dropping his trousers in that shop window, and my natural functions would clam up inside me. I had to have recourse to the most violent aperients, and soon came to exist in a state of constant physical misery.

Eventually I decided to take a fortnight's leave in a final effort to break the invisible grip. I went to Paris. Perhaps, I thought, completely different sights and sounds would get the nonsense out of my head. I would cut myself off from every familiar sight. Speak, read, think if I could, in a wholly different language. Surely then I would rid myself of the ever-nudging thought of Mr Idd.

But I was mistaken. It was in Paris that I saw Mr Idd once more.

I was in the Louvre, looking at Leonardo's *Mona Lisa*. After many years' absence I was seeking once again to get straight in my mind just what that enigmatic face had to say about the human personality, asking myself whether the great lady from the far past was smiling with gentle love or with the tinge of hostile contempt that I had sometimes felt emanated from her. Or, rather, I was attempting to do that. The crowd in front was, as always, impossibly dense. There must have been at least thirty people, craning and jostling to get their glimpse, most of them of course altogether ignoring every other wonderful work of art in the museum with, I suppose, the exception of the Venus de Milo. I remember, as I stood at the outer edge of the mob – no other word – that there came into my mind a travel article about Paris I had seen in some colour supplement in which the writer had happily claimed all that you needed in order to 'do' the Louvre was fifteen minutes to cross off those two masterpieces.

But at last I managed to get near enough, right up to the rope keeping sticky prying fingers away, to be able to see the picture whole. And it was just as I began to let flow into me that calm, if ambiguous, statement Leonardo put on canvas all those years ago that, first, I heard a twangy American voice proclaim, just to show she knew what had to be appreciated in the world-famed painting, 'Gee, what an antique smile', and, next, I was aware between myself and the picture of a blotting-out dull black form I somehow knew at once was Mr Idd. Then, immediately, there came a terrible, sharp rending sound.

The next moment Mr Idd was no longer there. Where he had gone, how he had dissolved among that thickly crowding mass of onlookers I could not say. But he had vanished. And the *Mona Lisa* was ripped from top to bottom.

You must remember, even though it was a good while ago, the sensation that act of desecration caused. What I remember, however, is quite another feeling. I found – try as I might to dissociate myself from it – that I was sharing with Mr Idd what I can only call a sense of holy joy at the sheer daring of the thing he had done. At its defiance. At the magnificent snook it cocked at all those gawpers and gapers.

And that made me fear more than ever the day when once again Mr Idd would be there. As I knew he would be. Knew with utter inevitability.

You will almost certainly have remembered that attack on the *Mona Lisa*, even though restoration work has long since obliterated every sign of it. What you may not remember, though it came not long afterwards, is the attack made on Sir Elton Dugbury.

You may not even remember Sir Elton. He was not, after all, a very important figure in the national life of Great Britain, even though he was a colourful personality who bounced and bullied his way over the years into several minor ministerial appointments. Outspoken if nothing else, and crudely photogenic with the embroidered waistcoats he chose to wear, he frequently figured in the headlines. There was his remark, made at the height of the Cold War, that none of the trouble need have occurred if both the Russians and the Americans had been taught to play cricket. Then there was the time he said there would be many fewer cases of rape if women would only learn to keep their legs together. And once he stated that there was nothing wrong with the arts that cutting off subsidies for everything except the Covent Garden opera wouldn't cure.

That off-the-cuff insult came shortly before Sir Elton was attacked. In the very Lobby of the House of Commons. I was there myself taking part in a protest, so angry – my work is in the field of the arts – that all my dread of encountering again the bogey that had come to haunt me had been chased for once from my head.

Sir Elton's contemptuous words – he was a junior Treasury minister at the time and might have had some responsibility for allocating arts funds – had seemed to epitomise everything I thought wrong with the ruling classes in Britain. Their insensitivity, that swaggering belief in whatever happened to come into their heads, any feeling for the finer things manifesting itself only when, like the opera, they cost a great deal of money. What happened was that Sir Elton, either not realising the demonstration was taking place or, perhaps more likely, delighting in brazening it out, had come down into the Lobby just when it was at its height. There was an immediate chorus of booing. Sir Elton – he certainly did not lack courage, whatever else was missing from his make-up – promptly got back up on to the steps leading into the Lobby and trumpeted out something about 'long-haired intellectuals'. It was difficult to hear exactly what. But the defiant shout sent a wave of angry protesters converging on him. I was among them myself, swept along whether I wanted to be or not.

And then the attack happened. A moment before I had become aware – emotions at once battered me back and forth – of a terribly familiar sight. There, in the front of the crowd sweeping towards the provocative figure in the pink flowered waistcoat, was Mr Idd.

How he had managed to smuggle a handgun through the security checks was something that caused a flurry of questions afterwards. But smuggled in it was, and within three or four feet of that flowered waistcoat it was fired.

But this time Mr Idd was unable to vanish in the way he had that summer evening in Regent Street, or later in St James's Street, or from that bathrooms shop with the pretty-pretty toilet bowl in its window, or even after he had desecrated the *Mona Lisa* itself.

No, this time he was caught.

He is in prison now. Broadmoor. The institution for the criminally insane. He is still his old self, despite such treatment as they give him. For long periods he is altogether quiescent, and then he breaks out. He plays some trick on one of the officers. Suddenly spitting in his face. Or pretending to be dead. There is not a lot he can do, but he is determined not to be totally suppressed.

You will ask how I know this. It is because, of course, I can still watch him.

But you must – you must – believe me when I say that all along I did truly see him as someone else. As someone I was able to observe from, as it were, a short distance away. You must believe that. You must.

The Birdman of Bow Street

JOAN LOCK

A remarkable character from the history of Bow Street Magistrates' Court: Sgt White, the chief jailer

Bow Street Magistrates' Court has never been a stranger to eccentrics, whether in the dock or on the bench, but one of its most remarkable characters was a policeman: Sergeant White, the chief jailer.

'Few jailers in the United Kingdom are better known,' *Police Review and Parade Gossip* told its first readers in 1893, and this was hardly surprising. At the time, the sergeant had twenty-two years' service, fourteen of them at Bow Street. He had never lost a prisoner, had developed a prodigious memory for faces, kept numerous pet birds on the premises – and he perfected the art of searching slices of bread and butter, by squeezing them between his fingers.

Over the years Sergeant White had come to expect small bottles of spirits to be hidden in jugs of tea sent in for prisoners by their families. Luxuries like tobacco and matches were also concealed in the oddest places. Once, he found some baked into a loaf of bread and, quite often, it was secreted in a thick slice of bread and butter. Prisoners also pencilled notes on the cuffs of their dirty shirts, collected by families.

All such forbidden items and practices gave Sergeant White and his trusty aids, Bush and Sloper, plenty to do. They duly peered at dirty shirts, stirred jugs of tea with long pencils and 'analysed' loaves.

The sergeant rarely forgot a face. Partly through a natural aptitude but mainly because he made it his business to remember. 'The study of a lifetime,' he called it.

'In my opinion,' he told *Police Review*, 'one of the principal duties of a man occupying my position is to study faces.'

To this end he watched every prisoner 'with the object of recognising him at any future period. I endeavour to get the face and form of every prisoner photographed, as it were, on my brain.' The only people who sometimes defeated him were criminals sent away for five years' penal servitude when young and who had aged considerably when they reappeared.

He was allowed some surprising latitude with his skill.

'Do you know the prisoner?' A magistrate once asked him of a man charged with indecent assault.

'Yes,' said White, 'I feel sure he was charged here about twelve years ago, and I think with a similar offence.'

'It was only eleven years ago,' complained the prisoner.

When he was not photographing faces on his brain and squeezing slices of bread and butter he was compiling a record of all the thieves' slang he came across.

Among the hundreds of entries in his notebook were 'lobsliding' (stealing a till) and 'fanning a scuff' (feeling pockets in a crowd).

Prisoners' terms for their sentences were also entered. Some you will recognise: 'a cadger's lagging' (seven days), 'two clean shirts' (fourteen days), 'a moon' (a month), 'a drag' or 'carpet bag' (three months), 'a stretch' (twelve months), 'a tubbing' (two years) and 'a lagging' (penal servitude).

Although the court and police station were housed in a splendid new building, the neighbourhood they served was largely a poor and criminal one. (In 1886 the toffs at Marlborough Street, another famous

Central London court, paid up over £2,000 in fines while Bow Street's clientele managed only £692 and went to prison instead.)

Model institution

Sergeant White had served in the new court since its opening in 1881. It was 'a model institution of its kind' thought the *Graphic* newspaper, though its acoustics left something to be desired.

Nonetheless, it had all the modern amenities, plus clean and well-ventilated cells and well-arranged and spacious rooms.

That mental magpie, Sergeant White, put his spacious room to good use, this time with a tangible collection. Every inch of the walls and every ledge was covered with pictures of past magistrates, well-known detectives and infamous prisoners who had passed through his court.

The *pièce de résistance* was a large frame containing photographs of the recently hanged Dr Neill Cream, who had murdered several prostitutes, and his solicitor, counsel and witnesses in the case. The sergeant had even kept the pencil with which Cream had taken notes during the summary hearing and the cardboard pad on which he had rested them.

Lion and the Lamb

Of course Bow Street produced the first 'stipes' and some of those in Sergeant White's time were contrasting characters themselves. There was the dapper and soft-hearted Mr Flowers (dubbed 'the lamb' by one magazine cartoonist) who, the *Graphic* decided, 'tempered justice with mercy perhaps too frequently', and the tougher, elderly Mr Vaughan ('the lion'). Mr Vaughan was not persuaded to retire until 1899 – when he was eighty-five years old! So, it was probably his short-sightedness, plus the poor acoustics, which caused the jackdaws to be banned, finally, from the courtroom.

Sergeant White not only kept birds but also allowed some of them the run of the spacious court rooms as the London *Star* reported:

When he had more spare accommodation at his disposal he used to keep as many as 40 birds here. With human prisoners to look after, he never imprisoned his birds when it could be avoided. His greenfinch and his canary were never in a cage, and when he held up his finger they would come and quarrel for the perch. Now his birds are only three in number, a blackbird of most beautiful plumage and two jackdaws.

It is purely their own fault that these jackdaws are caged while the court is actually sitting. They used to abuse their liberty shockingly. One 'beak' is generally considered sufficient for one court, but both birds were in the habit of introducing their own beaks as well, stealing quills and blotting paper, for the pleasure of pulling them to pieces, and pecking at the feet of those prisoners whose boots were of that particular fashion which left the toes protruding.

Apparently, things came to a head when 'one near-sighted magistrate' thought the noises one of the jackdaws was making emanated from a defendant whom he first warned for his impertinence and then had removed from the court.

Volatile jackdaw

A contemporary feature writer, F. W. Robinson, gives a glimpse of one 'knowing and volatile jackdaw' who had the run of the jailer's office. The bird hopped from desk to stool, stool to floor, taking stock of newcomers 'with the gravity of the inspector on duty'. He was 'altogether a general favourite of the staff'. Slightly less a favourite of Mr Robinson, one feels. He adds: 'It is declared that he is playful with old offenders, while he pecks viciously at newcomers.'

Police Review obviously felt quite honoured to obtain an interview with such an important man, but convenience and influence probably played a part in their early call since the offices were in Bow Street and their founder had been the court reporter.

All in all one wonders how Sergeant White got away with such goings on, particularly in an age of instant dismissals on sometimes flimsy pretexts. Of course the man was enthusiastic and devoted to his work and, seemingly, good at it. He looked good, too – young for his age – briskly striding the long corridors, and was obviously a good self-publicist.

However, apart from all his bull it is nice to record that he was also a kindly man. He had noticed that first offenders ('and innocent men') felt their degradation most keenly when they were put in the 'Black Maria'. He had seen it make strong men shudder.

'Sergeant White forgot to add,' said the *Police Review* reporter, 'that he never allows a man of this class to step inside the prison van without wishing them a cheery "Good night, sir!"'

That 'sir' must have meant a lot to them.

Someone Got To Eddie

IAN RANKIN

They paid me not to make mistakes. Not that I ever made mistakes, that's why I was the man for the job, and they knew it. I was cautious and thorough, discreet and tight-lipped. Besides, I had other qualities which they found quite indispensable.

He was lying on the living-room floor. He'd fallen on his back, head coming to rest against the front of a leather armchair. It looked like it might be one of those reclining armchairs, you know, with a footrest and everything, an expensive item. The TV was expensive too, but then I don't suppose he ever went out much. They don't go out much, people like him. They stay indoors where it's safe. The irony of this being, of course, that they become prisoners in their own homes, prisoners all their lives.

He was still alive, breathing badly through his wet nose, his hand sort of stroking the front of his T-shirt. There was a big damp stain there, and it was all his. His hair had gone grey in the past year or so, and he'd put on a lot of weight. His eyes were dark-ringed from too many late nights.

'Please,' he whispered. 'Please.'

But I was busy. I didn't like interruptions. So I stabbed him again, just the twice, probably in his abdomen. Not deep wounds, just enough to give him the hint. His head slouched floorwards, tiny moaning sounds dribbling from his lips. They didn't want a quick painless death. It was in the contract. They wanted something that was both revenge on him and a message to others. Oh yes, I was the man for the job all right.

I was wearing overalls and gardening gloves and a pair of old training shoes with the heel coming away from one of them. Disposable, the lot of it, fit for little more than a bonfire. So I didn't mind stepping in the small pools of blood. In fact, that was part of the plan. I'd put the overalls and gloves and trainers on in his bathroom. This was just prior to stabbing him, of course. He'd been surprised to see me coming out of the bathroom looking like that. But of course it hadn't dawned on him till too late. Always watch your back, they say. But the advice I'd give is: always watch your *front*. It's the guy you're shaking hands with, the guy you're talking to who will turn out to be your enemy. There aren't monsters hiding in the bushes. All they hide behind are smiles.

(Don't worry about me, I always ramble on when I'm nervous.)

I got to work. First, I dropped the knife into a plastic bag and placed the package in my holdall. I might need it again, but at this stage I doubted it. He wasn't talking any more. Instead, his mouth opened and closed soundlessly, like a fish in an unaerated aquarium. You hardly knew he was in pain. Pain and shock. His body was going to wave a white flag soon, but the brain was taking a little time to understand. It thought it was still in the foxhole, head down and safe.

Aquariums and foxholes. Funny the things that go through your mind at a time like this. I suppose it's to shut out the reality of the situation. Never mind virtual reality, this was visceral reality.

I was keeping the gloves on for the moment. I walked around the living-room, deciding how the place should look. There was a table in the corner with some bottles and glasses on it. They could go for a start. Hold on though, some music first. There had been no indications that any neighbours were at home – I'd watched outside for an hour, and since coming in had been listening for sounds – but all the same. Besides, music soothed the soul, didn't it?

'What do you fancy?' I asked him. He had a cheap little midi-system and a couple of dozen CDs and tapes. I switched the system on and opened the drawer of the CD player, slipped in a disc, closed the drawer and pressed 'play'. 'A bit of Mantovani,' I said needlessly as strings swelled from the small speakers. It was a version of the Beatles' 'Yesterday'. Good song that. I turned the volume up a bit, played with the treble and bass, then went back to the corner table and swept all the stuff on to the floor. Not with a flourish or anything, just a casual brush of the forearm. A couple of wine glasses broke, nothing else. And it didn't make much noise either. It looked good, though.

The sofa was next. I thought for a moment, then pulled a couple of the cushions off, letting them drop to the floor. It wasn't much, was it? But the room was looking cluttered now, what with the bottles and cushions and the body.

He wasn't watching any of this, though he could probably hear it. His eyes were staring at the carpet below him. It had been light blue in colour, but was now looking like someone had dropped a mug of tea (no milk) on it. An interesting effect. In the films blood always looks like paint. Yes, but it depends what you mix it with, doesn't it? Red and blue would seem to make tea (no milk). Suddenly I felt thirsty. And I needed the toilet too. There was milk in the fridge. I poured half a carton down my throat and was putting it back in the fridge when I thought, What the hell. I tossed it towards the sink. Milk splattered the work surfaces and poured on to the linoleum floor. I left the fridge door open.

After visiting the toilet, I wandered back into the living-room, took the crowbar from my holdall, and left the house, closing the door after me. Checking that no one was around, I attacked the door jamb, splintering wood and forcing my way back inside. It didn't make any noise and looked pretty good. I closed the door as best I could, tipped the telephone table in the hall on to its side, and returned to the living-room. His face was on the floor now, deathly pale as you might imagine. In fact, he looked worse than a few of the corpses I've seen.

'Not long now,' I told him. I was all but done, but decided maybe I should take a recce upstairs. I opened his bedside cupboard. Inside a wooden box there was a wad of folded banknotes, tens and twenties. I slipped off the rubber band from around them, chucked it and the box on to the bed, and stuffed the money in my pocket. Let's call it a tip. It's not that I wasn't being paid enough, but I knew damned fine that if I didn't pocket it, some dozy young copper first on the scene would do just the same.

It was a pretty sad little room, this bedroom. There were porn mags on the floor, very few decent clothes in the wardrobe, a couple of empty whisky bottles under the bed along with an unused pack of vending-machine condoms. A transistor radio lying on a chair with some dirty laundry. No framed photos of family, no holiday souvenirs, no paintings on the walls.

He'd been on medication. There were four little bottles of pills on the bedside cabinet. Nerves, probably. Informers often suffer from nerves. It comes of waiting for that monster to jump out of the bushes at them. OK, so after they've given their evidence and 'Mr Big' (or more usually 'Mr Middling') has been locked away, they're given 'protection'. They get new identities, some cash up front, a roof over their heads, even a job. All this comes to pass. But they've got to leave the only life they've known. No contact with friends or family. This guy downstairs, whose name was Eddie, by the way, his wife left him. A lot of the wives do. Sad, eh? And these informers, they do all this just to save themselves from a few years in the clink.

The police are good at spotting the weak ones, the ones who might just turn. They work on them, exaggerating the sentence they're going to get, exaggerating the prizes awaiting under the witness protection scheme. ('The Witless Protection Scheme', I've heard it called.) It's all psychology and bullshit, but it sometimes works. Often though a jury will throw the evidence out anyway. The defence counsel's line is always the same: can you rely on the evidence of a man who himself is so heavily implicated in these serious crimes, and who is giving evidence solely to save his own skin?

Like I say, sometimes it works and sometimes it doesn't. I went downstairs and crouched over the body. It *was* a body now, no question of that. Well, I'd let it cool for a little while. Ten or fifteen minutes. Now that I thought of it, I'd broken open the door too soon. Someone might come along and notice. A slight error, but an error all the same. Too late for regrets though. The course was set now, so I went back to the fridge and lifted out what was left of a roast chicken. There was a leg with some meat on it, so I chewed that for a while, standing in the living-room watching through the net curtains as the sun broke from behind some cloud. Want to know what blood smells like? It smells like cold chicken grease. I stuffed the bones into the kitchen bin. I'd stripped them clean. I didn't want to leave behind any teethmarks, anything the forensic scientists could begin to work with. Not that anyone would be working too hard on this case. People like me, we're seldom caught. After a hit, we just melt into the background. We're as ordinary as you are. I don't mean that we *seem* to be ordinary, that we make a show of looking ordinary, I mean we *are* ordinary. These hit men and assassins you read about in novels, they go around all day and all night like Arnold Schwarzenegger. But in real life that would get them noticed. The last thing you want to be if you're like me is noticed. You want to blend into the scenery.

I'm running on again, aren't I? It was just about time. A final lingering inspection. Another visit to the toilet. I checked myself in the bathroom mirror. I looked fine. I took my clothes back out of the holdall and stripped off the overalls, gloves, trainers. My shoes were black brogues with new soles and heels. I checked myself again in the mirror as I knotted my tie and put on my jacket. No tell-tale flecks of blood on my cheeks or forehead. I washed my hands without using soap (the fragrance might be identifiable) and dried them on toilet paper, which I flushed away. I zipped the holdall shut, picked it up, and walked back through the living-room ('Ciao, Eddie'), into the small hallway, and out of the house.

Potentially, this was the most dangerous part of the whole job. As I walked down the path, I was pretty well hidden from view by the hedge, the hedge Eddie must have considered a comfort, a barrier between him and prying eyes. At the pavement, I didn't pause. There was no one around anyway, no one at all, as I walked briskly around the corner to where I'd parked my car, locked the holdall in the boot, and started the engine.

Later that afternoon I returned to the house. I didn't park on a side street this time. I drew right up to the kerb in front of the hedge. Well, as close as I could get anyway. There were still no signs of activity in any of the other houses. Either the neighbours kept themselves to themselves or else they all had places to be. I gave my engine a final loud rev before turning it off, and slammed the car door noisily after me. I was wearing a black leather jacket and cream chinos rather than a suit, and different shoes, plain brown rather than the black brogues. Just in case someone *had* seen me. Often, witnesses saw the clothes, not the face. The real professionals didn't bother with hair dyes, false moustaches and the like. They just wore clothes they wouldn't normally wear.

I walked slowly up the path, studying the terrain either side, then stopped at the door, examining the splintered jamb. The door was closed, but suddenly swung open from inside. Two men looked at me. I stood aside to let them pass, and walked into the house. The telephone table in the hall was still lying on its side, the phone beside it (though someone had replaced the receiver).

The body was where I'd left it. He'd been so surprised to see me at his door. Not wary, just surprised. Visiting the area, I'd explained, thought I'd look in. He'd led me into the living-room, and I'd asked to use his loo. Maybe he wondered why I took the holdall with me. Maybe he didn't. There could have been anything in it, after all. Anything.

There were two men crouching over the body now, and more men in the bathroom, the kitchen, walking around upstairs. Nobody was saying anything much. You can appreciate why. One of the men stood up and stared at me. I was surveying the scene. Bottles and glasses everywhere, cushions where I'd dropped them, a carpet patterned with blood.

'What's happened here?' I asked unnecessarily.

'Well, sir.' The Detective Constable smiled a rueful smile. 'Looks like someone got to Eddie.'

Too Many Crooks

DONALD E WESTLAKE

'Did you hear something?' Dortmunder whispered.

'The wind,' Kelp said.

Dortmunder twisted around in his seated position and deliberately shone the flashlight in the kneeling Kelp's eyes. 'What wind? We're in a tunnel.'

'There's underground rivers,' Kelp said, squinting, 'so maybe there's underground winds. Are you through the wall there?'

'Two more whacks,' Dortmunder told him. Relenting, he aimed the flashlight past Kelp back down the empty tunnel, a meandering, messy gullet, most of it less than three feet in diameter, wriggling its way through rocks and rubble and ancient middens, traversing forty tough feet from the rear of the basement of the out-of-business shoe store to the wall of the bank on the corner. According to the maps Dortmunder had gotten from the water department by claiming to be with the sewer department, and the maps he'd gotten from the sewer department by claiming to be with the water department, just the other side of this wall was the bank's main vault. Two more whacks and this large, irregular square of concrete that Dortmunder and Kelp had been scoring and scratching at for some time now would at last fall away on to the floor inside and there would be the vault.

Dortmunder gave it a whack.

Dortmunder gave it another whack.

The block of concrete fell on to the floor of the vault. 'Oh, thank God,' somebody said.

What? Reluctant but unable to stop himself, Dortmunder dropped sledge and flashlight and leant his head through the hole in the wall and looked around.

It was the vault, all right. And it was full of people.

A man in a suit stuck his hand out and grabbed Dortmunder's and shook it while pulling him through the hole and on into the vault. 'Great work, officer,' he said. 'The robbers are outside.'

Dortmunder had thought he and Kelp were the robbers. 'They are?'

A round-faced woman in pants and a Buster Brown collar said, 'Five of them. With machine guns.'

'Machine guns,' Dortmunder said.

A delivery kid wearing a moustache and an apron and carrying a flat cardboard carton containing four coffees, two decafs and a tea said, 'We all hostages, mon. I gonna get fired.'

'How many of you are there?' the man in the suit asked, looking past Dortmunder at Kelp's nervously smiling face.

'Just the two,' Dortmunder said, and watched helplessly as willing hands dragged Kelp through the hole and set him on his feet in the vault. It was really very full of hostages.

'I'm Kearney,' the man in the suit said, 'I'm the bank manager, and I can't tell you how glad I am to see you.'

Which was the first time any bank manager had said *that* to Dortmunder, who said, 'Uh-huh, uh-huh,' and nodded, and then said, 'I'm, uh, Officer Diddums, and this is Officer, uh, Kelly.'

Kearney, the bank manager, frowned. 'Diddums, did you say?'

Dortmunder was furious with himself. Why did I call myself Diddums? Well, I didn't know I was going to need an alias inside a bank vault, did I? Aloud, he said, 'Uh-huh. Diddums. It's Welsh.'

'Ah,' said Kearney. Then he frowned again and said, 'You people aren't even armed.'

'Well, no,' Dortmunder said. 'We're the, uh, the hostage-rescue team; we don't want any shots fired, increase the risk for you, uh, civilians.'

'Very shrewd,' Kearney agreed.

Kelp, his eyes kind of glassy and his smile kind of fixed, said, 'Well, folks, maybe we should leave here now, single file, just make your way in an orderly fashion through – '

'They're coming!' hissed a stylish woman over by the vault door.

Everybody moved. It was amazing; everybody shifted at once. Some people moved to hide the new hole in the wall, some people moved to get farther away from the vault door and some people moved to get behind Dortmunder, who suddenly found himself the nearest person in the vault to that big, round, heavy metal door, which was easing massively and silently open.

It stopped halfway, and three men came in. They wore black ski masks and black leather jackets and black work pants and black shoes. They carried Uzi submachine guns at high port. Their eyes looked cold and hard, and their hands fidgeted on the metal of the guns, and their feet danced nervously, even when they were standing still. They looked as though anything at all might make them over-react.

'Shut up!' one of them yelled, though nobody'd been talking. He glared around at his guests and said, 'Gotta have somebody to stand out front, see can the cops be trusted.' His eye, as Dortmunder had known it would, lit on Dortmunder. 'You,' he said.

'Uh-huh,' Dortmunder said.

'What's your name?'

Everybody in the vault had already heard him say it, so what choice did he have? 'Diddums,' Dortmunder said.

The robber glared at Dortmunder through his ski mask. 'Diddums?'

'It's Welsh,' Dortmunder explained.

'Ah,' the robber said, and nodded. He gestured with the Uzi. 'Outside, Diddums.'

Dortmunder stepped forward, glancing back over his shoulder at all the people looking at him, knowing every goddamn one of them was glad he wasn't him – even Kelp, back there pretending to be four feet tall – and then Dortmunder stepped through the vault door, surrounded by all those nervous maniacs with machine guns, and went with them down a corridor flanked by desks and through a doorway to the main part of the bank, which was a mess.

The time at the moment, as the clock high on the wide wall confirmed, was 5.15 in the afternoon. Everybody who worked at the bank should have gone home by now; that was the theory Dortmunder had been operating from. What must have happened was, just before closing time at three o'clock (Dortmunder and Kelp being already then in the tunnel, working hard, knowing nothing of events on the surface of the planet), these gaudy showboats had come into the bank waving their machine guns around.

And not just waving them, either. Lines of ragged punctures had been drawn across the walls and the Lucite upper panel of the tellers' counter, like connect-the-dot puzzles. Wastebaskets and a potted Ficus had been overturned, but fortunately, there were no bodies lying around; none Dortmunder could see, anyway. The big plate-glass front windows had been shot out, and two more of the black-clad robbers were crouched down, one behind the OUR LOW LOAN RATES poster and the other behind the OUR HIGH INDIVIDUAL RETIREMENT ACCOUNT RATES poster, staring out at the street, from which came the sound of somebody talking loudly but indistinctly through a bullhorn.

So what must have happened, they'd come in just before three, waving their guns, figuring a quick in and out, and some brown-nose employee looking for advancement triggered the alarm, and now they had a stalemate hostage situation on their hands; and, of course, everybody in the world by now has seen *Dog Day Afternoon* and therefore knows that if the police get the drop on a robber in circumstances such as these circumstances right here, they'll immediately shoot him dead, so now hostage negotiation is trickier than ever. This isn't what I had in mind when I came to the bank, Dortmunder thought.

The boss robber prodded him along with the barrel of his Uzi, saying, 'What's your first name, Diddums?'

Please don't say Dan, Dortmunder begged himself. Please, please, somehow, anyhow, manage not to say Dan. His mouth opened. 'John,' he heard himself say, his brain having turned desperately in this emergency to that last resort, the truth, and he got weak-kneed with relief.

'OK, John, don't faint on me,' the robber said. 'This is very simple what you got to do here. The cops say they want to talk, just talk, nobody gets hurt. Fine. So you're gonna step out in front of the bank and see do the cops shoot you.'

'Ah,' Dortmunder said.

'No time like the present, huh, John?' the robber said, and poked him with the Uzi again.

'That kind of hurts,' Dortmunder said.

'I apologise,' the robber said, hard-eyed. 'Out.'

One of the other robbers, eyes red with strain inside the black ski mask, leaned close to Dortmunder and yelled, 'You wanna shot in the foot first? You wanna *crawl* out there?'

'I'm going,' Dortmunder told him. 'See? Here I go.'

The first robber, the comparatively calm one, said, 'You go as far as the sidewalk, that's all. You take one step off the kerb, we blow your head off.'

'Got it,' Dortmunder assured him, and crunched across broken glass to the sagging-open door and looked out. Across the street was parked a line of buses, police cars, police trucks, all in blue and white with red gumdrops on top, and behind them moved a seething mass of armed cops. 'Uh,' Dortmunder said. Turning back to the comparatively calm robber, he said, 'You wouldn't happen to have a white flag or anything like that, would you?'

The robber pressed the point of the Uzi to Dortmunder's side. 'Out,' he said.

'Right,' Dortmunder said. He faced front, put his hands way up in the air and stepped outside.

What a *lot* of attention he got. From behind all those blue-and-whites on the other side of the street, tense faces stared. On the rooftops of the red-brick tenements, in this neighbourhood deep in the residential heart of Queens, sharpshooters began to familiarise themselves through their telescopic sights with the contours of Dortmunder's furrowed brow. To left and right, the ends of the block were sealed off with buses parked nose to tailpipe, past which ambulances and jumpy white-coated medics could be seen. Everywhere, rifles and pistols jittered in nervous fingers. Adrenalin ran in the gutters.

'I'm not with *them*!' Dortmunder shouted, edging across the sidewalk, arms upraised, hoping this announcement wouldn't upset the other bunch of armed hysterics behind him. For all he knew, they had a problem with rejection.

However, nothing happened behind him, and what happened out front was that a bullhorn appeared, resting on a police-car roof, and roared at him, '*You a hostage?*'

'I sure am!' yelled Dortmunder.

'*What's your name?*'

Oh, not again, thought Dortmunder, but there was nothing for it. 'Diddums,' he said.

'*What?*'

'*Diddums!*'

A brief pause: '*Diddums?*'

'*It's Welsh!*'

'Ah.'

There was a little pause while whoever was operating the bullhorn conferred with his compatriots, and then the bullhorn said, '*What's the situation in there?*'

What kind of question was that? 'Well, uh,' Dortmunder said, and remembered to speak more loudly, and called, 'kind of tense, actually.'

'*Any of the hostages been harmed?*'

'Oh-uh. No. Definitely not. This is a . . . this is a . . . non-violent confrontation.' Dortmunder fervently hoped to establish that idea in everybody's mind, particularly if he were going to be out there in the middle much longer.

'*Any change in the situation?*'

Change? 'Well,' Dortmunder answered, 'I haven't been in there that long, but it seems like – '

'*Not that long? What's the matter with you, Diddums? You've been in that bank over two hours now!*'

'Oh, yeah!' Forgetting, Dortmunder lowered his arms and stepped forward to the kerb. 'That's right!' he called. 'Two hours! *More* than two hours! Been in there a long time!'

'*Step out here away from the bank!*'

Dortmunder looked down and saw his toes hanging ten over the edge of the kerb. Stepping back at a brisk pace, he called, 'I'm not supposed to do that!'

'*Listen, Diddums, I've got a lot of tense men and women over here, I'm telling you, step away from the bank!*'

'The fellas inside,' Dortmunder explained, 'they don't want me to step off the kerb. They said they'd, uh, well, they just don't want me to do it.'

'Psst! Hey, Diddums!'

Dortmunder paid no attention to the voice calling from behind him. He was concentrating too hard on what was happening right now out front. Also, he wasn't that used to the new name yet.

'Diddums!'

'*Maybe you better put your hands up again.*'

'Oh, yeah!' Dortmunder's arms shot up like pistons blowing through an engine block. 'There they are!'

'Diddums, goddamn it, do I have to *shoot* you to get you to pay attention?'

Arms dropping, Dortmunder spun around. 'Sorry! I wasn't – I was – Here I am!'

'*Get those goddamn hands up!*'

Dortmunder turned sideways, arms up so high his sides hurt. Peering sidelong to his right, he called to the crowd across the street, 'Sirs, they're talking to me inside now.' Then he peered sidelong to his left, saw the comparatively calm robber crouched beside the broken doorframe and looking less calm than before, and he said, 'Here I am.'

'We're gonna give them our demands now,' the robber said. 'Through you.'

'That's fine,' Dortmunder said. 'That's great. Only, you know, how come you don't do it on the phone? I mean, the way it's normally – '

The red-eyed robber, heedless of exposure to the sharpshooters across the street, shouldered furiously past the comparatively calm robber, who tried to restrain him as he yelled at Dortmunder, 'You're rubbing it in, are ya? OK, I made a mistake! I got excited and I shot up the switchboard! You want me to get excited again?'

'No, no!' Dortmunder cried, trying to hold his hands straight up in the air and defensively in front of his body at the same time. 'I forgot! I just forgot!'

The other robbers all clustered around to grab the red-eyed robber, who seemed to be trying to point his Uzi in Dortmunder's direction as he yelled, 'I did it in front of everybody! I humiliated myself in front of everybody! And now you're making fun of me!'

'I *forgot*! I'm sorry!'

'You can't forget that! Nobody's ever gonna forget that!'

The three remaining robbers dragged the red-eyed robber back away from the doorway, talking to him, trying to soothe him, leaving Dortmunder and the comparatively calm robber to continue their conversation. 'I'm sorry,' Dortmunder said. 'I just forgot. I've been kind of distracted lately. Recently.'

'You're playing with fire here, Diddums,' the robber said. 'Now tell them they're gonna get our demands.'

Dortmunder nodded, and turned his head the other way, and yelled, 'They're gonna tell you their demands now. I mean, *I'm* gonna tell you their demands. *Their* demands. Not *my* demands. *Their* de – '

'*We're willing to listen, Diddums, only so long as none of the hostages get hurt.*'

'That's good!' Dortmunder agreed, and turned his head the other way to tell the robber, 'That's reasonable, you know, that's sensible, that's a very good thing they're saying.'

'Shut up,' the robber said.

'Right,' Dortmunder said.

The robber said, 'First, we want the riflemen off the roofs.'

'Oh, so do I,' Dortmunder told him, and turned to shout, 'They want the riflemen off the roofs!'

'*What else?*'

'What else?'

'And we want them to unblock that end of the street, the – what is it? – the north end.'

Dortmunder frowned straight ahead at the buses blocking the intersection. 'Isn't that east?' he asked.

'Whatever it is,' the robber said, getting impatient. 'That end down there to the left.'

'OK.' Dortmunder turned his head and yelled, 'They want you to unblock the east end of the street!' Since his hands were way up in the sky somewhere, he pointed with his chin.

'*Isn't that north?*'

'I knew it was,' the robber said.

'Yeah, I guess so,' Dortmunder called. 'That end down there to the left.'

'*The right, you mean.*'

'Yeah, that's right. Your right, my left. *Their* left.'

'*What else?*'

Dortmunder sighed, and turned his head. 'What else?'

The robber glared at him. 'I can *hear* the bullhorn, Diddums. I can *hear* him say "What else?" You don't have to repeat everything he says. No more translations.'

'Right,' Dortmunder said. 'Gotcha. No more translations.'

'We'll want a car,' the robber told him. 'A station wagon. We're gonna take three hostages with us, so we want a big station wagon. And nobody follows us.'

'Gee,' Dortmunder said dubiously, 'are you sure?'

The robber stared. 'Am I *sure?*'

'Well, you know what they'll do,' Dortmunder told him, lowering his voice so the other team across the street couldn't hear him. 'What they do in these situations, they fix a little radio transmitter under the car, so then they don't have to *follow* you, exactly, but they know where you are.'

Impatient again, the robber said, 'So you'll tell them not to do that. No radio transmitters, or we kill the hostages.'

'Well, I suppose,' Dortmunder said doubtfully.

'What's wrong *now?*' the robber demanded. 'You're too goddamn *picky*, Diddums; you're just the messenger here. You think you know my job better than I do?'

I know I do, Dortmunder thought, but it didn't seem a judicious thing to say aloud, so instead, he explained, 'I just want things to go smooth, that's all. I just don't want bloodshed. And I was thinking, the New York City police, you know, well, they've got helicopters.'

'Damn,' the robber said. He crouched low to the littered floor, behind the broken doorframe, and brooded about his situation. Then he looked up at Dortmunder, and said, 'OK, Diddums, you're so smart. What *should* we do?'

Dortmunder blinked. 'You want *me* to figure out your getaway?'

'Put yourself in our position,' the robber suggested. 'Think about it.'

Dortmunder nodded. Hands in the air, he gazed at the blocked intersection and put himself in the robbers' position. 'Hoo, boy,' he said. 'You're in a real mess.'

'We *know* that, Diddums.'

'Well,' Dortmunder said, 'I tell you what maybe you could do. You make them give you one of those buses they've got down there blocking the street. They give you one of those buses right now, then you know they haven't had time to put anything cute in it, like time-release tear-gas grenades or anyth – '

'Oh, my God,' the robber said. His black ski mask seemed to have paled slightly.

'Then you take *all* the hostages,' Dortmunder told him. 'Everybody goes in the bus, and one of you people drives, and you go somewhere real crowded, like Times Square, say, and then you stop and make all the hostages get out and run.'

'Yeah?' the robber said. 'What good does that do us?'

'Well,' Dortmunder said, 'you drop the ski masks and the leather jackets and the guns, and *you* run, too. Twenty, thirty people all running away from the bus in different directions, in the middle of Times Square in rush hour, everybody losing themselves in the crowd. It might work.'

'Jeez, it might,' the robber said. 'OK, go ahead and – What?'

'What?' Dortmunder echoed. He strained to look leftward, past the vertical column of his left arm. The boss robber was in excited conversation with one of his pals; not the red-eyed maniac, a different one. The boss robber shook his head and said, 'Damn!' Then he looked up at Dortmunder. 'Come back in here, Diddums,' he said.

Dortmunder said, 'But don't you want me to – '

'Come back in here!'

'Oh,' Dortmunder said. 'Uh, I better tell them over there that I'm gonna move.'

'Make it fast,' the robber told him. 'Don't mess with me, Diddums. I'm in a bad mood right now.'

'OK.' Turning his head the other way, hating it that his back was toward this badmooded robber for even a second, Dortmunder called, 'They want me to go back into the bank now. Just for a minute.' Hands still up, he edged sideways across the sidewalk and through the gaping doorway, where the robbers laid hands on him and flung him back deeper into the bank.

He nearly lost his balance but saved himself against the sideways-lying pot of the tipped-over ficus. When he turned around, all five of the robbers were lined up looking at him, their expressions intent, focused, almost hungry, like a row of cats looking in a fish-store window. 'Oh,' Dortmunder said.

'He's it now,' one the robbers said.

Another robber said, 'But *they* don't know it.'

A third robber said, 'They will soon.'

'They'll know it when nobody gets on the bus,' the boss robber said, and shook his head at Dortmunder. 'Sorry, Diddums. Your idea doesn't work any more.'

Dortmunder had to keep reminding himself that he wasn't actually *part* of this string. 'How come?' he asked.

Disgusted, one of the other robbers said, 'The rest of the hostages got away, that's how come.'

Wide-eyed, Dortmunder spoke without thinking: 'The tunnel!'

All of a sudden, it got very quiet in the bank. The robbers were now looking at him like cats looking at a fish with no window in the way. 'The tunnel?' repeated the boss robber slowly. 'You *know* about the tunnel?'

'Well, kind of,' Dortmunder admitted. 'I mean, the guys digging it, they got there just before you came and took me away.'

'And you never mentioned it.'

'Well,' Dortmunder said, very uncomfortable. 'I didn't feel like I should.'

The red-eyed maniac lunged forward, waving that submachine gun again, yelling, '*You're* the guy with the tunnel! It's your tunnel!' And he pointed the shaking barrel of the Uzi at Dortmunder's nose.

'Easy, easy!' the boss robber yelled. 'This is our only hostage; don't use him up!'

The red-eyed maniac reluctantly lowered the Uzi, but he turned to the others and announced, '*Nobody's* gonna forget when I shot up the switchboard. Nobody's *ever* gonna forget that. He wasn't *here!*'

All of the robbers thought that over. Meantime, Dortmunder was thinking about his own position. He might be a hostage, but he wasn't your normal hostage, because he was also a guy who had just dug a tunnel to a bank vault, and there were maybe thirty eyeball witnesses who could identify him. So it wasn't enough to get away from these bank robbers; he was also going to have to get away from the police. Several thousand police.

So did that mean he was locked to these second-rate smash-and-grabbers? Was his own future really dependent on *their* getting out of this hole? Bad news, if true. Left to their own devices, these people couldn't escape from a merry-go-round.

Dortmunder sighed. 'OK,' he said. 'The first thing we have to do is – '

'We?' the boss robber said. 'Since when are you in this?'

'Since you dragged me in,' Dortmunder told him. 'And the first thing we have to do is – '

The red-eyed maniac lunged at him again with the Uzi, shouting, 'Don't you tell us what to do! *We* know what to do!'

'I'm your only hostage,' Dortmunder reminded him. 'Don't use me up. Also, now that I've seen you people in action, I'm your only hope of getting out of here. So this time, listen to me. The first thing we have to do is close and lock the vault door.'

One of the robbers gave a scornful laugh. 'The hostages are *gone*,' he said. 'Didn't you hear that part? Lock the vault door after the hostages are gone. Isn't that some kind of old saying?' And he laughed and laughed.

Dortmunder looked at him. 'It's a two-way tunnel,' he said quietly.

The robbers stared at him. Then they all turned and ran toward the back of the bank. They *all* did.

They're too excitable for this line of work, Dortmunder thought as he walked briskly towards the front of the bank. *Clang* went the vault door, far behind him, and Dortmunder stepped through the broken doorway and out again to the sidewalk, remembering to stick his arms straight up in the air as he did.

'Hi!' he yelled, sticking his face well out, displaying it for all the sharpshooters to get a really *good* look at it. 'Hi, it's me again! Diddums! Welsh!'

'Diddums!' screamed an enraged voice from deep within the bank. 'Come back here!'

Oh, no. Ignoring that, moving steadily but without panic, arms up, face forward, eyes wide, Dortmunder angled leftward across the sidewalk, shouting, 'I'm coming out again! And I'm *escaping*!' And he dropped his arms, tucked his elbows in and ran hell for leather toward those blocking buses.

Gunfire encouraged him: sudden bursts behind him of *ddrrritt*, *ddrrritt*, and then *kopp-kopp-kopp*, and then a whole symphony of *fooms* and *thug-thugs* and *padapows*. Dortmunder's toes, turning into high-tension steel springs, kept him bounding through the air like the Wright brothers' first aeroplane, swooping and plunging down the middle of the street, that wall of buses getting closer and closer.

'Here! In here!' Uniformed cops appeared on both sidewalks, waving to him, offering sanctuary in the form of open doorways and police vehicles to crouch behind, but Dortmunder was *escaping*. From everything.

The buses. He launched himself through the air, hit the blacktop hard and rolled under the nearest bus. Roll, roll, roll, hitting his head and elbows and knees and ears and nose and various other parts of his body against any number of hard, dirty objects, and then he was past the bus and on his feet, staggering, staring at a lot of goggle-eyed medics hanging around beside their ambulances, who just stood there and gawked back.

Dortmunder turned left. *Medics* weren't going to chase him; their franchise didn't include healthy bodies running down the street. The cops couldn't chase him until they'd moved their buses out of the way. Dortmunder took off like the last of the dodos, flapping his arms, wishing he knew how to fly.

The out-of-business shoe store, the other terminus of the tunnel, passed on his left. The getaway car they'd parked in front of it was long gone, of course. Dortmunder kept thudding on, on, on.

Three blocks later, a gypsy cab committed a crime by picking him up even though he hadn't phoned the dispatcher first; in the city of New York, only licensed medallion taxis are permitted to pick up customers who hail them on the street. Dortmunder, panting like a Saint Bernard on the lumpy back seat, decided not to turn the guy in.

His faithful companion May came out of the living-room when Dortmunder opened the front door of his apartment and stepped into his hall. '*There* you are!' she said. 'Thank goodness. It's all over the radio *and* the television.'

'I may never leave the house again,' Dortmunder told her. 'If Andy

Kelp ever calls, says he's got this great job, easy, piece of cake, I'll just tell him I've retired.'

'Andy's here,' May said. 'In the living-room. You want a beer?'

'Yes,' Dortmunder said simply.

May went away to the kitchen and Dortmunder limped into the living-room, where Kelp was seated on the sofa holding a can of beer and looking happy. On the coffee table in front of him was a mountain of money.

Dortmunder stared. 'What's *that?*'

Kelp grinned and shook his head. 'It's been too long since we scored, John,' he said. 'You don't even recognise the stuff any more. This is money.'

'But – from the vault? How?'

'After you were taken away by those other guys – they were caught, by the way,' Kelp interrupted himself, 'without loss of life - anyway, I told everybody in the vault there, the way to keep the money safe from the robbers was we'd all carry it out with us. So we did. And then I decided what we should do is put it all in the trunk of my unmarked police car in front of the shoe store, so I could drive it to the precinct for safe keeping while they all went home to rest from their ordeal.'

Dortmunder looked at his friend. He said, 'You got the hostages to carry the money from the vault.'

'And put it in our car,' Kelp said. 'Yeah, that's what I did.'

May came in and handed Dortmunder a beer. He drank deep, and Kelp said, 'They're looking for you, of course. Under that other name.'

May said, 'That's the one thing I don't understand. Diddums?'

'It's Welsh,' Dortmunder told her. Then he smiled upon the mountain of money on the coffee table. 'It's not a bad name,' he decided. 'I may keep it.'

The Writing on the Wall

VAL MCDERMID

I've never written anything on a toilet wall before, but I don't know what else to do. Please help me. My boyfriend is violent towards me. He hits me and I don't know where to turn.

Kick the bastard where it hurts. Give him a taste of his own medicine.

Get out of the relationship now before he does you serious injury. Battering men only batter with our consent.

I can't believe these responses. I asked for help, not a lecture. I love him, don't you realise that? He was raped and battered as a child. Are we just supposed to ignore damaged people?

If you don't get out of the relationship, then you're going to end up another one of the damaged people. And who will help you then?

Ask your friends for their support in dealing with him. When his violence begins, leave the house and go and stay with a friend.

I can't walk out on him. He needs me. And I can't tell my friends because I'm too ashamed to admit to them that I'm in a relationship with a man who batters me.

Sooner or later, they're going to notice, and then they're going to feel angry that you've excluded them from something so important.

How come you're the one who's ashamed, not him? He's the one dishing out the violence, after all.

Like I said at the start, fight back. Let him know what being hurt feels like.

He knows what being hurt feels like. He spent his childhood being hurt. And he is ashamed of his violence. He hates himself for his behaviour, and he's always really sorry afterwards.

Well, whoopee shit! That must really help your bruises!

This is the first time I've been in this loo, and I can't believe how unsupportive you're all being to this woman! Sister, there is counselling available. You deserve help; there's a number for the confidential helpline in the student handbook. Use it, please.

It's not just you that needs counselling. Tell your boyfriend that unless he comes for counselling with you, you will leave him. If he refuses, then you know his apologies aren't worth a toss.

Leave him; tell him you'll only take him back once he has had counselling and learned to deal with his problem in a way that doesn't include violence. Anything else is a betrayal of all the other women who get battered every day.

Thanks for the suggestion. I've phoned the helpline and we're both going to meet the counsellor next week.

> *I still say leave him till he's got himself sorted out. He's only going to end up resenting you for making him go through all this shit.*

I'm glad you've taken this step forward; let us know how you go on.

Sorry it's taken me so long to get back to you all. My lectures were moved out of this building for a couple of weeks because of the ceiling collapse. We've had three joint counselling sessions so far, and I really feel that things are getting better!

You mean he only batters you once a week instead of every night?

> *Now he's made the first step, you can tell him you're going to move out till the course of counselling has finished. You owe it to yourself and to the other victimised women out there to show this batterer that he is no longer in a position of control and power over you.*

Well done. Good luck.

I'm not moving out on him. I'm going to stick with him because he's trying so hard. He's really making the effort to deal with his anger and to resolve the conflicts that make him lash out at me. I love him, everybody seems to keep forgetting that. If you love somebody, you want to help them get better, not abandon them because they're not perfect.

Answer the question; is he still hitting you?

Oh for God's sake, leave her alone. Can't you see she's having enough of a struggle helping the guy she loves without having the holier-than-thou tendency on her back?

Save us from the bleeding hearts. If he's still hitting her, she's still collaborating with his oppressive behaviour. She should walk away while she can still walk.

So where's she supposed to go? A women's refuge packed with damaged kids and mothers isn't exactly the ideal place to study, is it?

Anywhere's got to be better than a place where you get hurt constantly.

And you think battering someone is the only way to hurt them? Grow up!

He hasn't hit me for over a week now. He's made a real breakthrough. He has contacted his mother for the first time in three years and confronted her with the abuse he experienced from his stepfather. He says he feels like he's released so much pressure just by telling her about it.

Surprise, surprise. Now he's found a woman to blame, he's going to be all right.

Yeah, how come he hasn't confronted the abuser? How come he has to offload his guilt on his poor bloody mother who was probably battered too?

Leave him. You are perpetuating the circle of violence. He will see your forgiveness as condoning his behaviour. Break out. Now. If you stay, you are as bad as he is.

Don't listen to them. Stick with him. You are making progress. People *can* change.

Bollocks. Been there, done that, got the bruises. Men who abuse do it because they like it, not because of some behaviour pattern they can change as easily as giving up smoking. The only way to stop being the victim of abuse is to walk away.

He is making changes, I know he is. It's not easy for him, and sometimes it feels like he hates me because I'm the one who persuaded him to confront his problems. He's started to get really jealous and suspicious, even following me to lectures sometimes. He's convinced that because I suggested the counselling, I'm seeing some women's group that is trying to talk me into leaving him. If he only knew the truth! Are there any women out there who have been through this, who would be prepared to do some one-to-one counselling with me?

Ah, the power of the sisterhood of the toilet wall! He's right, though, isn't he? We are trying to make you see sense and get out of this destructive relationship.

Sounds like you're swapping one problem for another. The guy is major league bad news. Sometimes if you love people the best thing you can do for them is to leave them.

I know what you're going through. I'll meet you on Saturday morning on the Kelvin walkway under the Queen Margaret Bridge at 10.30. Come alone. Make sure he's not with you. I'll be watching. If you can't make this Saturday, I'll be there every week till you can.

From the *Scottish Sunday Dispatch*:

BODY FOUND IN
RIVER KELVIN

Police launched a murder hunt last night after the battered body of a woman student was found floating in the River Kelvin.

A woman walking her dog on the river walkway near Kelvinbridge spotted the body tangled in the roots of a tree.

Police revealed that the victim, who was fully dressed, had been beaten about the head before being thrown in the river.

The woman, whose name is not being released until her family can be contacted, was a second-year biochemistry student at Glasgow University.

Police are appealing for witnesses who may have seen the woman and her attacker on the Kelvin walkway upstream of Kelvinbridge earlier yesterday.

A spokeswoman for the Students' Union said last night, 'This is a terrible tragedy. When a woman gets killed in broad daylight in a public place, you start wondering if there is anywhere that is safe for us to be.'

Social Work

WILLIAM G TAPPLY

I was lugging a bag of groceries back to my apartment when I saw her outside Greg's door. I tried not to stare at her, but she was very beautiful. She was wearing a short dark skirt and a matching jacket. She held a briefcase in one hand. She was bent forward at the waist and her head was cocked as if she were trying to hear through his door, and she didn't seem to notice me when I walked past her.

She tapped at his door and I heard her say, 'Greg? I know you're in there. Come on, now. We've got to talk.'

As I was bracing the grocery bag on my knee to open my door, she said, 'Excuse me, sir?'

I looked at her and saw that she was smiling at me. 'Me?' I said.

'Yes. Do you know if Greg's in there?'

'He's probably at work,' I said.

'Do you live there? Next door to him, I mean?'

'Yes, ma'am.'

She frowned. 'Well, I think he's in there. But he refuses to talk to me.'

'Greg's a pretty shy guy.'

She came over to where I was standing and said, 'I'm Andrea Castella.' She held out her hand. 'I'm Greg's social worker, and I've heard that he's lost his job so I need to talk to him.'

I put down my grocery bag and took her hand. 'Will Hobbes,' I said. 'Usually if he's in there you can hear him.'

Her hand was small and warm and soft, and she held on to mine for just an instant after I thought our handshake had ended. Her head was tilted a little to the side and she was looking directly into my eyes as if I were saying something extremely important.

'He talks to himself a lot,' I added.

She nodded and smiled. 'Have you seen him lately, Mr Hobbes?'

'Now that you mention it,' I said, 'I don't recall bumping into him recently. For a while there I'd run into him lugging his bike down the stairs about the time I'd be getting back from work – I'm on the night shift, you see, and – '

'That's when he was working at the fish market,' she said. 'He lost that job. Now he's supposed to be working for a carpenter.'

'Sure,' I said. 'I've seen him. Older guy. Comes by in his pickup. Greg waits for him in the stairwell.' I shrugged. 'I guess I haven't seen Greg for a week or two.'

She shook her head. 'Poor Greg,' she said. She smiled at me again. 'Well, thanks, Mr Hobbes.'

'Anything I can do to help, Miss Castella,' I said, 'don't hesitate to ask. I'm right next door here.'

She smiled quickly over her shoulder as she turned to go back to Greg's door. She tapped on it daintily with the knuckle of her forefinger, and said, 'Come on, Greg. It's Miss Castella. We've got to talk.'

I went into my apartment. I put away my groceries, piled up the magazines and newspapers that were scattered around the floor, and cracked open the windows to let some fresh air in. A few minutes later I heard a soft knock at my door.

I opened it, and Miss Castella was standing there. 'I wonder if I could use your phone, Mr Hobbes,' she said.

'Oh, sure. Come on in.'

She stepped in and looked around. 'Nice apartment,' she said.

'Thanks.' I knew she was being polite, but I liked her for it. My apartment is one of thirty-six identical units in a square brick building.

Not much compared to the six-room ranch I had lived in with Cathy and Bobby – seven rooms, if you count the knotty pine rec room in the basement. 'Phone's in there, on the wall.' I gestured in the direction of the kitchen. 'Want some coffee?'

She hesitated, then smiled. 'Why, yes. That would be lovely.'

I led the way to the kitchen and plugged in the coffee-pot, then went back into the living-room while Miss Castella made her call. I tried not to eavesdrop, but she made no effort to hide what she was saying from me.

'It's Andrea,' she said. 'Greg refuses to talk to me. I spoke to McMurtry, and he's had to fire him . . . Yes, the same thing again . . . Well, naturally, if he isn't working we lose the subsidy and . . . Yes, I know. I'll keep trying, but you know Greg. Look, I've got a couple more calls to make. I'll check in with you this afternoon.'

She came into the living-room, smiled quickly at me, rolled her eyes, sighed deeply, and sat on the sofa. 'Poor Greg,' she said.

'You like cream?'

'Pardon me?'

'In your coffee. Cream and sugar?'

'Just a little sugar, please.'

I poured two mugs full of coffee, spooned some sugar into Miss Castella's, and brought them back. She took the mug in both of her hands. 'Thanks a lot,' she said.

I took the chair across from the sofa.

She crossed her legs, and her skirt rode up her thigh. She tugged it down. 'How well do you know him?' she asked, peering at me over the rim of her coffee-mug.

'Greg?'

She nodded.

'I run into him now and then. I say "Hi" and he's always friendly. Doesn't say much. I don't suppose we've ever had a real conversation. He, um . . .'

'He's retarded,' she said abruptly. 'It's OK. You can say it.'

I nodded. 'I guess I knew that. But he seems like a nice guy, even so.

Quiet, shy. Keeps to himself. Oh, I hear him in there. He'll be singing or talking to himself. I mean, I assume it's to himself. I don't think he has much company.'

'No,' said Miss Castella, 'I don't think he ever has company.' She gazed up at the ceiling. 'I was so hoping this would work out.'

'He lost his job, huh?'

Her eyes came back to mine. She had fluffy black hair and a heart-shaped face with a small nose and a flowerbud mouth, and everything about her seemed tiny and delicate and perfectly formed. I tried hard to focus on her eyes, because she had kicked off her shoes and hitched her legs up under her so that she was sitting on them, and in that position she couldn't help exposing a length of soft pale thigh, even though she kept tugging at her skirt.

'I talked to his employer,' Miss Castella said. 'Greg's been a carpenter's helper. Minimum wage, but the Department subsidizes his pay as well as his rent. We try to get our clients out on their own. We figure if they're working, living independently, they feel productive and useful, and if we can give their self-esteem a boost – well, that's our job. We don't actually cure them. But we try to ease them back into the mainstream. As long as they can hold down a job, the subsidy continues.'

'But if they lose their job . . . '

She nodded. 'Then the subsidy is rescinded.'

'And then . . . ?'

'It's back to the home, I'm afraid.'

'Aw.'

'Well, Greg's lucky. Some of them are just thrown out on the streets, you know.'

'That's a bummer,' I said.

'So,' she said after taking a sip of her coffee, 'what about you, Mr Hobbes? You mentioned you worked a night shift.'

I nodded. 'At the Quik-Stop. It's a convenience store.'

'How interesting.'

I looked for sarcasm in her face, but saw none. 'I used to sell major applicances at Sears, before . . .'

She smiled softly. 'What happened?'

I shrugged. 'That was before my divorce. My wife – Cathy – she, um, she kicked me out. I've got a boy, my son. Bobby. He's three.'

Miss Castella had dropped her chin, and she was looking up at me, shaking her head slowly back and forth. 'I'm so sorry,' she said.

'After that – after Cathy – I just couldn't go up to people and try to talk them into buying refrigerators, you know? I didn't feel much like talking to anybody about anything, never mind trying to convince them to spend more money than they could afford on something they didn't need. So they fired me. Anyway, I like what I'm doing now much better.'

'Do you see your little boy?'

'I can. Saturday afternoon's my time. But that's when I sleep. I mean, I work Friday and Saturday nights – Tuesday night's the one I have off – so I have to sleep during the time I'm allowed to see Bobby.'

'But you could . . .'

'It's too hard.' I stood up. 'More coffee, Miss Castella?'

She smiled up at me. 'Please, Mr Hobbes.'

I took her mug, refilled it in the kitchen, and brought it back to the living-room. She had curled herself in the corner of the sofa. I sat beside her.

'How long have you been divorced, Mr Hobbes?' she said.

'A little over a year,' I said. 'She took up with this guy – Francis – he used to be a friend of mine – and she decided she loved him or something and so she told me she was getting a divorce and she was keeping the house and keeping Bobby. Just like that, all at once. No warning. That's how it happened. I'm paying her fifty bucks a week, which is a big hunk of what I make at the Quik-Stop. She keeps the house and Bobby and I pay her so she can . . . can be with Francis.'

'No-fault divorce,' murmured Miss Castella.

'Yeah, no fault. My lawyer said it was the best deal we could make. One afternoon a week with Bobby when I have to sleep, fifty bucks a week, she keeps the house, because she decides she – she likes Francis better than me.' I looked up at her. 'I'm sorry,' I said.

She reached toward me and patted my arm. 'It's OK, Mr Hobbes,' she said softly. 'I'm a social worker. You can talk to me.'

She took a long swig of her coffee, then stood. She smoothed her skirt over the front of her thighs, then bent and slipped on her shoes. 'Well,' she said, 'unfortunately, I've got to go. I really appreciate the coffee, and the use of your phone, and the nice conversation. It's a pleasure to talk to normal people once in a while.'

I stood and walked with her to the door. She opened it, then turned. 'If you notice anything going on with Greg, would you mind calling me?' she said.

'Sure.'

She fumbled in her purse and pulled out a business card. Her fingers brushed mine as I took it from her.

'I've got to talk to him,' she said. 'Try to patch things up with Mr McMurtry or find him another job. Or else . . .' She shrugged.

'I'll do what I can,' I said.

The only other person in the entire apartment building that I knew besides Greg was Freddy Bellino, two doors down across the hall. Freddy was a construction worker who'd lost his job and was hoping to get a disability settlement. He had two elementary-school kids and a wife who had a decent job, so Freddy mostly loafed around his place watching TV while the kids were at school. He did the cooking and the laundry and seemed pretty content with his life as father and househusband, and I kind of envied him, even though Jolene, his wife, was crabby and not even that attractive. Sometimes I picked up coffee and doughnuts on my way home from work and Freddy and I had breakfast together.

One morning a couple days after my encounter with Miss Castella I told Freddy about it, and he grinned and said, 'You shoulda moved on her.'

'What do you mean?'

'She was askin' for it, man. Don't you know nothin'? Broad comes into a guy's apartment, it means only one thing.'

'She needed to use my phone.'

He blew out a loud breath. 'She ask to use *my* phone, man, I don't sit there politely telling my life story and drinking coffee with her, know what I mean?'

'You think so?'

'Damn straight. She's askin' you all those personal questions? Why you think she was doin' that?'

'She's a social worker, Freddy,' I said. 'It's her job to be interested in people.'

'Boy, you can be awful dumb sometimes. She's comin' on to you and you blew it, man. Listen, Willie boy. Next time she asks to use your phone, you just send her down here, hey? You tell her ol' Freddy's got a phone and a story he'd like to tell her.'

'It's not like that,' I said. 'She's a classy well-educated lady who knows her way around. She trusts people, that's all.'

Freddy rolled his eyes and shoved a big hunk of doughnut into his mouth. 'You tell her she can trust Freddy Bellino.' He grinned around his mouthful of doughnut. 'She can trust him to know what she's after, see?'

After I left Freddy and went back to my apartment, I took Miss Castella's business card from where I'd stuck it behind my phone. Andrea Castella, MSW, it read. It had two phone numbers on it. One was her office. The other I thought might be her home. I considered calling her, inviting her to come by to talk about Greg. I tried to think up a story about Greg that would convince her to come over. I could offer her a glass of wine instead of coffee.

But I couldn't think of a story to tell her. So I didn't call.

A week or so later I was coming back to my apartment from picking up the mail downstairs. As I passed Greg's door I heard his voice inside, talking to himself, I assumed. I figured this would give me an excuse to call Miss Castella. I'd tell her Greg was home, talking to himself, and maybe she'd like to come over. I paused there in the corridor, trying to understand what Greg was saying. Then I heard her. I couldn't make out what she was saying, but her voice was calm and professional and Greg's was low and subdued. It sounded like they were getting things straightened out.

I went into my apartment and put on some coffee. I stood by my door so that when I heard her leaving I could step quickly into the corridor as if I just happened to be going out. I'd act surprised and say, 'Oh, Miss Castella. Hi.' And if Freddy was right, she'd give me a big smile and ask to use my phone.

Then we'd see.

So I kept an ear cocked for the click of the latch on Greg's door and her voice in the corridor. I kept remembering her huge blue eyes and the softness of her hand when we shook and her sympathetic smile and the way her thigh showed when she sat on her legs in the corner of my sofa. 'You can talk to me,' she'd said.

When I heard her scream, at first it didn't register.

But she screamed again from next door, and not even in the movies had I ever heard a human voice with as much terror in it. She wasn't yelling for help. She wasn't screaming words. It was just a high, piercing cry, primitive like a wild animal, and I envisaged a rabbit with a hawk sinking his talons into its neck and the way it might scream, knowing it was being killed.

I slammed out of my apartment, and from the corridor her scream came louder, high-pitched, just one long terrible inhuman sound. I tried Greg's knob and the door opened into his kitchen. Miss Castella was cowering with her back against the sink, hugging herself, screaming, those beautiful blue eyes wide and her little flowerbud mouth round, screaming and screaming, and Greg was crouched there in the middle of the room facing her, his legs wide and bent and his arms out like a wrestler circling his opponent, and then I saw the knife in his hand.

I didn't even think about it. He could easily have pivoted round and sliced me or sunk that big blade into my stomach, but at the time all I could think of was Miss Castella and that scream of hers that filled my head. I grabbed Greg round the neck and spun him around and threw him against the wall and then I hit him in the face. I kept punching him until he dropped the knife and fell to the floor with blood pouring from his nose.

I kicked the knife away from him, and he looked up at me and mumbled, 'I'm sorry.'

'Don't move,' I said to him. 'Don't go anywhere or I'll kill you.'

His eyes were wet. 'I'm sorry,' he said again.

Miss Castella had slumped on to the floor. She was crying and sobbing. Her breath came in great shuddering gasps. I knelt beside her and put my arm around her. 'It's OK,' I said. 'It's OK now.'

She pushed her face against my chest and grabbed my shirt in both of her hands. Her body was trembling, and I held her tight, patting her back and murmuring, 'It's OK, it's OK.'

After a few minutes she took a deep breath and looked up at me. 'Thank you,' she whispered.

I glanced at Greg. He was on his hands and knees, blood all over his face, looking up at us with big frightened eyes.

I helped Miss Castella to her feet. She clutched on to me, and I think she would have collapsed if I hadn't held her up. 'You stay there,' I said to Greg. 'Don't you move.'

I helped her back to my place and led her to the sofa. She sat there hugging herself. 'Do you want some coffee?' I said.

'Do you have any brandy?' She had stopped crying now, and I thought she might be in shock or something. Her eyes were wide and unfocused and she just held herself and rocked back and forth.

'I've got some bourbon.'

She nodded. 'OK.'

I splashed some bourbon into a glass and brought it to her. She took the glass and held it in both hands. I sat beside her. 'Take a sip,' I said. She looked up at me as if she were surprised to see me there.

I touched her hands and guided the glass to her mouth. 'Sip some,' I repeated.

She shut her eyes for a moment, then tilted up the glass and let some bourbon slide into her mouth.

'I'm going to call the cops,' I said.

'No.' She gripped my arm. 'Don't.'

'Yes. He could've killed you.'

'I'm his social worker,' she whispered. 'It's my fault.'

'It's not your fault. He attacked you. I'll be right back.'

I dialled 911 and told them what had happened. The cop I talked to seemed to know who Greg was. He said they'd be right over.

I went back and sat beside Miss Castella on the sofa. I put my arm across her shoulders and she huddled against me holding the glass of bourbon in both hands until we heard the sirens. Then I got up and went into the corridor. Three uniformed officers came up the stairs. 'He's in there,' I said.

They opened the door. Greg was still crouched on the floor. He stared up at us with his bloody face.

One of the cops whistled. 'What happened?'

'I heard the screams. He had a knife. I came in and hit him.'

'Well,' he said, 'that's good work.'

They got Greg to his feet. They twisted his arms behind him and handcuffed him. I went back into my place and sat beside Miss Castella. 'They've got him,' I said. 'They'll take care of him. It's OK now.'

'You saved my life,' she whispered, staring at me. Here eyes were still a little unfocused.

'I just – reacted,' I said.

She leant over to me and kissed me softly on the cheek. 'Thank you,' she said.

A minute later there was a tap on my door. I got up and opened it. It was one of the cops. 'Can I talk to you for a minute?' he said.

He came in. I took him to my living-room. He asked Miss Castella what had happened. Her voice was shaky, and she kept hesitating, and once or twice tears welled up in her eyes. But I put my arm around her and she managed to get her story out.

She had come to tell Greg that since Mr McMurtry had fired him and refused to hire him back, they were taking his subsidy away and he'd have to leave his apartment. They would have to readmit him to the hospital for another evaluation. He got angry, picked up a knife, and she started screaming. That's when I came in.

The cop asked her a few more questions, but it was a simple story. Then he asked me to tell my side of it, and I did, and the cop seemed mainly interested in the fact that Greg had a knife in his hand.

'Well, Mr Hobbes,' he said to me, 'I guess you're a hero.'

I shrugged. 'I didn't really think about it. I just did it.'

'That's what makes heroes,' he said.

After he left, Miss Castella and I sat there for a long time. I had my arm around her and she had her arms around herself, and she leant against me and neither of us said anything. She sipped at her bourbon, and once in a while she shuddered.

Finally she said, 'I've got to call the office.'

She went to the phone, and I overheard her say, 'I've counselled with Greg. I'll tell you about it when I get there. Call Mrs Berman and cancel my appointment with her, will you? I'm not going to be able to make it.'

When she came back she looked better. 'I don't know how to thank you,' she said.

I shrugged. 'You don't have to.'

'I should've known better than to see him alone. But there's nothing in his records to indicate he'd be violent. He's not schizophrenic or psychotic. He's just retarded. If you hadn't been there . . .'

'I'm glad I was.'

She smiled. 'Me too.'

'You blew it,' said Freddy when I told him about it later. 'You had her, man.'

'She was in shock, for Pete's sake,' I said. 'What'm I supposed to do – '

'Afterwards,' he said. 'After she'd calmed down. That's when you should've moved on her, man.'

I stared at him. 'You are a pig,' I said.

＊

I never get letters. Bills and throwaways is about all I ever find in my mailbox. But a few days after Greg attacked Miss Castella, a small envelope with my name written on it in green ink came in my mail.

I took it upstairs and sat on my sofa to open it. 'Dear Will,' it read. 'I can never thank you enough. You are a true hero. I owe you my life. I will never forget.' She signed it, 'Fondly, Andrea Castella'.

It was the first time she had ever used my first name.

I held the note to my face, and I don't think the scent of her that I smelt on it was my imagination.

A few weeks passed. I put in my shifts at the store, six nights a week with Tuesdays off, came home in the morning, read the paper, slept in the afternoon, watched television until it was time to go to work, sent fifty bucks a week to Cathy, and tried to decide if I should go to see Bobby on a Saturday afternoon some time.

I stopped bringing Freddy doughnuts. I realised he wasn't the kind of guy I wanted for a friend, that I'd be better off with no friends at all than with one like him.

I wouldn't say I forgot Miss Castella, but the image of her had faded in my memory. I kept her note taped to the door of my refrigerator, and I read it often. Any trace of her scent had disappeared from it, though.

So when I heard someone tapping at my door, I figured it was probably Freddy, because I couldn't think of anybody else it might be. But it was Miss Castella.

'Hi, Will,' she said.

'Oh, gee, Miss Castella,' I stammered. 'Want to come in?'

She smiled that big blue-eyed smile of hers. 'Why yes, thank you.'

She was wearing a pale yellow silk dress. It was cut low in front and it fell loosely over her hips, and as I followed her into my living-room I couldn't help noticing how it clung to her so that I could see her body move under it. She trailed a wake of that same scent I'd detected on her note.

She had called me Will.

'Want some coffee, Miss Castella?'

'That would be lovely.' Another smile. 'And since you saved my life, I think you ought to call me Andrea, don't you?'

I shrugged. 'I guess so, Miss – Andrea.'

I made some coffee, and when I brought the two mugs back into the living-room she was kneeling in front of my stereo looking at my tapes. 'You like jazz, huh?' she said, looking up at me.

'I don't listen to it much anymore.'

'Can we listen to this one?'

She held up *Kind of Blue*. Miles Davis. It was one of the tapes Cathy and I used to play after we'd gotten Bobby settled down for the evening. We would sit close to each other on the sofa in the knotty pine rec room with our shoes off and our feet up on the coffee-table, sipping wine, relaxing, drifting on the music. That was back when things were good between us, before Francis.

I thought it was a significant coincidence that Miss Castella had picked that Miles Davis tape for us to listen to.

I got the music started. Then I sat beside Miss Castella on the sofa. She moved close beside me. Her hand moved on to my leg and she leant her cheek against my shoulder and sighed deeply. Miles Davis's trumpet sounded blue and sexy. I put my arm around her shoulder and she cuddled against me. Her fingernail drew little circles on the top of my thigh. 'Oh, Will,' she said.

'Are you OK now?'

She tilted her head and rubbed her cheek against my shoulder. 'I dream about it,' she said. 'Sometimes I'll be driving or just sitting there at my desk and it will suddenly come upon me. That feeling of absolute terror. But then you're there, and I feel . . . peaceful . . . safe . . . everything's all right.'

I held her. I just wanted to hold her that way forever.

Her fingernails were moving on my leg. I closed my eyes.

I felt her hand on my jaw. 'Will?' she murmured.

I didn't want to open my eyes. 'Yes?'

I felt her breath on my cheek. Then her lips were moving on my face. She kissed my forehead and my eyes and my nose and then her mouth brushed softly against mine. 'Oh, Will,' she whispered, and she snuggled against me. 'Do you like me, Will?'

I nodded. I didn't trust my voice.

'I like you,' she said. 'You're my hero.'

'Do you – do you want more coffee?' I said.

She laughed. 'Why sure. I guess so. Let me get it.'

'I can – '

'I'll get it, Will. Let me.'

She got up and went into the kitchen. I didn't open my eyes. I was afraid she wouldn't come back.

But she did. She squirmed against me and her hand went to my leg and squeezed it and moved on the inside of my thigh. She was kissing my face. Her mouth was wet, and her tongue licked and prodded, and her whole body was rubbing against mine, and she was murmuring, 'Please, Will. Please want me, oh.'

I gripped her shoulders and tried to push her gently away. 'Wait,' I said. 'Please.'

Her eyes were wild and she was shaking her head. 'I *want* you,' she said.

'No, wait.'

I held her away from me. She stared wide-eyed at me. 'What's the matter? Don't you want me, Will?'

'It's just – too fast.'

'Don't you like me?'

'I do. I like you.'

'Don't you want to . . . ?'

'I do, but – '

'You *don't* like me, do you?'

'Please don't talk that way. I like you a lot. It's – '

'Don't lie to me.'

'I'm not. I just – '

'I'm not attractive, is that it?'

'No. You're beautiful.'

'I'm ugly.'

'No.'

'You think you're too good for me. You're still hung up on that wife of yours. You think she's prettier and smarter and sexier than me and that I'm just this ugly boring little social worker. I – '

I squeezed her shoulders. 'Please. Stop it. Don't talk that way.'

'You hate me.'

'No, no, it's not like that,' I said.

Her face had changed. Her eyes had narrowed and her little mouth was twisted. 'You,' she hissed. 'You're all the same. All of you.'

And that's when I saw the knife in her hand. My kitchen knife. She raised it as if she was going to stab me. I grabbed her wrist and twisted it, and we tumbled on to the floor. I bent her wrist until the knife fell out of her hand. I picked it up and she scrambled to her feet and backed against the wall. Then she started screaming. Her screams paralysed me, those same primal wild-animal screams, full of raw terror. She crouched there staring wide-eyed at me, screaming and screaming, and I stood there in the middle of my living-room facing her and I couldn't move. Her screams filled my head, and I was only vaguely aware of my door crashing open. And then I was knocked flying and something smashed into my face and I was on the floor and he was kicking my ribs and my chest and my head.

'Don't you move, you crazy sonofabitch.' Freddy was standing over me. 'If you move I swear I'll kill you.'

I crouched there on my hands and knees and I watched him go to Miss Castella. He knelt beside her and bent his face to hers and whispered to her, and then he put his arm around her. After a minute he helped her stand up. She was sobbing and holding on to him, and he turned to me and said, 'Just don't move. The cops'll be here in a minute.'

'He had a knife,' Miss Castella said to Freddy.

'I know, babe,' he said. 'It's OK now.'

He led her out of my apartment with his arm around her, and she leant into him with her head against his shoulder. I could see her body shuddering with her great racking sobs, and I waited for the police to come.

CLEWSEY'S CLICHÉS

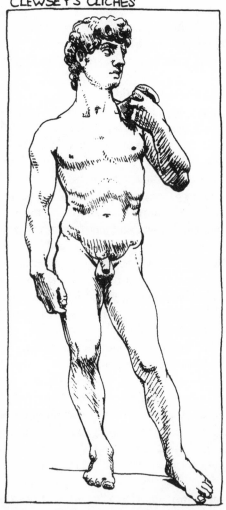

"IT HAS LONG BEEN AN AXIOM OF MINE THAT THE
LITTLE THINGS ARE INFINITELY THE MOST IMPORTANT."

Six in the Morning

MAXIM JAKUBOWSKI

He was headed towards middle age in low gear, going nowhere in no particular rush. Life was easy, rather quiet, unspectacular. He candidly thought he had left all the storms and the rage well behind by now.

And then she came into his life with no word of warning.

Eddie of the tousled blonde hair, the long white legs, the crooked teeth, the wide child-bearing hips, the dark brown eyes that looked at him with their peculiar mixture of wonder, interrogation and vulnerability.

An ill-advised letter, a few drinks, an Indian meal and a torrid episode of flesh against flesh in his empty office after dark, and he was soon a prisoner of the republic of desire, an almost-forgotten world of the excitable past, where he felt like a college kid all over again waiting for the phone to ring to hear her voice: 'Hello, it's Eddie', girlish, shy, bashfully lustful.

Her blondeness eternal.

The hours, the days spent apart from her felt as if they lasted ages, thinking in silence of all the things she might be doing out there in south London. What she was wearing, how much her husband touched her in bed – he had already ascertained in conversation that she usually wore nothing to sleep, and the thought both excited him wildly and fanned his jealousy.

Over a Bank Holiday, she went to stay with her parents, and he imagined her frolicking beautifully in a Surrey garden of polished lawn and carefully pruned roses, back at night alone in the room she had grown up in as a child, and then as a rebellious adolescent, with her long-abandoned scruffy dolls as sole companions. He would close his eyes and feel like crying, as the lust grew so overwhelming, as it mingled deceitfully with the fear of ever losing the little he possessed of her.

A long weekend without seeing her, alone with his thoughts, sunny, unending days looking for things to do to carry his mind elsewhere, away from mental images of her face, her body.

Criminal Scenario One

Life has worn him down slowly. A marriage of affection, where both partners are now weary of each other's foibles, jobs lost, mortgages, claustrophobic rooms, bright but rebellious pig-headed children who insist on answering back. When he grows all too easily irritated with his family, it reminds him awfully of the way his father was with him when he was a teenager. Eddie is there outside, flying luminously through his other life, and he feels he must act, do something. He reads in the newspaper of a murder in Oxford of all places, shades of Inspector Morse. He kills wife and children with a hammer. The blood is everywhere. Now I am free, he says.

Sunlight slivering through the drawn curtain of the window of an anonymous chain hotel room near Charing Cross station. Eddie on her side, her flank partly in shadow, the oval shape of her breast rising gently over the sandy dunes of her body. An image he memorises for ever. A still life of his lover embedded in his neural circuits like the flash of a thousand cyberpunk suns.

He sort of wonders what he's got himself into. How does one

conduct an affair, what are the ethics, the etiquette, the sheer human mechanics of extramarital liaisons?

He's read too many novels. He feels he's trapped in a bad story. He knows that with Eddie it's very special, but then again they would think that, wouldn't they? All illegal couples do. And the flies on the wall are probably falling over themselves laughing at the absurdity of the situation and the desperate seriousness they have made their own. Classic fools all.

He sees himself as a figure of ridicule. The archetypal middle-aged guy who has fallen for the sweet smile of some young bimbette. Lolita redux. She is after all twenty years younger. But no, he tries to convince himself, she is different. He can feel it inside, remembering how when they lay together, cradled against each other, she would gently kiss his upper chest, while her cold fingers skimmed over his shoulders.

They don't know where they are going. It's an open boulevard of dreams, like an American highway in those road movies he likes so much. 'We'll see how it goes. Take one step at a time,' they assure each other, grasping for reassurance. They swear they do not wish to harm, to hurt others through their irresponsible actions, but she says he turns her on so much, does all the right things, and he just can't get her out from under his skin, he's literally entranced by her natural, unassuming, beautiful spell.

He should be suffering from scruples, feeling all sorts of deep and tortured remorse, but some days he just feels light-headed, serene, surprised he can shoulder the guilt so lightly.

What comes next?

Criminal Scenario Two

On a 6.23 train from St Pancras to Nottingham to a conference he would much rather not attend, he meets this strange guy who insists on starting a conversation. The stranger pulls a gleaming metal liquor flask from his coat and pours him a perfect shot of malt whisky. Later, past Leicester, relaxed, it all comes out, how he wishes his life would change but this other woman he's going out with is married, and so is he and he doesn't know what to do. The stranger on the train suggests they do it like in the movies. He will take care of his wife, and her husband. And you only have to do it once. Two for the price of one, hey? A bargain. Almost amused, he provides the unknown guy with names and addresses.

The longer the clandestine affair went on, the more being apart from her felt unbearable. One-sided telephone conversations when one adulterer or another could not really say much, because of others standing around in their open-plan offices, would just add to their mutual frustration; snatched drinks in crowded pubs and hotel bars populated by inebriated foreign businessmen; unending weekends spent torturing each other with thoughts of what the other might be doing a few miles away across the river; meeting mutual work acquaintances and bursting to tell them the truth, all the truth just to see the look of surprise on their face at the idea of him and Eddie being together: 'No, surely not, I didn't know you even knew each other. But what about . . .'

The pace of their passion quickened. Barely a few hours after making love in some forbidden place, both would, independently of each other, clumsily inserting themselves back into the real world, yearn like crazy for the other, bodies crying out during the crowded night in the company of loving ones, once genuinely cared for.

They were coming together in sheer overdrive, losing control of the situation, their feelings, their day-to-day lives. Scared, confused, elated, depressed.

Monday mornings were often the worst, separately emerging from a weekend of missing madly, assaulted by doubt, by the possibility that something might have happened somehow to pull them apart, bringing spouses back into the eternal equation. A telephone conversation was then enough, reassuring like a warm blanket; checking that the miracle telepathy had worked again, they had been thinking the same things, feeling the same painful emotions, suffering the same irritations about the pettiness of the world and all it contained.

They would feverishly make plans, to steal an evening, a whole night, only to come crashing against the same old wall of fear. 'No, this is going too fast, we've only known each other eight weeks, we must slow down, be less intense, act like the grown-ups we know we are.' But their senses scream out a different tune, and they know they are just kidding themselves. This is a road to nowhere; impulsive, out of control, he knows that should he perhaps step on the brakes, the whole edifice will come crashing down over him like a wall of flames.

Criminal Scenario Three

Her husband gets an anonymous letter in the mail. 'Your wife is cheating on you. Where do you think she is on those evenings when she gets home so late? And that weekend at the TV symposium in Leamington Spa when she didn't want you to come and join her for the Saturday night?' it says, in a square old-fashioned manual typewriter face she cannot recognise. He is shattered, angry, badly hurt. Eddie responds blankly to the accusation, as surprised by the turn of events as he is. This is not the way she wanted it to be. She wonders who it can be. That woman in the office who's never liked her? But how could she have found out? Or was it her lover himself, his patience eroded by the combined assault of all the hours they have not managed to spend together, desperately attempting to precipitate events? Her husband walks out of the cramped, claustrophobic flat, drives off into the south London night in a rage. Ten minutes later, he rushes through an orange light near Blackheath Park and collides with a heavy goods lorry which had right of way. He dies instantly.

He is in awe of her naked body.

As she sheds her black dress slowly, revealing the sheer Irish whiteness of her flesh, he gazes at the amazon beauty of her body.

Her hair tumbles like a blonde fountain around her pale face, undomesticated Medusa-like curls reaching across her forehead to her deep-set brown eyes. Her mouth is a slash of red lipstick, lips thick and sensual, ripe forbidden gates to her teeth and throat, to the distinct smell of her breath. The sleeve slides down across her right shoulder, unveiling the length of her arm. Her brassière is sheer black gauze cupping her breasts in delicate bondage; she slips it off and her nipples harden slightly under the strange caress of the cold ambient air.

His gaze moves lower to her navel. Her stomach is flat, like a marble table, the straight cliff of her belly descending like a sheer precipice towards her pubic area, where her thatch is much darker, curling wildly at the edges and projecting thick tufts at its centre, which he will have to part later to reach the unencumbered lips of her cunt to reveal the pink, obscenely textured walls of her moist sexual innards.

Her high pelvis circles out slowly in languorous curves from hips up to stomach, her unending legs beginning their journey downwards from its equator. Others might argue that her rear is too big, ever so slightly out of proportion, even to her tall frame, but he doesn't care in the slightest. He finds the whole lavish spectacle of her wondrously attractive, luminous even. He feels she was born to be nude like this; she should be painted, her long limbs spreadeagled over white drapes in pornographic poses; if only he knew how, he would take a hundred photographs of her, for private consumption, close-ups of her thighs which bruise so easily, enlarged studies of the pale brown moles and small beauty spots criss-crossing the ocean of her white skin, one slightly above the left breast, another at the onset of her cleavage, yet another beneath the right shoulderblade; yes, Polaroids of her toes, of her half-open scarlet lips revealing a few teeth out of conformist alignment, of the puckered hole of her arse when she lies down on the bed on her stomach and opens her legs and rear to his exploratory caresses.

She has a manly walk, a gawky posture, but he adores the way she strides nude from bed to bathroom, the way her hips swivel as she turns to avoid the corner of the bed and another bruise.

Her body, her soul, an object of desire.

'I missed you.'

'Me too.'

'You look great.'

'Flattery will get you everywhere. Come here, hold me, I want you inside me.'

And he moves towards her, as nervous as the first time in his office. He wipes the red away from her lips, delicately twists the wedding and engagement rings off her finger, picks up her handbag from the floor, opens it and pulls out the golden-coloured lipstick tube and mashes the tip gently against her nipples; if he isn't capable of painting her portrait, at least he can adorn her breasts the colour of blood ruby.

Criminal Scenario Four

He returns home late one night after sex with Eddie. Following their exertions, they had washed as best they could at the minimal office sink. He is tired, his back hurts from the embraces on the hard floor and he goes straight to bed, forgetting to shower. His wife joins him soon, after completing the administrative update on the files she will require at tomorrow's surgery. He is dozing, half in reality, half in dreamland, she takes his hand to kiss him goodnight and smells Eddie's cunt still lingering on his fingers. Immediately, she feels violently sick. They have a flaming row. She makes dire threats. The next morning, while she is still sobbing in the bedroom, he feels he has no alternative and quietly walks over to the garage where he drains the hydraulic fluid from the brake system. There is a steep hill running downwards on the way to his wife's practice.

You've read all about in in books, newspapers and magazine articles in the lifestyle sections. You've seen so many movies. You thought it was easier than this. You were damn wrong.

How in late twentieth-century contemporary London do married folks engineer affairs of the heart or of the body electric? How do they manage it? According to published statistics and reputedly accurate surveys, he and Eddie were not the only ones involved in this ridiculous game; there were supposed to be a million or so others out there, also lying, deceiving, being furtive and madly discreet, conducting the precise business of crazy passions and also thinking it didn't show on their face, in their eyes. Surely, all these other sexual adventurers planned things better. But where do you obtain the right book of adulterous etiquette? With the do's and don'ts, the handy tips, the practical explanations, the coded map revealing in which public spots it is possible to kiss openly and not be recognised by acquaintances, the welcoming bars or cafés willing and able to harbour illicit lovers, the pubs where the muzak doesn't play too loud and drown the sweet nothings and the frequent embarrassed silences. He would have paid a fortune for such a book of revelations. She would willingly have commissioned a documentary programme on its rationale.

It was like learning to walk all over again.

You thought clandestine sex was easy. It isn't. You must beware of not biting her in the throes of passion when the only impulse coursing through your body is to consume her in one gulp, to bring her closer in an act of gentle violence, chewing on the flesh of her breast, digging your fingers into the pillowed softness of her thighs (remember, she bruises easily), nibbling the taut skin of her neck. No bites, no marks.

You must remember, after washing the sweat, the dried come, the smell of her off your body in the kitchen sink out there in the office corridor, the grimy one which the office tea-lady normally uses for cleaning the mugs, to dress so carefully again in the penumbra. Beware of putting your socks on again inside out, of not hooking her brassière at the back together again as it was when her husband helped her dress that very morning. And what else might you have forgotten? Think. Hard. This is a dangerous road you're treading, my boy.

This is how you enter the twilight world of sin.

You find a small hotel in Bloomsbury towards the back of the British Museum, and you both blush intensely when enquiring whether they have a day rate. Both holding your mostly empty attaché cases like talismans of probity. You know the receptionist knows. Eddie blushes even deeper, a red hue of guilt painting her pale white skin from forehead to cheeks. Or it's a bed and breakfast in south Clapham, where the carpet on the stairs smells of cheap cologne, and you must both use a pay-phone in the entrance hall to call respective offices and beg off sick for the day.

Naturally, you always pay cash. Credit card vouchers, and of course later monthly bills, are a dead giveaway. Aren't they?

But they were fast learners, oh yes, they were.

And whenever the need grew so intense he couldn't bear it any longer, he would wait in ambush at ten to nine in the morning in the side street round the corner from her office, and surprise her striding jauntily towards the television station from her tube exit. Seeing him, she would lower her eyes, in false modesty.

'I want you badly. Take the day off,' he would order.

Sometimes she would, sometimes she just couldn't. An important meeting, a visitor, a screening. But most times she would.

Criminal Scenario Five

The affair with Eddie is now two and a half months old. They have managed seven carnal encounters. He is an inveterate list-maker; he checks in his office diary the coded entries: over the course of their days and early evenings he has penetrated her sixteen times. Every time they part, it just gets harder to let her go. He wants her totally, selfishly. One autumn evening when it's already dark by six or thereabouts, he lurks outside the financial newspaper where her husband works. He recognises him from a photograph he had glimpsed in her handbag while she was in the hotel bathroom putting her make-up back on. He follows. Through wet streets on to the suburban train from Victoria station. When the moment is right, shortly after the station, in the shadow of Blackheath Common, he hits him from behind with a steel bar he'd earlier found in the corner of his garage. The husband is taller, but he has the benefit of absolute surprise. Dazed by the first blow, her husband slips to the ground. Once there, he no longer stands a chance. Overwhelmed by thoughts of Eddie's childish face, he hits him again and again with the improvised weapon, kicks him violently in the stomach, in the head. Soon, the husband is no longer moving. Or breathing. He steals his wallet to make it look like a routine mugging.

'It's usually at six in the morning when I wake up and the house is all silent, that the pain is at its worst,' he tells her in an Italian coffee bar at equal distance from their respective offices. Once you deduct seven minutes' walking time each way, they have barely three-quarters of an hour left to talk to each other before the lunch break is over. She cradles a hot cup of cappuccino. He nibbles a plate of tuna salad. She lowers her eyes.

'I know, sometimes I wake up three or four times at night, thinking of things, of you,' Eddie replies. 'I just don't want you to be unhappy because of what is happening.'

'OK,' he admits, 'sometimes I am unhappy, even bloody miserable, but then again I wouldn't want to exchange the few good times, when we are together, for anything else in the world. I'll accept the pain and the misery, it's still worth it, Eddie.'

'What are we going to do?' she asks him.

'I don't know.'

'You know, there are times in the morning when I'm on the commuter train coming into town, I sort of wish, dream that I might impulsively do something crazy, jump on to another train, go to India, leave everything behind.'

'I know the feeling,' he confirms. 'I want to go away too, take you with me and damn the rest of the world. I want to take you to New York, book into the Algonquin where the rooms are too small but the old furniture is nice, walk out into the winter cold of Madison Avenue and treat you to bagels and lox for breakfast. Later, we'd walk down to the Village and spend hours foraging in the basement of the Strand for cheap review copies of new books, have lunch off Bleecker in a Mexican restaurant. I can imagine you naked in the Algonquin room, Eddie, a silly game show on the silent television screen, the curtains drawn and your body all mine.'

'Sounds nice,' she says, 'but there's just no way I can get away for a whole week, you know that. And neither can you.'

He sighs. 'Or New Orleans, where the drunkards roll down Bourbon Street holding their plastic beer glasses, and the riverboats are docked on the Mississippi near the Jackson Brewery. Or Paris, where there must be a hotel on the Left Bank where the lift to the upper floors would barely be large enough to accommodate the two of us. Yes, couscous meals, and good wine, and you and you and you.' He smiles kindly, warming to the idea of their dreams of escape.

She looks up from her cup. Her long fingers move to his hand over the table-top, brush lingeringly over his lower arm.

'Jesus, Jesus,' she says.

Criminal Scenario Six

Although he has promised Eddie he will never do anything rash, the anxiety, the impatience are just gnawing away at the fabric of his gut, like a plague rat on the rampage. One evening, he is sitting morose watching golf on TV, when his wife walks into the room and complains that his socks smell. He hasn't bothered putting his slippers on since his return from the office. The sheer pettiness of her irritation bugs him. He ignores her remark. Soon they have a major argument on their hand. It inevitably veers out of control and when he least expects it, he somehow blurts out the existence of his

*affair with Eddie (although he is careful not to mention her by
name, even though his wife has never met her or heard of
her). The recriminations continue for hours. That night, while
he is sleeping, exhausted by the pressures and their release, his
wife quietly goes out by the back door to the garden, locks
herself in the garage, connects a rubber hosepipe to the Volvo's
exhaust and commits suicide.*

What about the sex? I hear you ask.

It was good.

There was something aloof about Eddie in general, and with every
new encounter he could feel himself removing brick after brick in her
wall of remoteness. And as the emotions were released, the embraces
became tighter and all-consuming, born of sheer desperation, hemmed
in by the obligatory time restrictions that bound the two of them.

And as the love grew stronger, the emotions moved ever more out of
control.

Although she would never say so, he felt that she always wanted the
fucking to be harder, more violent. It wasn't his style, but there were
moments when, moving in and out of her, his hands would
involuntarily rise towards her throat and hold her tighter, press against
her skin ever so slightly, evading the mad temptation to squeeze. And
Eddie would gasp and gaze at him with that unfathomable look in her
sad eyes.

She was one of the few women he had ever been with who would
keep her eyes open during the lovemaking, drinking it all in,
scrutinising the spasms of pain and pleasure in his face. At first he
found this somewhat unsettling, but he grew to like it and wouldn't
have swapped the intensity of the experience for anything in the
world.

Shards.

The way she would gently wet her fingers with saliva before taking
his penis in her hand and later her mouth.

The uncontrollable waves of pleasure that coursed through her like electricity when he touched her wet arsehole and timidly inserted a finger there, afraid of scratching her, harming her as he distended her reluctant opening and his mind wandered over pornographic and illegal horizons of buggery.

This evening she was still having her period and she agreed to remove her tampon. They made love on the dark carpet, joined by the blood, and later had to rush out to a night chemist to purchase some cleaning material to erase the stain from the office floor.

The shocking intimacy the first time he penetrated her mouth with his tongue.

The time she burst out in uncontrollable giggles when he licked between her toes.

Radiant Eddie.

Criminal Scenario Seven

Finally, they overcome the guilt and flee their respective marriages. They find a small flat in a part of London neither of them really knows well. For a couple of months things go swimmingly, as they overdose on the joy of whole nights together, love in the morning when the sun rises and on weekend afternoons on the sofa with Italian soccer on television. Financial matters are complicated: extracting themselves from previous commitments, house payments and attempting to do the right thing vis-à-vis their previous partners, without resort to greedy lawyers. The pressures soon grow. He picks his nose in bed. She is a bit of a slob when it comes to housework and refuses to iron his shirts. The season of quarrels is soon with them, aggravated by the inner knowledge that they have burned their bridges and there is no going back. One day, when one of them returns home late with a flimsy explanation, the other jealously suspects the worst: isn't this how their own story began? Once you've betrayed a spouse, surely the second time is easier. After the ugly words, they come to blows. A head falls violently against the table corner and one of them dies.

A grey Chelsea morning. Lingering pain in his heart for what is missing. Downstairs in the corridor, the doorbell rings insistently.

'Coming, coming,' he shouts.

Slightly out of breath, he opens the door.

Two young men in bad haircuts and grey trench coats stand there with a menacing look on their face. 'I'm sorry to disturb you, sir. We're police officers. I'm afraid we have some rather serious questions to ask. I must advise you that anything you say may be taken in evidence. Can we come in?' the shorter one moves forward through the door and past him.

'Are you acquainted with a Mrs Edwina Cambridge?' the second police office asks, following the first one in.

'Yes, I am,' he replies. What else could he say?

The Hand That Feeds Me

MICHAEL Z LEWIN

It was one of those sultry summer evenings, warm and humid and hardly any wind. The sun was just going down and I was grazing the alleys downtown, not doing badly. It never ceases to amaze me the quantity of food that human beings throw away. Especially in warm weather. The only real problem about getting a decent meal is the competition.

When I saw the old man poking in a barrel I said to myself, 'Here's trouble.' I was wrong, but I was right.

The old guy was grazing too and at first he didn't notice me. But when he did, though I couldn't make out the words, he was obviously friendly. And then he threw me a piece of meat.

It's not always smart to take meat from strange men, but this guy seemed genuine enough. I checked the meat out carefully, and then I ate it. It was good. Topped me up nicely.

I stayed with the old guy for a while, and we got along. I'd root a bit, he'd root a bit. And we'd move elsewhere.

Then he settled down to go to sleep. He patted the sacking, inviting me to sleep too, but it was early so I moved on.

A couple of hours later it was semi-dark, like it gets in the town. I didn't go back down the old guy's alley on purpose. Things just worked out that way. There are forces in a town at night. They push you this way, they push you that.

I could tell immediately that something was wrong. I approached cautiously, but nothing happened. Nothing could happen. The old guy was dead.

There was blood on his face. There was blood on his clothes. Someone had given him a terrible beating. Beatings are something I know about.

I licked one of the wounds. The blood was dry on top, but still runny under the crust. The old guy's body was pretty warm. Whatever had happened wasn't long over.

Nosing around, I picked up the scents of three different men. They were all fresh, hanging in the tepid air. Three men together, three against one. One old man. That could not be right.

I set out after them.

They had headed away from downtown. Curiously, they had stuck to the alleys, these three men, though they hadn't stopped at any of the places I would have. The places my dead acquaintance would have.

The only time I had trouble finding the spoor was where the alley crossed a street near a couple of stores. Seems they went into one of the stores, then headed back for the alley.

After another block I began to find beer cans they had handled.

At first I picked each can up, carefully, and I put it where I could find it again. But once I had one can from each of the men, I ignored the rest. I followed the trail with increasing confidence. I figured I knew where they were going.

The long, narrow park by the river is popular on a summer's night. I could tell immediately that it was teeming with life, and not just because so many scents crossed that of the trio I was following. All you have to do is listen. A dozen human beings, not to mention the other creatures.

But my trio made it easy again. They were down by the riverside, whooping and hollering and throwing things into water.

I was extremely cautious as I drew close. I wasn't quite sure what I would do. I only knew that I would do something.

I saw them clearly enough. Young, boisterous men, rough with each other and loud. They picked up stones and swung thick sticks to hit the stones into the river. Already drunk and unsteady, most of the time they missed, but when one connected they would all make a terrible din to celebrate the crack of stick on stone.

Lying in the grass behind them were more cans of beer and a pile of jackets. There was also a fire. A fire! On a hot night like this.

It wasn't until I crept near that I realised that in the fire they had been burning something belonging to the old man. The old man who gave me meat. The old man they had beaten to death.

I was sorely tempted to sink my teeth into the nearest one, maybe push him over the bank and into the water. But I was self-disciplined. A ducking was too good for these three, these murderers.

I edged close to the fire, to the beer cans. To the jackets.

The idea was to grab all three garments, but just as I made my move, one of the louts happened to turn around and see me in the light from the embers.

He yelled ugly things to his friends, and they reeled back towards me. I am not a coward but they did have sticks. And I am considerably bigger than a stone.

I grabbed the top jacket and ran for it.

They chased for a while, but they were no match for me running full out, even lugging the flapping jacket. And this was no small, lightweight thing. It was a heavy, leather, and *not* clean.

But I got 'clean' away, and the last I heard of the three young killers was what I took for loud, angry swearing as it floated across the humid night air.

I went straight back to the body of the old man. I laid the jacket down by one of his hands and pushed a sleeve as best I could into its forceless grasp. I spread the jacket out.

I left the old man three more times. After each trip I returned with a beer can. Each can reeked of a killer. Other men might not be able to track them from the smell, but each of the cans bore a murderer's finger marks.

Then I sat and rested. I didn't know what it would look like from higher up, but from where I sat the scene looked as if the old man had grabbed the jacket of one of the men who had attacked him. Beer-drunk men. The old man had grasped and wouldn't let go. They, cowards that they were, ran off.

Cowards that they were, if one of them was brought to justice from his jacket, he would squeal on the other two from his pack.

I was pleased with my justice.

I raised my eyes to the moon, and I cried for the dead man. I cried and cried until I heard living men near the alley open their doors. Until I heard them come out into the still summer night. Until I heard them make their way to the alley to see what the fuss was.

Once I was sure they were doing that, I set off into the darkness.

The Butcher of St Pierre

SUSAN KELLY

P aris, 1954

I know her at once, the girl sipping *café au lait* at the next table, although she has nothing of her mother about her, nothing except that full, pink, treacherous mouth. She was ten when I last saw her and is now a self-contained young woman of – what? twenty-two? She is the daughter of the Butcher of St Pierre. She was not the problem, though. It was her mother that was the problem: the wife of the Butcher of St Pierre . . .

She was lovely. I was barely eighteen and she was thirty-four but She made the girls look unfinished. It wasn't just a question of red-gold hair and blue eyes, of a generous and treacherous mouth, of a slender and languorous body. Her ankles enslaved me and Her feet. Before the war She had silk stockings and dainty shoes from Paris, but even bare-legged in peasant clogs they were the feet and ankles of an Empress of all the Russias: very long and very narrow and very white, the tawny crescents of the nails standing out like drops of dried blood on a linen bridal sheet. She did not pinch them in pointed toes or spoil the angle of Her calf muscles with silly heels like spikes. They were as healthy and as soft as the feet of a baby.

Her husband was the butcher. The thought of his meat-cleaver hands fumbling those feet distressed my nights. He prospered: a village needs meat, even in time of war. He was proud of Her and dressed Her, with his profits, like a queen.

They had that one daughter, Solange, as if one experience of the disfigurement of pregnancy and the indignity of childbirth had been enough for Her. Solange was her father's daughter: the pork butcher's child. She had his thrusting nose and prominent eyes, nothing of her mother's except that mouth. She played in the shop after class and swept up the bloodied sawdust and her stomach never turned.

The war, paradoxically, freed me, or kept me idle, as others put it. Out of school, movement restricted, I was not taken for war work since it was generally agreed that I was not quite all there; that my mother, bearing me in her forty-sixth year, had cut things a little too fine.

The Germans accepted that; they were not all insane geniuses.

So I walked the hills with my binoculars watching the birds migrate and if I happened to witness and report back troop movements or carry a message to a distant farmhouse, it was nobody's business but my own. I was undersized, could pass for fourteen, could run, crouching, through a field of corn without raising a ripple. I carried birds' eggs in my pocket as excuse and on the one occasion that the troops stopped me, I babbled and showed off my prizes, grinning and gibbering, and they boxed my ears and trampled my unborn birds and sent me away without searching me.

A new man arrived that spring and the village absorbed him. They called him Lucien. I did not engage him in conversation for fear he would betray himself. It was not that he had an accent – nothing so definite – he was just different. Not that the Germans would be able to tell, but there are always one or two of our own people who ought to be on our side, but aren't. So I would say 'Bonjour' simply to him and once he patted me on the arm in passing and slipped a piece of paper to me and I took it to the woman who called herself Jeanne and who was the Dusserts' long-lost cousin from Limoges.

Lucien was tall for a Frenchman and very fair. He wore blue overalls like everybody; he smoked Gauloises like everybody; he rode a boneshaker bicycle like everybody. He was like nobody. He was pale and beautiful and there was in his blue northern eyes something which might have been fear as he found that it was not, after all, a jolly exciting game.

He lodged with the Vidals who were old and vague and had already forgotten why he was there. Sometimes in the village shop they would cluck their tongues over his nocturnal comings and goings as if he were the son of the house and I would drop a jug of milk on the stone flags and be scolded for it.

The Vidals kept pigs in the hills but were now too frail to tend them. Lucien would walk that way each day to feed them and scratch their backs and move them occasionally so the Germans didn't steal them. The grazing was poor that year after a hard winter and the pigs had rooted their way to the summit where they enjoyed the sunshine and sheltered in the woods at night. I saw them often while running errands that way for gentle, discreet Jeanne.

It was one such errand that took me out in mid-July. There had been fresh troop movements in the area following the successful sabotage of the munitions factory on the Lyons road and I moved through the woods with more than my usual stealth.

I picked my way soundlessly among bracken and branches to the clearing where the pigs now grazed. They ignored me, happily absorbed in their fresh slops and with scratching their hides against the stumps. They had nothing to do but grow fat and end their days on the butcher's slab.

The foliage was dense enough to make a dim green tent of this natural hallway. I stumbled on a root and reached my hand out for safety and found myself clutching the fistful of rusted iron which was Lucien's handlebars. I heaved the bike upright and examined it, puzzled. Had Lucien met with some accident? Why should he abandon his *vélo* like this?

Where the bicycle lay was the beginning of an overgrown path which led to the abandoned quarry. I wrenched a branch from a young ash and

stripped the fresh leaves bare and beat at the overgrowth, which parted
easily enough before me. I tiptoed into the greenness, ducking low
branches and smoothing away nettles.

I could have made a good deal more noise for all they cared. I could
have danced a Grenoble jig and bellowed an old Lyonnais drinking
song; I could have fired a gun or set off a cannon. Supporting myself
against a great oak, gazing down into the damp hollow, I saw no more
and no less than I had begun to expect: a lying mouth devouring young
white flesh, pale straw hair wet with sweat and dew, a cat's cradle of
limbs.

I gripped my ash stick in my free hand and bit my teeth hard into the
bark to keep from crying out. But it was he who cried at that moment -
Lucien, the defiler - in words I could not recognise or understand:
traitorous, barbarous, English words, and all movement ceased. Except
for those feet, Her feet, rubbing themselves up and down the length of
his naked thighs in the siesta-time silence. He groaned and spoke some
more English words but She stopped up his treacherous mouth with
Her own - the instigator, wiser than he.

The sows had littered well. Next year's herd was assured and the
autumn slaughter could begin: pork, bacon, ham, sausages - the
butcher's day was full as he brought the boars down one by one from
the hills. Solange fetched water and ground stale bread and mixed
spices. By the end of September he had disposed of the whole herd.

I slept little. The nights were lively: more factories had gone up in
flames and the red roar on the night horizon was my weekly cinema, my
entertainment. The dull hum of army lorries was less customary
entertainment, though, and brought me from my bed one Friday night.
Two muffled lorries full of troops swung through the centre of St Pierre
and I dragged on my clothes and boots and shadowed them.

They stopped in front of Père Vidal's house and a dozen armed men
rattled out into the night, caring no longer what noise they made. They
circled the house, dragged out the occupants. Lucien, sleepy, with eyes
already dead, watched as they shot the old man, who died without a

whisper. I knew that he would cry out, Lucien, when they beat him, would not be able to help himself from shouting out the English words of fear and pain which would sign his death warrant and gentle Jeanne's and how many others'? Or did he have a cyanide capsule? And had he hidden it well enough? And did he have the guts to swallow it?

I reached Jeanne before they did, though, and kept her and her wireless set safe in the hills for six days and waved goodbye to her from a remote flat field in the dark quarter. In my thirty years on earth, that is the one thing I have done of which I am proud.

I wanted to ask her before she left to take a message back to those faceless uniforms in unknown England and ask them what they thought they were doing, sending shy schoolboys to a messy death, reducing them to telegrams of regret. Why had they not warned him to leave the native women alone? But the moment passed and the question remained forever unanswered.

Messy and degrading and unncessary; a beating with an ash switch would have sufficed or, if death alone could satisfy honour, a lonely ambush with a boning knife.

If it had been any other woman.

Many of the villagers had sons of that age – hiding with the Maquis or safe in unoccupied France. They thought it too harsh a penalty to pay for a boyish infatuation; they thought they knew where to look for justice and revenge. Lucien's supposed betrayer was executed after a trial and a sentence which were secret even to the accused. I found the Butcher of St Pierre early one morning, his throat cut with one of his own knives, dumped in the stream, below the village where he wouldn't pollute the drinking water. Someone had carved a Cross of Lorraine on his meaty palm.

And She? It was not long before those tender feet, silk-stockinged once more, were whispering their endearments to a German major's thighs. But She knew the mood of the village better than Her husband and left before the tar was warm and the feathers gathered. She took Solange south and died, so I heard, in a boating accident in 1944.

And so I obtained my release . . .

*

War is the ideal background for a murder: what is one body more or less when thousands are dying every day? And murder is easier at one remove - the anonymous note, the whispered word. I had put that time behind me until today, in a pavement café four hundred miles and twelve years away. I could feel no remorse for Lucien, although I have felt the occasional pang for Old Vidal and the butcher – those innocent bystanders – and how many others?

If it had been any other woman.

Solange has finished her coffee, the froth a lingering moustache on a generous lip. Her companion laughs and reaches across to smooth it away with his napkin in a gesture of spontaneous tenderness which makes the plain creature pretty. He takes her hand and raises her cheap engagement ring to his lips and I throw a few coins on the table to pay my bill and get up and go. For Solange is not her mother, she is not her father, and lies and treachery are not inherited.

At least I don't think so: I have never put it to the test and fathered a child of my own.

❧❦ *The Great Tetsuji*

SARA PARETSKY

O nce upon a time there lived a philosopher in the middle of a large city. He was a quiet man who lived strictly by rules of logic. A friend asked him once what he considered the most important value in life. The philosopher replied: 'That nature is rational brings me much comfort.' The philosopher, whose name was Marcus, took what came to him in life, whether pain or pleasure, with equal grace. He considered that all events in life came from nature. When they were good, he rejoiced, when they were bad, he sorrowed – but he took nothing personally, for nature is impersonal. He did not believe in bad luck or good luck, but in how one lived in reaction to an impersonal, random nature.

While Marcus tried to be totally rational, he was not without passion. In fact, his major passion was for the game of Go. When he broke his leg one day falling down the stairs, Marcus accepted the injury philosophically – for did it not come from nature, which was impersonal? But when he lost game after game of Go to the noted strategist Dr Kim, he was beside himself with anguish. When he devised a tactic that defeated Dr Kim, his joy knew no bounds, and he could talk of nothing else for days.

In Marcus's country, most people practised a religion which involved the worship of trees. They felt that nature was divinely created and inspired, and that the spirits of the gods inhabited trees. They believed, too, that when people died, their souls came back in the trees and shrubs and grasses of that country.

Marcus's friends generally shared this tree-worship. But Marcus did not. While not scoffing at it – for he, too, revered nature – he felt that the existence of the world every day was a miracle, and that to worship spirits was a blasphemy against the wonder of nature. At death, one's bones lay in the ground and gradually returned to dust. One's friends and relations could not been seen in the surrounding greenery (although a vine in his back yard that tried strangling his oak tree did remind Marcus of his mother).

Marcus lived in this quiet, rational way for many years. But as his life moved through the cycles of nature, and he went from fifty towards sixty, he began to be troubled by his lack of prowess at Go. He studied day and night, and all the works of the greatest Go masters lay by his bedside. Yet he could not make the breakthrough to sho-dan, or first rank.

At first he took his failure philosophically. In the course of nature he had not learned Go as a child, and in a rational nature, his brain circuits as an adult were just not adapted for Go brilliance. This act of nature was no more personal than when he fell and broke his leg. It was there, it was rational, it could not be fought.

As time passed, however, Marcus no longer could react so calmly to the victories of Dr Kim. There were days when he wished passionately that he believed in a spirit world – if so he would implore the gods to give him that tiny missing ingredient that would make him sho-dan. Instead, he pored more and more intensely over the Go teachings of the great masters.

Marcus began neglecting his students – he had no time to teach philosophy. Every moment with his students was a moment torn from Rin Kae Ho or the great Tetsuji. One day the master of the school came to him and sadly told him they would no longer be able to pay his salary if he did not return to teaching.

Marcus looked up briefly from his study of the joseki. 'What use do I have for money? I have no needs, other than to become sho-dan.'

His friends stopped coming to visit. Whereas before Marcus could always be counted on for a friendly evening's chat, now he spoke to no one. He sat madly working problems out on the board in front of him, consulting this master, that master.

Occasionally he would exclaim, 'Now I understand!' then race off to the Go Club where he would challenge Dr Kim to a game. At first his new strategy would work. He would win three games and lower his handicap to six stones from seven. But then Dr Kim would figure out his new tactic and change his own strategy. Marcus would once more start losing and be forced to return to his home and renew his studies.

After a while, he had to sell his house, a fine old mansion, in order to live. For it was not true that he needed only the joseki to survive – he had to eat and he had to order new Go journals. So he sold the house and moved into a tiny apartment – one room for his Go books and boards, one room for cooking, eating and sleeping.

At this, his friends grew so concerned that they begged him to seek professional help.

'But I am studying the great professionals,' Marcus protested.

'No, Marcus,' his oldest friend Sara told him. 'We do not mean the Go professionals. We mean some professional, a diviner or a seer, who can help cure you of this obsession.'

'But nature is truly rational,' Marcus said. 'No diviner can help me.'

'Nature may be truly rational, Marcus,' Sara responded. 'But you are not. A diviner might return you to your former state, where your friends as well as the dead master Tetsuji had time with you.'

After she left, Marcus did not think about what she had said - Sara was always nattering on about something. But in the night, in his dreams, her words wore themselves into a new pattern in his brain. Why should not a diviner help him? After all, he was obsessed. Sara was right – he was no longer rational. Perhaps nature was not so rational after all.

The next day he consulted the Yellow Pages for diviners. There were hundreds and hundreds of them. How could he choose? He did not want to call his friends – they would only scoff. Since in his heart of hearts he still thought nature was rational, he did the rational thing – he chose a diviner at random.

Johannes Michaelensis had the perfect diviner's office. It was an attic room in an old house in a part of the city Marcus had never visited before. Indeed, the winding street was only two blocks long, and Marcus had trouble finding it on the city map. He walked past the house twice before finally saying to himself, 'After all, nature is rational; what can happen to me here other than an afternoon's entertainment at the vagaries of human nature?'

He walked the four flights of stairs to the attic door. It was shut. On it was carved a wondrous display of trees and shrubs with a half-moon rising above them - all magical signs in the religion of Marcus's people. As he stood hesitating, a voice called from the other side, 'Enter. You are a doubter but you are a friend.'

Marcus opened the door with more boldness than he felt. In front of him lay another set of stairs, very steep. They led to the attic room where Johannes Michaelensis practised his craft.

The diviner sat on a stool in front of a high draughting table, whose top was a sheet of clear glass. He did not look up when Marcus entered the room, but continued to stare into the glass. An owl was perched on his left shoulder; its plumage blended with the long golden beard which hung almost to the diviner's waist. On Johannes Michaelensis's head was a pointed hat decorated with more mystic signs.

'I have seen you coming in my glass for many weeks now, Marcus Aurelius.'

The philosopher was startled, then he reminded himself: he knows who I am because my picture was in the papers many times in my days as a philosopher. And he is trying to prove his prescience to me by pretending that he was expecting me.

The diviner spoke as though listening to his thoughts. 'I know you doubt my powers, O philosopher, O would-be sho-dan. Yet so great is your need you are willing to test them. When you thought you chose my name at random from the Yellow Pages, the great spirits were really guiding your finger: for had you chosen one of my brother diviners, O Marcus, they would have cursed you to the ground and turned you into a withered stump for putting the divine powers to the test.

'But to me these powers speak differently. To me they say: all men are truly trees, whether they believe it or not. Therefore help the troubled philosopher that he may bloom in harmony with nature once again. So, would-be sho-dan, tell me your mind.'

The philosopher was startled. He knew there had to be some magician's trick here, but he didn't have enough time to figure it out. 'You seem to know my mind, O diviner. Can you not tell me what I seek?'

The diviner nodded, still looking into the glass. 'I see it clearly, O philosopher. But unless you speak it, you may not have it.'

Marcus thought a long minute. Then he shut his eyes and said rapidly, 'I would like to commune with the great Tetsuji. I would like to speak to his spirit beyond the grave. I would like the secret from him of how to become sho-dan.' After he had spoken, he felt as though he had been running many miles at top speed. Now that the words were out, he was ashamed and wanted to cry.

The diviner saw nothing wrong with his request. 'You have spoken your wish, O philosopher. It has been painful, and that is the price of a true wish. You have sacrificed much for your desire – your peace, your home, your friends, your job.

'Now if your desire were a shameful one, the great spirits would tell me your sacrifices were the just torment for a wicked man. But they tell me that the price you have already paid is heavy enough. Come close to me, Marcus Aurelius. Look deep inside the glass, and do not speak until the spirit speaks to you. Do not move until I tell you the spirits have left.'

The philosopher walked on unsteady feet next to the magician. I know this is a trick, he said to himself, but I still feel its power.

He stood next to the diviner. Despite the man's golden beard, his face was wrinkled like an old man's or a gnarled tree. The diviner lifted his left arm so that it lay behind Marcus's shoulder, close but not touching. The green drapery of his long sleeves brushed the back of the philosopher's cloak.

Marcus stared into the glass. At first he saw only the dark table-top underneath. Then gradually the glass misted over. Figures formed in the swirling mist. Out of them, a face took shape. It was white, not ghostly white, but the white of aspen bark. From behind the bark, two black eyes peered with fierce liveliness.

'You have called to me many nights, Marcus Aurelius,' the spirit said. 'But you left me no channel to answer you. Now that I can speak to you, you may ask me what you wish this one time. But then you must leave me in peace. Tell me your mind, Marcus Aurelius.'

'Oh, great Tetsuji. Please share with me the secret of sho-dan.'

The aspen bark seemed to laugh. 'It is no secret, Marcus Aurelius. It lies in the patterns of the mind. Remember, O philosopher: nature is rational, and so are the patterns of Go.'

It did not say any more, and Marcus felt terribly disappointed. He almost turned to leave, but the diviner's robe brushing his shoulder reminded him not to move.

In his disappointment, he had stopped focusing on the glass for a moment. Suddenly he realised that it was changing, that it was forming shapes and patterns under his eyes. At first he did not understand what he was seeing. It looked familiar, yet strange. Then he realised: he was watching the patterns of Go. Not the moves, not the strategies he had studied so diligently, but the shape of the game which lay behind it, the shape which Tetsuji saw more clearly than strategy.

While he stood, he lost all track of time. But when the magician touched his shoulder and told him he was free to leave, a day and a night had passed. It was lunchtime of the next day.

Marcus paid the diviner's fee. When he left, he felt relaxed and relieved – and a little disappointed. His obsession with the study of Go had vanished. He had lived with it so long that he missed it.

But the day was bright, the air inviting, and he thought of his friends for the first time in many months. He called on Sara on his way home and asked her to eat lunch with him.

That night, he went to the Go Club, and faced Dr Kim. He laid down his seven handicap stones. Dr Kim played on the two-three point in the near corner. Confidently, without thinking, Marcus responded. As the game progressed, he was seized with a great joy: through the lines on the board he could see the patterns of the game, the shape of the stones themselves. He abandoned joseki and fuseki and played to the shape of the game. And when he had by dawn reduced his handicap to even stones with Dr Kim, he felt no gloating triumph, but only the remarkable wonder of the shape of the stones.

As he walked home through the starlit streets, Marcus thought, 'For the trees are part of nature, and they make the Go board. And the stones are part of nature: they come from the oceans. So why should I not become a master of Go, when nature is truly rational.'

❧ *Cryptic Crime Acrostic*

SARAH CAUDWELL AND MICHAEL Z LEWIN

The diagram on the following page, when filled in, will read as a quotation from a book. All the letters appearing in this quotation have been used to make up a series of 26 words, phrases and names. These words, phrases and names are indicated by the numbered blanks beside cryptic clues A to Z on pages 118 and 119. The number beneath each blank shows where that letter fits in the diagram. In addition, the first letters of the answers to the clues spell out the name of the author and title of the book from which the quotation is taken. In each diagram square, the letter in the upper righthand corner shows which clue that square may be filled from.

1 T	2 J	3 I	4 A	5 Z		6 B	7 D	8 E		9 C	10 G	11 W		12 I	13 M
14 P	15 L	16 S	17 C	18 N		19 R	20 L	21 K	22 Z		23 D	24 F	25 V	26 L	27 U
28 J	29 R	30 K	31 G	32 B		33 P	34 I		35 A	36 M	37 T		38 H	39 S	40 B
41 A	42 I		43 R	44 K	45 G	46 T		47 K	48 C	49 Q	50 G		51 T		52 S	53 Y
54 R	55 Q		56 Z	57 I	58 F	59 R		60 B	61 G		62 T	63 C	64 A		65 G
66 V	67 Z	68 I	69 F	70 K		71 X	72 C		73 B		74 D	75 N	76 B	77 U	78 Y
	79 P	80 X	81 C	82 E			83 K	84 H	85 U	86 C	87 R	88 Y	89 X	90 S	91 E
92 F	93 T	94 B		95 Q	96 D	97 Z	98 G		99 S	100 R	101 F	102 H	103 L		104 E
105 T	106 S	107 V	108 G		109 P	110 D	111 C	112 R	113 F	114 W	115 H		116 G	117 T	118 O
	119 D	120 Z	121 Y	122 E	123 P	124 H		125 O	126 P	127 L		128 C	129 K	130 I	131 U
132 Y	133 J	134 V	135 X	136 P		137 M	138 W	139 F	140 C	141 N	142 K	143 J	144 T	145 V	146 B
	147 A	148 M	149 X		150 T	151 X	152 L		153 F	154 C		155 B	156 V	157 L	158 D
159 E		160 N	161 K	162 O	163 I	164 R	165 Z	166 B	: :	167 G	168 C		169 J	170 T	171 F
	172 M	173 G	174 L	175 N	176 U	177 K		178 E	179 P		180 N	181 T	182 A	183 C	184 Z
185 K	186 O	187 L	188 D	189 I		190 J	191 X		192 P	193 H	194 L	195 D	196 V	197 C	198 S
199 W	200 N	201 T	202 B	203 L		204 F	205 L	206 R	207 X	208 O	209 H	210 D	211 C	212 Q

A $\overline{182}\ \overline{64}\ \overline{147}\ \overline{35}\ \overline{41}\ \overline{4}$ Wimsey's first to break into safe for beermugs etc.

B $\overline{76}\ \overline{166}\ \overline{32}\ \overline{155}\ \overline{6}\ \overline{146}\ \overline{60}\ \overline{94}\ \overline{40}\ \overline{73}\ \overline{202}$ Where Holmes saw Watson had lately been
in a fight as an irregular.

C $\overline{111}\ \overline{48}\ \overline{86}\ \ \ \overline{9}\ \overline{128}\ \overline{140}\ \overline{17}\ \overline{197}\ \ \ \overline{81}\ \overline{72}\ \ \ \overline{154}\ \overline{211}\ \overline{183}\ \overline{168}\ \overline{63}$ To get large liquid asset
across the border, run off thither hotfoot – no coming back, too dodgy.

D $\overline{195}\ \overline{96}\ \overline{210}\ \overline{110}\ \overline{119}\ \overline{23}\ \overline{158}\ \overline{7}\ \overline{188}\ \overline{74}$ Terrible charge may be made by one furious I
scorn her love.

E $\overline{122}\ \overline{159}\ \overline{104}\ \overline{91}\ \overline{178}\ \overline{82}\ \overline{8}$ 'Stir' – one term initially for locking inside.

F $\overline{204}\ \overline{24}\ \overline{113}\ \overline{69}\ \overline{92}\ \overline{171}\ \overline{139}\ \overline{153}\ \overline{101}\ \overline{58}$ Exchange letters on corpse doctor dissected.

G $\overline{173}\ \overline{98}\ \overline{65}\ \overline{45}\ \overline{31}\ \overline{108}\ \overline{167}\ \overline{61}\ \overline{10}\ \overline{50}\ \overline{116}$ In Europe or Asia, perhaps, unable to control
oneself.

H $\overline{38}\ \overline{115}\ \overline{193}\ \overline{124}\ \overline{102}\ \overline{209}\ \overline{84}$ Opposing doggerel gets beheaded for it.

I $\overline{130}\ \overline{34}\ \overline{12}\ \overline{189}\ \overline{163}\ \overline{68}\ \overline{57}\ \overline{42}\ \overline{3}$ Jewel of a book from Collins, a second on the way
before one finishes.

J $\overline{190}\ \overline{169}\ \overline{28}\ \overline{133}\ \overline{143}\ \overline{2}$ When taking part in prowl I should like a hooter.

K $\overline{177}\ \overline{161}\ \overline{142}\ \ \ \overline{129}\ \overline{30}\ \overline{83}\ \overline{44}\ \overline{185}\ \overline{47}\ \overline{70}\ \overline{21}$ Find solution to mysteries in TV series.

L $\overline{15}\ \overline{26}\ \overline{187}\ \overline{127}\ \overline{152}\ \overline{194}\ \overline{174}\ \overline{205}\ \overline{157}\ \overline{20}\ \overline{203}\ \overline{103}$ I espy loot – gem hidden in
philosopher's study.

M $\overline{172}$ $\overline{148}$ $\overline{36}$ $\overline{137}$ $\overline{13}$ Only partial backing for alibi Hastings gives upper-class Englishman . . .

N $\overline{200}$ $\overline{141}$ $\overline{75}$ $\overline{175}$ $\overline{160}$ $\overline{180}$ $\overline{18}$ . . . and his lady, meeting old Greek charcters in city beside the Nile.

O $\overline{208}$ $\overline{186}$ $\overline{125}$ $\overline{118}$ $\overline{162}$ American woman's one of the family that fell for Edgar.

P $\overline{79}$ $\overline{136}$ $\overline{14}$ $\overline{109}$ $\overline{123}$ $\overline{33}$ $\overline{126}$ $\overline{192}$ $\overline{179}$ Saying no, not yes, to Jersey going back to cine production.

Q $\overline{55}$ $\overline{49}$ $\overline{95}$ $\overline{212}$ American lawyer hits town to shed new light on everything.

R $\overline{100}$ $\overline{29}$ $\overline{164}$ $\overline{19}$ $\overline{112}$ $\overline{206}$ $\overline{43}$ $\overline{54}$ $\overline{87}$ $\overline{59}$ Complex for real men, yet not for Holmes.

S $\overline{106}$ $\overline{198}$ $\overline{39}$ $\overline{16}$ $\overline{99}$ $\overline{90}$ $\overline{52}$ Seeing colour of blood round bite, was almost sick.

T $\overline{51}$ $\overline{46}$ $\overline{1}$ $\overline{201}$ $\overline{117}$ $\overline{144}$ $\overline{93}$ $\overline{62}$ $\overline{170}$ $\overline{181}$ $\overline{105}$ $\overline{150}$ $\overline{37}$ I, the Saint, am in trouble, needing hay fever cure.

U $\overline{77}$ $\overline{27}$ $\overline{85}$ $\overline{131}$ $\overline{176}$ Even setting the French against the Spanish.

V $\overline{134}$ $\overline{196}$ $\overline{66}$ $\overline{107}$ $\overline{145}$ $\overline{25}$ $\overline{156}$ Article you and I and several more find dreadful.

W $\overline{138}$ $\overline{114}$ $\overline{11}$ $\overline{199}$ Whimper from beginner after catcall . . .

X $\overline{71}$ $\overline{207}$ $\overline{191}$ $\overline{149}$ $\overline{89}$ $\overline{80}$ $\overline{151}$ $\overline{135}$ . . . from the wings and stagehands starting to hoot 'Derivative'.

Y $\overline{132}$ $\overline{53}$ $\overline{78}$ $\overline{121}$ $\overline{88}$ Tong leader ran away back to China.

Z $\overline{22}$ $\overline{67}$ $\overline{120}$ $\overline{5}$ $\overline{184}$ $\overline{56}$ $\overline{165}$ $\overline{97}$ Sap has been fleeced rotten, losing last three notes.

The Train

STEPHEN MURRAY

The regular snicker was Granny's needles flickering in the kitchen below. The scraping noise was Grandad's chair on the flagged floor, followed by the dull chink of the bottle meeting the rim of the cracked glass. From the village beyond: a dog barking; a door banging; a burst of cursing abruptly cut off. Laughter. From the encircling forest: only silence.

It was not always so. There were times when it moaned like a living creature in torment. Sometimes the whole village was engulfed by its roar as if transported to a tropical isle where endless surf crashed on to a coral reef. But when Paul thought of the forest at all he thought of its silence. Winter nights of frozen stillness when you could hear a distant bough creak with the weight of snow before shedding it with a gentle *crump*, and the sound was no more than a pebble vanishing into a bottomless well. And long summer nights lying in bed listening for the snap of a fallen branch beneath a careless footstep a kilometre away, and the squeal of an animal caught in a snare. It was such a night tonight.

Which was why as the chair creaked below as Grandad reached for his tobacco pouch, Paul stared at the beams over his head and pondered the phenomenon of the whistle.

He had heard it twice.

The first time had been three weeks ago and he had almost written it off as one of those dreams which dimly registers even as it fades on waking. But last night, in the small hours, he had heard it again, carrying clearly over the still forest like the shriek of a rabbit when it feels the talons of the owl rip through its skin; clear and high and sharp.

A train whistle.

Which was not impossible. The railway to the capital passed ten or twelve miles away, and on hot summer's nights sound carried freakishly, bouncing off layers of air high in the atmosphere. But Paul was sure this whistle had been closer. Night, when sleep came with difficulty if at all, was a good time for pondering mysteries, and while he kept his limbs carefully immobile his mind busily teased at the problem.

Mentally he ranged over the village and the area immediately around. The single street. The houses scattered along the road and in the fringe of the wood. The school. The wood-yard where Grandad worked and where . . . where Dad . . .

Paul sniffled and set his jaw.

Then there were the farms, hacked out of the forest, where the crops were beginning to sprout again under the inexpert cultivation of the women and the old men. And further off the Hall, which gossip said had been requisitioned and was enjoying a last blaze of activity, surrounded by a rash of temporary hutments, the parkland ploughed up for potatoes. And the quarry . . .

The quarry was served by a narrow-gauge railway line. Indeed, such lines threaded through the forest in several places; used for extracting timber and stone, they took lime and coal to the farms and carried away produce. How had he come to forget those little railway lines? Probably just because they were such an established part of his local geography. Obviously, there was the explanation of the whistle. Only a smaller mystery remained of why, when the summer days were so long, someone should transport stone or lime or anything else in the few truly black hours of night.

Down below, Grandfather knocked out his pipe against the bars of the fire. The poker rattled and the hod banged as Granny shook slack on to the coals for the night. Soon their slow steps would ascend the wooden staircase and the door of their room creak shut. They rarely spoke. He hadn't told them about hearing the whistle. They would have replied that the night was for sleeping, or told him it was a dream, or in some way slighted his truthfulness.

The real reason they would discourage curiosity – Paul felt very adult as he acknowledged it – was that they were afraid. He sometimes thought everybody in the village was afraid, these days, except the stupid and the stupidly brave. And most of those, like his father, were dead.

The days were too much like each other. Great events happened elsewhere: feats of bravery and conquest; desperate struggles, loudly trumpeted victories, heroic retreats. News of all these reached the village. And the village itself was not untouched, though nobody bothered now to remark upon the absence of able-bodied men.

Paul was not untouched.

For almost two months after the episode in the wood-yard he had been the object of fascinated curiosity. Then in a glorious, hopeless fight in a distant country, six of his schoolmates were bereft of their fathers and attention turned to them. There had been many deaths since, so that his father's was almost forgotten. Even for Paul life went on. Dreary lessons with the worn-out drudges, too old to fight, who attempted to teach them. The ritual playground games according to season which even the war could not displace. But it was a dull life.

Paul sensed that the grown-ups found it worse than dull. Arguments broke out more frequently and flared into feuds. He became familiar with the sound of women fighting, and with the aura of carnality which hovered like marsh gas over first one house, then another. Paul's grandparents avoided talking of these matters, even when the police had to be called to Mrs Becker's and took away the one-legged man, Thomas, still in his vest, his braces round his waist, his trouser leg flapping empty. Sometimes it was difficult to remember any other sort of life, yet Paul clung to his faith that this precarious, febrile affair was not normality. There were a good many things one knew without needing to be told these days; if one was wise.

After lunch next day he slipped quickly from the table and was out of the door while Granny was still chewing her turnip. He supposed he loved them for all their weakness, but he knew he could do pretty much what he chose and the whistle worked on his mind.

The forest was not featureless, though it would have seemed so to any stranger. It was crossed by tracks, pierced by glades, punctuated by quarries worked or derelict; even inhabited here and there. Paul walked without anxiety for several hours, but equally without profit. Gradually the urgency of his excursion dwindled and he began to ramble, and then to saunter. He was far from the village: maybe five kilometres, which was as good as five hundred in this wooded continent; in an area which he had not visited for some time, and never on his own. It had an air, almost a smell, of novelty, and he wandered contentedly, savouring the sights and the birdsong and the sensation of being so far away from all that was familiar and secure.

It was late afternoon when he stumbled out into a broad ride. Tree stumps poked through lime-green fronds of uncurling bracken, and nuthatches sang on piles of brushwood half submerged in new growth. To right and left the ride stretched away, curving like the rim of a giant wheel.

Every two hundred metres stood a post bearing a notice. Paul waded through the dense blue shadows of the forest fringe until he stood opposite the grinning skull and crossbones and read the stark warning. He stared out across the carpet of greenery trying to imagine the mines lurking beneath, and wondered how often a deer or a wild pig triggered one off. The far side of the ride presented a blank wall of pines. The silence was more, not less, profound for the small noises of birds and mammals about their business. The brightness of the sun in the cleared ride and the flitting butterflies and darting dragonflies made the war seem impossibly far away. Paul found a spot where a tree on the fringe of the forest had fallen naturally, leaving an inlet of sunlight, and lay full length on the infant, soft-stemmed bracken and daydreamed of heroism and mystery and long-limbed girls casting covert looks from beneath silken lashes.

The coolness of his skin woke him. The sun had dipped behind the trees, whose shadows slanted out towards him across the ride like striding giants. As he watched, a puff of smoke appeared above them. He judged it was about half a mile distant.

Grandad and Granny would long ago have noticed his absence. Paul started off around the fringe of the ride, whose huge arc must eventually bring him nearer to the village. It was in his mind at first that the smoke he had seen might be that of a train, *the* train, but after its initial appearance it steadied and darkened in a way that suggested the burning of refuse.

The sun was weaker now and much lower, and dusk was overtaking the countryside, blurring the trees on the inner side of the cleared ride into one grey mass. The birdsong slackened and ceased. He tried to work out how far he would have to walk to complete half the circumference of the ride. He thought of cutting across and taking the direct line past where the Hall must lie to the village; but every three hundred paces brought him opposite another post with its message of death grinning out of the thickening dusk; and he didn't know what further deterrents there might be inside this puzzling ring: dogs, perhaps; and guards trained to shoot on sight. Different birds began to call, the night-dwellers; and once or twice he heard the sound of heavier animals pushing through the undergrowth. It was not, after all, so fanciful to believe that wolves roamed the forest. He began to listen for their moaning call and to look over his shoulder at every unexpected noise.

Something hard met his advancing foot. He tripped and fell to his knees in the pine needles.

The moon was riding high, casting a baleful eerie glow over the landscape, creating nonsensical shadows, turning every pile of brushwood into a revetment manned by helmeted figures. By its light Paul saw what he had tripped over: a length of steel, rusty at the sides and dulled on top. Beyond it was another, tied to the first by baulks of timber which had settled deep into the litter of the forest floor. Crude, little used, not even properly laid, weaving in and out of the trunks before issuing forth to cross the ride – but he had found the railway.

The railway became his daily destination. He supposed his grandparents imagined him to be playing with the other village children when he slipped from the table after dinner and through the open door into the long summer evening, or absented himself when school finished at midday on Saturday to reappear only as the dusk fell suddenly – the forest stole the sun like a jealous lover - late in the evening. Georg the slater remarked that Paul visited him less often, and asked him if he had a girl.

Georg had been last summer's discovery. Paul had roamed then too, though less widely; and coming one afternoon to the rim of a quarry, drawn by a rhythmical tap-tapping that echoed through the forest, he had looked down and seen the slater on his low stool, the slab of stone between his leather-clad knees, working with his beetle and wedge round the perimeter until the perfect laminates came free, to be stacked at the end of the row that switchbacked against the quarry wall behind him. And Georg had stretched and reached for his tobacco pouch and looked up and seen the boy standing on the rim of the quarry, and their eyes had met, and the slater, with a jerk of his head, had invited Paul down and shown him his slates and his tools and finally, one day, his caravan. After his father died, it was to the quarry that Paul ran. It became his refuge, and in Georg he at last found one friend who could be depended upon for strength and no condemnation.

At first Paul went back whenever he could to that place where the rails snaked through the trees and emerged into the ride. But the rust on the rails turned cherry red, and Paul lost interest, and the next day he visited

Georg instead and persuaded him to bring his ferret out for a run on the caravan floor.

But that night, after dark, Paul heard the whistle again. Next morning he played truant from school and slipped in among the trees and ran. And when he came to the edge of the ride he knelt down and ran his hand along the surface of the rails and felt the smoothness of the steel, and shaded his eyes against the sun's dazzling reflection off those two bright stripes from which the rust had vanished, and felt a perplexed elation.

Thereafter Paul came doggedly every afternoon. He brought a book, and what he could find in the way of food, and lay, where the sunlight dappled the fringe of the ride, in the fresh and tender bracken fronds a hundred metres from those two enigmatic bands of steel, reading, dreaming of love, and waiting.

And one day the train came.

To be precise, it was already there. He heard the hiss of steam as he approached through the forest; and with it, a low undulating murmuring that sounded animal in origin. He slowed as he came near, and suddenly there it was, through the trees.

The trucks were ancient: worn-out antiques dragged from siding ends; four-wheeled box-vans that might once have carried fresh fruit, and closed cattle trucks, with planks nailed over the outside. He could hear the baying and lowing and smell the feral stink of beasts crowded too long together. The engine was out of Paul's sight, located by a smudge of dirty smoke hanging over the trees and the muffled hiss of steam leaking from decrepit joints. Paul turned to walk parallel to the trucks with the idea of finding the engine and maybe exchanging a word with the driver. He might be invited up into the cab. Last year, or the year before, when people were still easygoing, it would have been a matter of course. He could ask.

But as he made his way through the trees, keeping a dozen metres inside the forest where the smell of pine resin conquered the reek of the cattle trucks, with a deep, creaking groaning the train began to move. As it did so the groaning and lowing inside stirred into renewed life. Paul watched the rusty wheels turn protestingly and lurch over an uneven joint in the rails, jolting each truck in turn. Then he pressed closer behind the nearest tree as the closed trucks gave way to a flatbed with soldiers on it and a machine gun on a tripod. Lastly came a shabby carriage, in which more soldiers were visible. And then the train was past, and Paul stepped silently out of the trees and watched the end of the coach recede in the direction of the ride, until it turned a bend and disappeared. A foul odour like the smell of a neglected chamber-pot remained when the train had gone. Paul wandered forward, interested in the way the rails now had a shiny stripe running along their edge, a new, somehow purposeful air. He turned and walked back, following the tracks, stepping on the sleepers.

And then he saw the bundle lying between the rails.

It was perhaps twenty metres distant. He had good eyesight but the trees fractured the light into deceptive shafts of sun and shadow, so the bundle was difficult to discern. But it lay between the rails. It must have been run over by the train.

Paul wondered what happened when a train ran over you. If you stayed between the rails so that it didn't cut your head off, what happened then? He thought of lying there looking up, and seeing all the bits normally hidden. And as he considered it, the bundle moved. And he saw, as he had known all along, that it was a body. If it moved, it was not a dead body; and no bits seemed to be left on the ground. Reassured, a dark figure against the dark forest background, Paul stood still and waited to see what would happen next.

It stood up. Its clothes were rags wrapped peasant-like round its limbs and head. They looked stiff, and very dirty, like the sacks and greasy cloths that the old women of the village wore, that gave off fetid odours as they shuffled into Mass. But something about the way the figure moved told him this was no old woman, nor peasant either.

It looked cautiously both ways, then walked back to where the railway line crossed a track a few metres away. It stood indecisively.

He's lost, Paul thought suddenly. He doesn't know where he is. He's frightened, too. He's jumped off the train to get away from the guards with the machine gun.

The figure looked this way and that, and finally turned in the direction which led, eventually, to the village. Paul stepped forward, the pine needles deadening his footfalls, and said, 'You'd better go the other way.'

The tattered figure gathered up its skirts and ran, and Paul saw that its skirts really were skirts, and it ran with the gait of a woman, but fast for a woman. And as abruptly it halted, snatching quick glances all round, tensed for further flight.

Yes, she's scared, he thought. Of whom? There's only me. And so he knew for the first time in his life what it was to have the power to evoke fear. And then he thought, Or she thinks there may be others with me. And that was more comforting, because the idea that she feared him was pregnant with a dark intoxication that he was not yet ready to confront.

'There's no one with me,' he said. 'Granny and Grandad are at home. I'm on my own. You could come home except they're a bit queer about strangers.' And then he said: 'I've got a piece of bread if you're hungry.' He fumbled in his pocket and held it out on the flat palm of his hand, as one offers a carrot to a shy horse. And the woman began, as if drawn against her will, to inch forward.

It was like dealing with one of the flea-ridden cats that scavenged the fringes of the village. He watched the same instincts warring in the woman: food and flight. He held his hand out very still with the slab of ryebread on it. The woman's eyes flashed from the food to his face and back again. He was sure he saw her tremble within the noisome rags that covered her. Now she was closer, barely three metres away, and the rank smell of her enveloped him, the same stink that had oozed from the cattle trucks. The conclusion of that logic hit him like a blow in the stomach. The trucks had been filled with people, like this one. But he had no leisure for horror and packed it away for future digestion.

He studied the woman; not disgusted so much as fascinated, never having met before a human so nearly in the state of a beast. Her face was filthy, her hair matted and wild, and her eyes bored at him out of dark caverns. Her legs were bare beneath her tattered skirt, bare and wasted and discoloured with dirt of every hue. He did not need to be told that she was outside the law. It was that which had made him call out to her in the first place: the knowledge that she was on the run and must be warned that the village was hostile to strangers. The words had been out before he thought about them. It was the ethic of the playground - fugitives were not to be delivered into the hands of authority. But it was more than that. Something infinitely more serious than a playground game was in question. Instinctively he had declared his allegiance; and it was not to the village.

The remembrance of what had happened to his father flickered across his mind and for the first time he stopped it and looked it straight in the face, and as he did so he knew that he had accomplished another piece of growing up. That instant of bleak acceptance was as necessary as pulling out milk-teeth is necessary. A child could not help the woman before him: so he must not be a child. It was as simple as that.

Certainly she must not go to the village. She would be betrayed in a moment, with no thought and no compassion, as the villagers battered harmless grass snakes and slow-worms to death. And with the certainty came shame. This is the sort of people I live with, he told himself bleakly. Cruel people, petty people, ready – eager, happy – to betray and kill. Granny and Grandad as much as any of them. And Dad? And me?

There was a dry scrabbling on his extended palm, like the darting of a squirrel, and she was stuffing the bread into her mouth, eyes on him dark and . . . and wet, yes, with tears, because they began to spill over and run down her cheeks leaving pale streaks. Paul felt the pricking of tears behind his own lids: tears of incredulity that someone could be so grateful for so mean a gift; tears of pain at her pain. He blinked them back, but perhaps those sharp dark eyes had noted their presence, for he felt a current of sympathy flow between them, frail, tentative but warm.

The sun was not visible here beneath the forest canopy but Paul had spent his life within these purlieus. It was suppertime, and in all this wilderness of trees there was a real chance that some home-going woodman or quarryman would happen along. Deep among the millions of conifers you were given no warning of people's arrival. He must get the woman away from the track. At the same time a dozen more problematic matters were besieging his brain. Already, before he had consciously arrived at the need for a plan, let alone the plan itself, he was aware that food, shelter, secrecy, water, warmth, all were going to be needed tonight. And perhaps for many days and nights. Perhaps for as long as the war endured.

And then he thought: for we will lose the war. That is why I know that she need only be protected until it ends. He had never thought of the outcome of the war before; it was just 'the war', a state of existence which had overtaken them all. The woman was stuffing the last mouthful of black bread into her mouth, and he thought: in between her first bite and her last I have grown up.

Up to now she had not spoken, and it was only when she glanced up and croaked a word he did not understand that he realised that he had not expected to understand her anyway. He said 'I'm sorry', and spread his hands apologetically. But she was more resourceful, trying what was obviously the same word in different languages. He recognised it at the third or fourth try: it was 'thank you'. He was curiously touched. In the village duty and gratitude were strictly preached, but only towards adults. Thanks did not often come his way. It was only after this thought had passed through his mind that he realised that the word he had understood was in the language of the enemy. Was she, then, an enemy, a prisoner of war? Had the train perhaps been taking her to jail? But it was not her own language, he could tell that. So then he wanted to believe that she had been captured by the enemy – my enemy's enemy is my friend – but logic would not let him, for the soldiers on the train had been in the uniform of his own country. My country's enemy is . . .

'Water.'

She was watching him attentively. Paul frowned and then, seeing her confidence falter and her limbs tense for flight, tried and humiliatingly failed to convey that he was only exercised by the problem of finding water in the forest. It was fear he saw in her darting eyes and her poised limbs: fear of him; and now the thought, instead of exhilarating him, brought indignation. She believes that I shall give her up! And skulking at the rear of his consciousness was the awareness that there would be a reward for betraying her, and most of the villagers would not even think such an act one of betrayal.

Stumbling over the words, and reinforcing his meaning by gesture, he told her to follow him and turned away into the trees. She stepped lightly and the thick layer of pine needles muffled her footsteps, so that several times he was certain she had slipped away into the trees; but when he turned she was behind him still. He risked a smile of encouragement, and she responded with an urchin grin that illuminated her pinched face even through the grime, so that he thought: she's no older than me.

They came out on to a road, which they crossed, and shortly after reached a disused quarry. The trees fell back round a scrubby waste, and a rock wall towered before them in a horseshoe. The light penetrating into the clearing had called forth a profusion of plant life on the old spoil heaps. Butterflies flitted among the patches of nettles, and the tinkle of falling water added a final touch of refreshment and peace. Momentarily Paul perceived the abandoned quarry as a place of beauty, and when he turned he read the same appreciation in the woman's eyes and fellow-feeling engulfed him.

He led her by the faint path that wriggled round and over the piles of debris until they came to the foot of the cliff, where the clear water issued from a fault in the rock and ran splashing down a series of tiny precipices into a roughly hollowed basin before spilling over and forming a stream that vanished into the lush vegetation.

She knelt down to drink like the pictures in his Sunday School primer of Gideon's alert four hundred, thirstily scooping handful after spilling handful of water to her mouth.

He said, clumsily in the alien language, 'It's all right.' And she turned to him, a clear ring round her mouth where the water had washed away the filth, and smiled, a flash of white teeth. She pushed herself to her feet and came towards him, hand outstretched in a curiously formal gesture of thanks, and her smell preceded her. Involuntarily Paul's mouth wrinkled and she faltered and he was ashamed.

She spoke a word that meant nothing to him, then gestured; and Paul at last grasped her meaning and turned his back, feeling his cheeks warm. He heard her feet shifting on the broken slate and knew she was – you could hardly call it undressing, in those rags . . . Then came the swirl of water as she stepped in and thrust towards the far side, where under the miniature cataract the pool was almost a metre deep.

He heard the sound of the waterfall change as she stood beneath it, and knew she was naked, only a few metres from him; and saw a blue butterfly he did not recognise, and concentrated hard on it, following its jerky flight from clump to clump of nettles, and felt a tingling like pins and needles in his body and knew it was because of her presence, though there was scarcely a girl in the school he had not seen naked in the stream that passed by the village, where they all swam every summer's afternoon when school was done. The sun felt very hot now, and his flesh was hard, painful against his leather shorts, so that he was doubly glad he had his back to her.

'You can turn round now.'

She had wrapped herself in her shawl, and the rest of her clothes were stretched out on the slabs of rock at the basin's side, sodden but already steaming. Her limbs where the shawl did not cover them seemed very white. He saw her glance take in his ludicrously peaked shorts and the laughter bubble up in her face. But then she said again, in that alien language, 'Thank you', and Paul realised that normal judgements did not apply. He was sure she wasn't more than a year or two his senior, but she possessed a maturity that had nothing to do with years, forced upon her by experiences he could not even guess at; so that he saw that in some circumstances experience could coexist with innocence, and forgave her amusement.

She sat down on a slab of slate where the slanting sunlight played and then lay back, rearranging the shawl to let her long pale legs be warmed by the sun, and her delicate shoulders and the tops of her breasts. She patted the rock beside her and he sat down; and slowly, in the language of their enemy, stumblingly, almost idly, they began to tell each other things.

And at some point the wind changed and Paul's ears picked up, faint but distinct, the familiar tap, tap, tap from among the noises of the forest, and he knew that it was all right. Suddenly he felt sure of himself and in charge of events. The familiar sound of the slater's hammer had provided him with the answer.

Two days later he came over the rim of the quarry, where the juniper bushes grew, and saw Georg's head lift and then bend back to the stone between his knees. The chink, chink of the hammer echoed in syncopated rhythm round the bowl of the quarry as each blow was overtaken by the next. As Paul scrambled down the final incline he saw the stone fall in two and by the time he gained the quarry floor, strewn with waste, Georg was stacking the slates at the end of a new run and selecting a fresh stone, turning it deftly in his hands so that the grain ran true and setting it between his leather-clad knees. The girl was nowhere to be seen; Paul felt a surge of affection for the slater, and wondered how he had contrived her escape.

Georg greeted him with heartiness. 'Well, now, Pauli! You should be in school. You know that? You should be in school. Finest time of your life.'

Paul ignored this, except to note with puzzlement the slater's loquacity. It was the jolliness of adults who curry favour with children, and he and Georg had never stood in those positions.

'Where is she?'

Georg made the first taps round the circumference of the slab of stone to separate the laminate. It seemed to take his whole attention. When he arrived back at his starting point he glanced up from under his black matted hair. 'She's safe. Least said, soonest mended.'

'But she's gone? You found a way?'

'Always in a rush, aren't you, Pauli? Everything has to be done yesterday.' There was an edge of harshness to the reproof. The slater gestured with his head towards the end of the quarry, where the caravan was parked under the scanty branches of a brace of tenacious rowans. 'She's in there.'

Paul was disappointed. He had not imagined, when he brought the girl here, that his hero would be so unimaginative as to hide her in the very first place that any searcher would look for her.

'Go and talk to her. If you can get any sense out of her. Though if I were you, I'd forget all about her and nip back to school.' He gave the wedge a sharp, practised tap with the hammer and the slate split away. As he lifted it free, it fractured in his hand and fell in two. Georg swore harshly and threw the two halves skimming to the quarry floor. Paul felt the hostility in the air. It was directed at him; rare in Georg, and a new experience, to be the source of something stronger than mere anger to a grown man.

Georg was afraid.

The revelation burst upon him, dazzling and bewildering. Georg was afraid!

Paul crossed the quarry floor towards the caravan. Shards of slate crunched under his boots. It was like walking on the moon.

Because he had been in before (treasured times, playing truant from school, taking refuge with a man who asked no questions and made no demands) Paul was ready for the atmosphere that prevailed in the caravan. It was a deep, undersea atmosphere, compounded of the dimness of the light filtering through grimy windows that looked out only on to the looming quarry wall, the effulgence of the stove that grumbled all through the year weeping trickles of wood smoke through the joins of the flue pipe, and the presence of Georg himself, lingering like a discarded suit of clothes even when he was bodily absent. It was evocative of his life in the caravan: the meals fried in the black pan; the long winter nights in the fold-down bed; the games of patience. The ferret in its wooden crate on a top shelf at the back of the caravan added its own sharp contribution to the atmosphere; and sometimes a bad-tempered scrabbling could be heard, or a glint of angry red eye discerned behind the air holes drilled in the front of the crate.

All this was familiar; but as Paul pushed open the door other smells, which because they were not familiar made a more immediate impression, met him: an unquantifiable vaguely piscine sharpening of the atmosphere that accorded with the undersea quality of the light. And a similarly unquantifiable disturbance of what Paul had always thought of as the essential peace of the caravan. It was no longer the refuge untouched by the horrors and cynicisms of the rest of the world. Its carapace had cracked. The outside world had inserted a fingernail and was prising away the shell which had formerly seemed impregnable.

And as all this passed through Paul's mind, and as he docketed it for later inner debate, he made out the girl against the shadows.

If he had not known, from the circumstances, that there was no other girl it could be, would he have recognised her?

She was cleaner; much. Her hair was combed and roughly trimmed and held back by a slide. Her clothes were not the rags that had been roughly tied round her when Paul found her in the forest, but proper women's clothes, though their mix of styles looked ludicrously antiquated even to Paul. Nevertheless, she wore them with an attempt at bravura. She even wore a little make-up. Paul, remembering with a pang her innocent nakedness beside the pool, felt there was something a little too practised about her. She resembled, not the frightened wood nymph he had then thought her, but one of the girls of the vullage who hung around in gangs flaunting themselves at the soldiers, and who sometimes went off blatantly arm in arm with them towards the trees, shouting shameless remarks over their shoulders to their mates. He no longer felt able to help her; she was too far beyond him in hardness and sophistication.

And yet he felt again the urgency of his attraction to her; and in another of the flashes of recognition that seemed to be tumbling over each other's heels he realised: I want her. As a man wants a woman, and for the same reasons: for the way her skirt hangs over her calves; the way her hair curtains her neck; the way her breast swells and the shadowed cleft where the blouse lies open; for the secret places beneath her skirt which summoned his hunger. It was not that Paul had been at all ignorant before. This, he thought fleetingly, explains things. Knowledge has nothing to do with desire.

She seemed glad to see him. Yet they had, in these new circumstances, little to say to each other. They both, as if acknowledging that they were bound by a special bond that demanded the effort, attempted to talk as they had by the pool that first day; but the words that came out were stilted and empty.

He thought she was worried.

'Is he . . .'

She seemed to have difficulty formulating the question, and eventually came out with a word which he knew must be in her native language, grimacing with frustration. He shook his head helplessly and then said, half-guessing her meaning, 'He's my friend.' And even as his lips formed the word he experienced a pang of doubt – which was not really doubt but a new, adult awareness that Georg was not what he had seemed only last week when Paul had been a boy. And with new, adult eyes, as with an organ barely formed and still unreliable in its function, he looked beneath the slater's joviality and saw something which was not honesty.

It was too late now to wonder whether he had done right in bringing the girl here. But the idea that he had led her into peril, not safety, frothed sourly in his stomach.

Meanwhile, the girl had restructured her question. 'Will he do what he has said?'

'What has he said?'

'That he will hide me.'

'Here?' He looked around the little caravan in dismay. How could the slater keep her here? For one night, a fine night, he could sleep under the stars and surrender to her the bunk with its frowsty quilt. But he would not do that for more than a night or two; and then how could they both live here? Where would she sleep? Brothers and sisters shared the same room – the village houses were small, the families large, but decency could be contrived. But Georg and the girl were not brother and sister.

And then he despised his childish obtuseness. Adult truths hung heavily in the air between them. He shouldered them brutally aside. The question she had asked was the only one that mattered. Would Georg keep his word?

'What has he promised?'

His voice was harsh and must have sounded censorious. She pointed her chin and said, 'You are only a boy.' But her eyes were anywhere but meeting his. And he thought: this is what it means to be a fugitive. And he recalled the Meyers leaving the village barely two years before, in a hurry . . . in the night. And how Dad wore a new watch after they had gone, and the Meyers' furniture appeared in neighbouring houses. He had never questioned how they came to be eating off plates that he knew had been the Meyers'. He had preferred to believe that they had given their things away before they left.

Now he told himself: this was the way it was. When you were a fugitive you had to let other people take whatever you had. And if you were a woman with nothing else, you still had one thing that men wanted. You gave the only currency you had in exchange for promises you did not more than half believe would be kept.

The assurance she wanted, which might have let them talk easily, he could not give; and shortly he muttered an apology and turned and left the caravan. He climbed the quarry wall by a different path, away from the slater at the other end still working with beetle and wedge, and the tap, tap, tap of the hammer seemed to follow him to the very edge of the village.

He stayed away from the quarry after that. As long as he stayed away he could believe that everything was all right. Indeed, it *was* all right. The girl was living with Georg as his mistress, in exchange for his protection, and why, Paul asked himself roughly, should he lament that? But he could not bring himself to see the two of them together. And it seemed kinder not to inflict on her a witness to her – he could not say 'shame', for in the desperate situation in which she had been, such notions had little meaning - say rather, her necessity. Instead, he made his way each day to the edge of the ride, where the sun flooded the soft growth of fern and grass, and there he passed miserable hours and days, lying full length, the insects in his hair, spinning daydreams of might-have-been, and dreams of still-shall-be, when the war should be ended, when her long limbs might lie here by *his* side; and the finches alighted on the marker posts and the sun bleached the colour from the skull and crossbones, and the rabbits washed their whiskers above the buried mines and from time to time dirty, greasy smoke smudged the sky beyond the further margin of the trees.

But he came to the quarry sometimes just to look, from the concealment of the bushes that grew to the rim, down into its bowl as into the home of some busy caged creatures that go about their business untroubled in a zoo. Just to confirm, from small signs and occasional glimpses, that Georg was there; and that the girl was there too.

The summer peaked in somnolent magnificence, as if oblivious to the cold, relentless news of the war. Men were dying; fathers, husbands; more of them, less splendidly, more often, more futilely. Paul knew it, as everyone in the village did. The war, which in its first years had rolled away into the distance, into far countries and even continents, was contracting and would soon become a neighbourly matter once again. It was a summer, meanwhile, of a splendour and a languor such as Paul had not known in his life. Old women spoke of long-dead summers, and of earlier wars.

On a day of such perfection that it seemed to have arrested time itself, when the blood flowed sluggishly and the brain floated on sun-saturated fantasies, Paul made his way - it might have been five, eight, ten o'clock - from the ride to the old workings where the pool shimmered and the waterfall splashed, removed his few clothes and his heavy boots and waded into the water where she had waded, that day when he had done so much growing up. The water lapped silkily at his shins, at his thighs, at his genitals, at his hips; and in his imagination she was with him. The forest seemed ineffably still.

Afterwards he put on his clothes and continued to the rim of Georg's quarry. Not to see her; just to know that she was there; still there.

The quarry was deserted. Then with a bang the door of the caravan shut and there was Georg, crunching the debris of generations of slaters beneath his boots like the tramp of a regiment as he crossed to his work. With a casualness that raised a prickle of apprehension in Paul he stooped and turned over the lumps of slate until his practised fingers settled on one suitable for his purpose. Then he squatted down on his stool, lifted the beetle and wedge, and began the preliminary tapping round the perimeter of the slab of rock. As if it were a day like any other.

But after a moment he paused, set down the beetle, and took something from his pocket: a leather tobacco pouch, which he unfurled, and a briar pipe. As Paul watched, the slater filled the pipe with every indication of pleasure and lit it and began to puff happily, the work abandoned. Then he fetched out a squat bottle, uncorked it and tilted it to his lips.

He drinks when he has money, Paul said to himself. When the contractor has been and the stacks of slates have gone, on the little trucks behind the puffing, grunting engine.

But the stacks of riven slates stood behind Georg as he sat smoking his pipe; running four high in a brown switchback twenty metres long.

Georg sat and smoked. Behind him, fifty metres away, was the caravan, and it was something more fundamental than the mere absence of movement at the window which proclaimed to Paul: I am empty.

He wriggled back from the perimeter of the quarry until he could stand up unobserved, and made his way home. The forest was silent: empty of that tap-tap-tap.

Georg was setting charges. Paul checked the caravan first, quietly, knowing she would not be there but punctilious in ensuring he did not condemn in error. She was not there; and her smell, the clean female smell of her that had always been there even beneath the crusted dirt of their first encounter, that smell which he could not have described and had not known he had even noticed, had gone. On the shelf above the bunk five bottles stood in a neat row like dutiful servants. Paul turned away and looked across the quarry floor to the broad back of his friend where he went about, tamping explosive and cutting fuses from a hank at his belt.

The slater looked round when he heard the crunch of Paul's footsteps, and grinned. He greeted Paul cheerily as he had so often, so that Paul marvelled that he had never understood the emptiness of that bonhomie. He read the new, uneasy wariness in the slater's eyes. He knows, Paul told himself, that he has betrayed a trust; but he isn't sure I know.

And then Georg saw the shotgun and the grin faltered and died.

'Does your Grandad know you've got that, Paul? Guns are dangerous, you know.'

The platitude, and the *de haut en bas* air of admonition with which it was delivered, almost made Paul laugh out loud. But fear shook the slater's attempt at reproof and that was as it should be. True adulthood beckoned on the horizon, and he ran to meet it eagerly. He raised the gun with no further doubt.

Georg had taken a step forward, his clasp-knife in his hand; now, as Paul held the gun level, he took another backwards. Paul followed, and they began a little ridiculous movement, step and pause and step, always nearer the rock face.

'Put it down, Paul,' the slater said. And then: 'I've something in the caravan you'll like. Some chocolate. Where do you think I got chocolate, eh?' And then: 'That's an old gun, boy. You don't know what you're doing. A gun like that can kill you.' Which made Paul laugh inside.

The crunch of his boots on the bigger debris that lay at the foot of the quarry wall seemed to alert the slater to where they were. He glanced behind him, to the brown towering rough rock face, pierced by the shot-holes, from which hung the fuses, like the tails of rodents, trailing towards the place where they joined to the main line of fuse. He frowned, and brought the knife up, his eye held by the barrel of the shotgun.

Paul had known he could not kill a man while looking him in the face. Not this first time. Before he could think he let the barrel of the ancient gun droop until it was pointing at the slater's legs and pulled the trigger against the weak pressure of the rusty spring. As the shot exploded in a black cloud the gun kicked until it stood almost vertical, wrenching his wrist brutally. At first Georg seemed to have vanished; then the sooty gas wisped aside and there he was, lying in a heap at the foot of the quarry face. He thought with contempt: he's wet himself. But the great dark stain spread rapidly down the trousers and up the shirt, and he knew it was blood.

He let the gun fall. The barrel was split, a bulge along its length. Georg's mouth gaped, his eyes rolled, but if he was screaming Paul was deaf. He walked past him, stooping to collect the slater's knife as he passed. The matches were in Georg's discarded jacket. Paul held the flame to the end of the fuse, seeming to hear the slater's voice: No need to rush, boy. I always use a fifteen-minute fuse. Plenty of time to get clear. It's rushing that kills quarrymen, because you don't get it properly alight, and it smoulders, and you go back and – pouff!

He made sure; watched a centimetre or two of the fuse wither and crumble, then turned his back and left the quarry, and the caravan, and Georg lying there at the foot of the wall of rock.

He had reached the perimeter of the forest and was among the first trees when he heard the crack of the explosion and the rumble of rock and the crying of the birds. He walked on, deeper into the forest, away from the village. Somewhere ahead he became aware of a deeper rumble that might have been distant gunfire. After a while he came to the railway and followed the metals. Late in the afternoon he came to where it crossed a road, and heard the sound of a vehicle approaching. From the shadow of the trees he watched the vehicle stop and a soldier get down, shouldering a rifle. The vehicle moved off, and the man remained, watching the crossing. Soon Paul heard a train whistle, and after a long delay an ancient engine wheezed over the crossing, towing a string of creaking, closed trucks that moaned and stank.

After it had passed the guard relaxed, walked up and down, then turned under the trees and unbuttoned his trousers. Paul walked up behind him on the carpet of pine needles and stabbed him in the back, as near as he could judge level with his heart. The soldier fell, spurting blood and urine. He had a holster at his side, and there was a pistol in it, which Paul took, together with the rifle. The man wasn't dead, but he left him there and walked on into the forest. Some time later he heard shouts and shots from behind him, but they died away. The rumble of gunfire was continuous now, and he wondered how far away it was and how long it would take to come closer.

He began to count the trees. When he got to ten thousand he lay down with the rifle and slept.

❧❧ *Fancy*

BILL JAMES

'Yes, I'm around places like this at night a lot – and waste ground, several London stations, heaths, student accommodation.'

'Same myself. Funny we've never met.'

They were sitting at opposite ends of a wooden bench in this Hampstead bus shelter. It was after 1 a.m., and no bus would come.

'Better than idling at home.'

'Every few nights I need this sort of outing.'

'Call me Charles. Obviously, not my real name.'

'I'm Vernon. As it were.'

Charles said, 'Frankly, I'm the Wolfman rapist you've read of in the press, doubtless.'

'That's a laugh.'

'I'm telling you. Seven women hereabouts. I itch somewhat for Number Eight tonight.'

Vernon's voice rose in rage: 'You've got what I'd call a steaming cheek. You're talking to him, old son: me, I'm Wolfman.'

'You're what?'

'You heard.'

Charles said, 'He's nearly six feet tall and thin. Pointed, cruel face - well, like a wolf's. Obviously. All the girls say that. You're a chubby, gross little object, for God's sake.'

'I don't like your tone.'

'Lump it, then.'

'Anyway, Wolfman's got a refined, super-cool accent,' Vernon replied. 'It's been frequently mentioned in the press. Listened to yourself lately? You're slum rubbish.'

'I can turn on class. It's a cover.'

'I'm much, much taller than you'd think,' Vernon said. 'And slimmer. It's the way I'm sitting.'

'You know what? You're sick, that's all,' Charles said. 'Who the hell claims to be a rapist when he's not?'

'You.'

Charles stood angrily. 'You push your luck. I'll see you off.' He took a step towards Vernon, who also rose. 'You're standing now?' Charles enquired.

'The Wolfman rapist's got a word tattooed on his – on his person,' Vernon replied. 'This has been observed by victims and publicised by police, in case it's fortuitously noted in, let's say, a Turkish bath.'

"Excelsior". I'll show you. There's light enough.'

'Yes, and *I'll* show *you*.'

In a moment Charles snarled, 'You had that done after hearing of it.'

'You can talk. You're pathetic. Just a mimic.'

'Sod, I'll – '

They began to fight then, punching each other's face and head ferociously. Charles was cut over the eye. Vernon's nose and lip bled heavily.

A young blonde woman, in miniskirt and bulging blouse, suddenly appeared from the road. Her heels towered. Rushing forward, she pulled the two apart and flung them casually to separate ends of the shelter, where each folded down exhausted on the bench.

'Zip your trousers, boys,' she said. 'You'll get chilled. Then out of here, smartish.'

'Who the hell are you?' Vernon asked, standing again, his voice pugnacious, lip wound or not.'

'Police,' the woman said.

'You what?' Charles replied.

'Decoy for the Wolfman rapist. I have to lure an attack. Goons like you will mess it up.'

'You've struck lucky, girl,' Charles said, 'for I'm Wolfman.'

'Take no notice, officer,' Vernon told her. 'I am he.'

'With "Excelsior" on your respective members?' the woman sighed. 'Blokes like that here every night, acting out their would-be sex lives, haunting his ground. Everyone to his own kicks. It's harmless. One tattooist's bought a Porsche from extra work. Off you go now, gents.'

As they walked away, Charles said, 'Some fool, that one.'

'Too true.'

'It's because you were there.'

'How?' Vernon asked.

'She saw straight off you couldn't be Wolfman and decided we must both be nutters. Thus, despite a brazen confession, I outwit the fuzz once more.' Charles chuckled rather heartily.

'And I'm a nutter?'

'What else?'

'I'll show you what else, you lying prat.'

They began to fight again in a side street but, when the policewoman neared on her stilts, they stopped and made their way towards an all-hours coffee bar. At one table a couple of pretty girls sat talking, and, in a while, the redhead drifted over to sit with Vernon and Charles.

'My friend and I think you two must be boxers on your way home from a late-night tourney,' she said. 'The marks on your faces. Though not unbecoming by any means. I believe they're called tourneys.'

'Tourney's fine. You should have seen the other guys,' Vernon replied.

'I knew it,' the girl cried, thrilled. 'My name's Louise.' She turned and called her friend: 'Oh, we were right, so right, Elaine! A tourney. Elaine's absolutely mad about boxers.'

Elaine, dark-haired and taller, joined them.

'I'm Rocky Blaze,' Charles remarked.

'Jabs Bison,' Vernon said.

'We're nurses,' Louise explained.

'Jabs really flips for nurses,' Charles said. 'He's famous for it in the fancy – as we pros call boxing.'

'What about you, Rocky?' Elaine asked, leaning over and gently touching one of his cuts.

'Whoever comes,' Charles answered.

'Oh, invariably,' Elaine said.

Towards 3 a.m. they made their way to the nurses' home and sneaked in through a ground-floor window. Charles went with Elaine to her room and Louise took Vernon to hers. The men arranged to meet near the same window again later.

When they rendezvoused at 5 a.m. it was still dark. For a moment, the two stood tidying themselves. Charles, gazing from the window, suddenly said, 'My God, I saw someone dash through the grounds and disappear near the front of the building. It's the hunt. The fuzz has traced me after all. I'm a golden prize.'

'Louise is eager to meet me again,' Vernon replied.

'Same with Elaine and me.'

'But I'm not sure,' Vernon said. 'I'm so busy.'

'I told Elaine similar,' Charles replied.

'I didn't say why, naturally, but being Wolfman – there's so much preparation and lying in heated wait,' Vernon explained, 'with buckets of excitement burned up.'

'Oh, for Christ's sake, you're not still on about that? Honestly, can't you understand, you're not Wolfman? It's a delusion, all in your tortured dreams, like being Jabs Bison. For I'm the Wolfman rapist. If anyone's been traced, it's me.'

'Like hell,' Vernon said.

'Excuse me, but did she comment on "Excelsior"?' Charles asked.

'It was dark. I didn't mention same as I was not on Wolfman duty.'

'Me, too,' Charles said.

'But you never are on Wolfman duty, you foul fraud.'

Charles punched him in the ear and once more they were about to fight when a series of brilliant searchlight beams slashed the blackness, playing fiercely on the nurses' home. A loudspeaker voice blared: 'Come out, Wolfman. This is the police. We saw you enter. You're surrounded. Your raping nights are over.'

Vernon and Charles climbed out jointly, bravely, competitively, through the window and four harsh beams swooped on them. They walked with dignity towards the cordon. When they reached it, a uniformed sergeant genially took each by the arm. 'Get out of the way, laddies, will you,' he said. 'The Wolfman rapist's trapped in there. Heard of him? Big stuff. Yes. You've had a bit of nurse nooky? You'll be needing your prunes and Cornflakes, I expect.'

Vernon and Charles stood behind the cordon and watched. After not very long, a thin man about six feet tall, and with a narrow face, came out from the front of the building and strolled smiling defiantly in the lights towards the police. 'It's a fair cop. I've had a decent run,' he drawled. 'Pity Wolfman couldn't enjoy one last fling, though, damn it, you fellows.'

'I don't like this at all, Vernon,' Charles said, 'Life's lost its purpose.'

'It's going to kill my evenings out stone dead, Charles, if he drops from the news.'

'There's Elaine, of course.'

'And Louise,' Vernon remarked.

'They're very nice, but I need something with, well, a bit more substance,' Charles said. 'Something for the mind.'

'I know what you mean, Rocky. Look: don't forget the fancy.'

'Right! Maybe a bit of road work together and sparring, Jabs?'

'Sounds good to me, Rocky. We could be contenders.'

The Crumple Zone

JOHN MALCOLM

The carcass of the car parked on the garage forecourt next to the pub was a model example of precision wreckage. One half of the bonnet was still intact, pristine and shiny; the other half was a smashed mess piled into the off-side windscreen, which had shattered into cobwebs of pendent splinters. The driver's area was still perfect but the front wheel on the near side had been impacted into the dashboard bulkhead. An exposed engine block was draped with wires and broken pipes like mangled mechanical spaghetti. The two halves could not have been more professionally contrasted; the sight was like an advertisement for safety equipment of some sort.

I gesticulated at the battered remnants with a smile at my companion. 'Rupert's been at it again,' I said.

Henry Battersby gave me a perplexed and rather impatient look. 'Rupert?' he queried, with a frown.

I nodded affirmatively. 'Rupert Fletcher. Local farmer. Tremendous boozer. Apparently he drove into the narrow railway bridge at Wood's Corner, about a mile up the road, the night before last. Hell of a smash. He was driving home from this pub, of course. He claims that a car came through the arch against the signs – it's narrow and only one way – so he had to swerve into the brick support column to avoid it. The other fellow – if there was one – didn't stop. So he says. And there you have it: one side of the car squashed in completely. Head-on impact.'

'Good heavens,' Henry said in awe. 'Was he terribly badly hurt?'

'Lord, no. Not Rupert. Drunkard's luck, as always. He was on the driving side. Had his seat belt on. Got straight out, swearing agricultural blue murder, and walked back here for a drink. He stayed out of the way until the garage collected the car – it's by no means the first time and the police will soon lose their patience with him, even though he's a local bigwig - and downed a few hard ones to get his nerve back.'

'Amazing.' Henry was impressed. 'Miraculous, almost.'

'It's the crumple zone, you see. These cars are designed for it. They're always advertising the fact. A few others do the same. The front gracefully collapsed where it hit the bridge but Rupert's side was undamaged. Brilliant, really.' I peered at the dislocated wheel. 'Not sure what a passenger might have got, though, if there'd been one. Fortunately Rupert hadn't picked up any willing local ladies that night.'

Henry shivered. 'Come on,' he said, turning his gaze away. 'Let's have that beer. I need it.'

I chuckled and led him into the pub. Our local is not a very successful or inviting place but Henry was keen to go out. He and his wife Jean had hardly arrived, on one of their rare visits *en route* to Dover, before he made it clear that he needed a noggin, causing a surreptitiously raised eyebrow from my wife Mary and a look I can only describe as nettled from Jean. She gave me a glance that implied that I was the cause of leading him astray. This behaviour, the look said, would not normally have occurred. Jean did not approve of pubs, not for Henry anyway. I smiled to myself at this, because men visit pubs for many reasons and I am not a great pub man, as Mary would confirm. It was not as though I was rushing Henry away so that the men could chat manly chat at a bar together; the initiative definitely came from Henry. A determined look had come to his face.

'Well,' Mary said, anxious for the visit to be a success, 'of course there's time for you to have a beer at the pub before we eat. You two boys run along; Jean and I have a lot to catch up on.'

Jean gave me a rather wintry smile and put her camera equipment down carefully in the hall. Henry led the way out to his car and we unloaded their cases – quite a few of them – before we strolled along to the pub. They were on their way to the Channel ferry and were stopping with us overnight in a way they had not done for a while. Tensions are bound to occur when long-married couples travel together; I am always careful to plan any trips Mary and I take very carefully. Women, as a rule, want to stop randomly to see sights whereas men, almost always, are anxious to reach a destination. These conflicting desires can cause problems which it requires a sophisticated approach to resolve. Something, quite clearly, was slightly off key between our guests. It made me wonder how Jean's new life was affecting them.

When Jean started to write her travel guides Henry took a very tolerant view of the whole enterprise. I remember thinking, at the launch of her first book up in town, that Henry was very relaxed about the prospect. They had gone to the continent together to research her first effort – it was a guide to Brittany – and he proved invaluable to her; a handsome acknowledgement adorned the first page. At the launch they looked bronzed because they had just come back from some fieldwork in researching the second volume - publishers drive hard once a series is under way – which had taken them to Alsace-Lorraine. It was something Jean had always wanted to do; she said that the existing guides did not provide nearly enough information aimed at the woman traveller and holidaymaker, so a series of little books, illustrated with her own photographs, would provide more carefully for feminine needs. She specialised in visiting select areas of the continent not too heavily trampled by tourists and the idea had caught on well. Her publisher – a woman, of course - was delighted. There were several in the series by now. Jean also contributed articles to some of the glossier magazines and odd Sunday supplements. Her name was becoming known. Mary was delighted for her. Middle age is a difficult time and Jean was an example of the sort of renaissance that many dream of having. She was very professional – she'd been a journalist when she married Henry - and dedicated to the field she had chosen. Their two children were at university and almost off their hands; the series provided the transition from mother and housewife back to a career that most would envy.

'Pint of bitter,' Henry said in response to my query. The saloon bar was almost empty and the landlord was pleased to see me. 'I haven't had a pint in a pub for ages.'

I nodded affably at the landlord as he drew the pint, and got a gin and tonic for myself. 'Let's sit by the garden window,' I suggested. The interior décor of the pub – modern reproduction with false oak beams – always put me off my drinking, but Henry didn't appear to notice.

'Oh great,' he said enthusiastically. 'You are so lucky down here, Jimmy. The suburban pubs around us are frightful. Look at that wistaria; this is the country for you.'

I smiled quietly. To Mary and me the area was becoming congested, nothing like what it was when we moved in, but all of life is relative and I'd no doubt our landscape was emptier than Henry's part of Surrey.

'Cheers, Henry,' I said, raising my glass. 'Long time it's been.'

'Cheers.' He drank a deep draught and sighed. 'What a relief. You're a lucky man, Jimmy.'

I raised an eyebrow just a little at this second invocation of luck. Luck has never been a forte of mine. I eradicated it from my thinking a long time ago. To rely on luck, or to believe in it, is a grave mistake.

'Come, come,' I riposted. 'Surely you're the lucky one? Off on a continental jaunt while we all toil on at home. A jaunt, what's more, which you can legitimately claim on expenses. Fully tax allowable. This time tomorrow you'll be in the Vosges, or near it, staying at a good French hotel with a splendid meal in prospect. It sounds more like good fortune than anything else to me.'

Fortune, of course, had nothing to do with it. It never has. Henry's jaunt was the result of Jean's work, of careful planning and meticulous research. The success of Jean's guides lay in the detail she so scrupulously wove into them and in the photographs she took. She had a real eye for a picture. In her guides there were the most unusual shots of local interest, brilliantly taken, which made the places she captured on film seem fascinating. Whether it was a charming *colombier* of unusual style or a group of labourers engrossed in an esoteric craft, her pages were enlivened by things that made you want to see them in the flesh. Her technical proficiency with equipment was remarkable. Much of the material was women's stuff, of course: weaving textiles and cooking buns, that sort of thing. But I had to admit that it was well done; several reviewers had commented on the fact.

Rather than nodding his agreement Henry frowned again, revealing a preoccupation that would perhaps be exposed in more detail soon. I noticed now that his face looked tired, or stressed, from some source which was draining his normally healthy complexion.

'It's not what you think,' he muttered. 'No beer and skittles in this caper. Chief cook and bottlewasher isn't exactly my idea of fun.'

I gave him a querying look. His remark was difficult to follow. I knew that Jean praised the way he made things easy for her – driving much of the way, navigating, seeing to the arrangements and foreign exchange, helping with the camera equipment, that sort of thing – and had assumed he derived enjoyment from their excursions, but his expression was not happy. The role of a man on motoring holidays can be one of heavy responsibilities. There is anxiety about the enjoyment which must be derived from what is a relatively expensive expedition. Opportunities must not be missed. The needs of each partner are different. This can lead to many resentments and tensions. For myself, when travelling with Mary, I am careful to release her for those shopping hours which seem to be so necessary for her enjoyment of a trip, that dawdling in craft markets peering at bogus local handiwork which she finds so satisfying and which bores me to death. Most continental cities, particularly the French ones, cater for a man's amusements very adequately. My known interest in early porcelain enables me to slip off, ostensibly to museums, while Mary spends her time in her own way without feeling she is taxing my patience. It is a very civilised arrangement which allows me to relieve the possible frustrations of attendance on her by dallying with an available lady of professional practice in the right part of town for an hour or so, returning relaxed and cheerful to escort my wife on to the next stage of our sortie. My philosophy in everyday life has been very similar; an occasional visit to London, to a reliable blonde in Soho or Shepherd Market, has prevented many an outburst that might have damaged an excellent marital relationship. Travel concentrates the demands of partnership tremendously; my solution has always been to apply suitable remedies at judicious moments.

'These bloody guides,' Henry said suddenly, interpreting my look of query, 'have become a real pain. I hate the bloody things. Jean is completely taken over by them. Nothing else matters. Nothing. It's become an absolute obsession.'

I produced a surprised but sympathetic expression. I had known Henry for a long time, perhaps not intimately but certainly quite well. He was a conventional enough sort of man for nowadays: a good father, an understanding husband, reliable, and supportive of Jean during the time she stayed at home to bring up the children. He was a bit unlucky in that his semi-academic job, with its secure pension arrangements, had led him into a cul-de-sac, an impasse where he was pretty well stuck even though it seemed to have the advantage that he could take a number of weeks' holiday at regular intervals. It requires considerable flexibility to adjust to a wife with a new role, one which dilutes the concentration on husband and home, and Henry had become rather set in his ways. In my case I have always been sanguine about what Mary would do once our offspring went on their way and it has proved advisable to be so; she much enjoys her return to teaching and, fortunately, the school holidays are long enough to ease the absences and occasional neglect our domestic circumstances have to endure.

'I'm sorry to hear that,' I said, gravely. 'I rather thought you both enjoyed your jaunts and fieldwork, so to speak.'

'We did. To start with. It was great. Well, Jean was very busy with things of course, so it meant that she was tired in the evenings when we might have, well, when we had finished for the day. I could understand that. But you know what journalists are like; they get so self-important about what they're doing and now Jean things it's all so bloody vital, damn it. As though nothing else matters.'

'Well,' I said mildly, 'it is very important to her, I'm sure. And she's a very thorough person. Always has been.'

'It's as though there's nothing else.' For a moment I thought he hadn't heard me. 'And it's not as though it earns all that much. I mean, it's useful, of course. But Jean acts as though she's become the major earner or something.'

I looked reflectively into my glass, which was becoming empty. The revelation of marital stresses always disconcerts me. I do not think I have ever confided anything to another man in the way that I was sure Henry was about to do with me, and I felt embarrassed. It is not only a question of loyalty; to allow such inside knowledge to reside in someone else is to give a hostage to fortune. One never knows when the acquisition of personal knowledge may be used to one's detriment.

'You've finished your beer,' I said. 'Let me get you another.'

'No, no.' He was fiercely vehement. 'It's my round.'

He took the glasses to the bar and ordered seconds, his gaze going out through the opposite window to the garage forecourt where, out of my view, the result of Rupert Fletcher's latest escapade stood forlornly crumpled on the concrete. I turned back to look at the wistaria in the other direction. It was going to take some time for Henry to adjust to things but, I thought, he was a tolerant man and theirs was a long marriage. When, in years to come, he looked back at this period and realised that they were only halfway through at most, he would smile and realise that the earlier, conventionally family-oriented period was the transitory part, not this one. I am very fond of my children but I have always kept a balance about these things. One has to see life in an overall perspective; I've often smiled to myself at the way Mary fondly asks about the porcelain I've seen in some local museum when, apart from a quick glance at its contents to establish credibility, I've actually spent the time in pleasurable bed-based contortions too unseemly to be practised in respectable married life. One needs one's own crumple zone, to use a bad pun, for the relief of those frustrations it is not fair to dissipate upon one's lifetime partner.

'I'm sorry to be such a grouch.' Henry smiled quickly at me as he returned with the drinks. 'I'm sure you don't need to listen to my grumbles about these trips. It's just that this one has started out somehow worse than ever. Jean's been so peremptory. Really bossy. But we'll be better once we're on our way. She's always so anxious that we get everything done in the time available that it tells on her at the start. It's been marvellous to break our trip here as we used to, and to relax over a beer in a country pub with you. I get a bit wound up, you see, about all the hassle of travel and I insisted that we stop here because I haven't seen you for ages. Jean wanted to get straight on to Dover but we don't get much chance to catch up with you these days. You look just the same as ever. How are things?'

I smiled and raised my glass in acknowledgement of his round. 'Not too bad,' I said, modestly. 'Weathering the difficulties of modern life. Mary's very keen on her teaching now, you know. It's made for changes, of course. You and I, Henry, have got to get used to this sort of shift in circumstances. I cook quite a good casserole, myself. Iron the odd shirt. Help out in that sort of way.'

This was true. I didn't like it, of course, no one does, but it was my concession to Mary's return to work. It made me feel less guilty, too, about my little trips to Soho and Shepherd Market. If anything, I now realised, they had increased in frequency since Mary went back to work.

'Oh, I do all that sort of thing, too,' Henry said, falling to a frown again. 'Most evenings Jean's writing up some guff or another for a guide or one of her articles. Someone has to keep the household going. And she diets so much these days – they all do, don't they – that she says she doesn't want anything to eat at night. Then she looks at me, one of those sorts of looks that says I shouldn't want to eat anything either, so I go and cook myself a good fry-up just to make a point. With a stiff drink or two. Or three. I mean there's not much else to enjoy these days.'

'Oh dear,' I said, sadly.

'It affects the travel, too. You said that tomorrow we'd be having a splendid meal at our hotel. Jean hardly ever does that because of the diet thing. And I hate eating alone.' He scowled, and I noticed that he'd almost finished his second pint already. 'To be honest, Jimmy, travelling with Jean is just a microcosm of life with Jean. You buy the tickets, do most of the driving, read the map, carry the bags, change the money, help with the bloody camera, take the crap if anything goes wrong, stay off the booze and food and, at the end of the day, Jean gets into her own little bed and goes straight to sleep. Leaving me thinking what the bloody hell am I doing, damn it?'

'Oh dear,' I said again. This was embarrassing. Worse than I'd expected. It was as though the break at the bar had temporarily lifted him, but then my injudicious remark about helping in domestic circumstances had put everything back. Resentment seethed in his tones. Here certainly was a beleaguered breadwinner, not only threatened by his partner's rise in career but also advising me in no uncertain terms that he was being deprived of what he obviously regarded as his marital bedtime rights. One has to be so careful about making assumptions in that direction, especially when travelling abroad in circumstances which can lead to heightened expectations which are not always shared by one's long-standing partner. For this reason my own quietly accomplished escapades during the day reduce the chance of stresses of that sort. I take care not to overimpose myself on Mary when travelling, just as I am circumspect at the end of one of her working days. The signals are clear enough and when they are negative for too long I find an alternative essential.

'You're so lucky with Mary,' Henry said, glaring from his now-empty glass out in the direction of the garage. 'You and she are such a well-integrated couple. She's such a pleasant girl. Always has been. I often cite you two as an example of how to get on.'

'Ah,' I said. 'How kind of you. Let me get you another drink.'

I bought him another pint but confined myself to a simple tonic water, wondering what version of events was being related to Mary. He downed the third pint less hastily and seemed to recover a bit.

'Come on,' I urged him. 'Cheer up. You and Jean can work out a system to suit the both of you. Talk to her about it. If it's causing such a strain you must be open with each other.'

Hypocritical advice is dreadfully easy to dispense; I felt a pang of self-reproach as he nodded sombrely and thanked me. 'Actually, you're right,' he said. 'I'll do that as soon as possible. Mustn't let these things fester.' Then he downed his beer with a flourish and we set off back to dinner before our absence could lead to recriminations. When Mary lays out a special meal it is prudent not to arrive late.

Fortunately the walk back seemed to revitalise Henry without the overemphasis that drink can induce. His manner was positive. He spoke to his wife cheerfully and was attentive to Mary. The evening passed off well; we talked of uncontentious things like our children and the news of old friends. Jean was cordial to me, perhaps in reaction to the mood in which I had brought back her husband from the pub. We retired to bed in jocular spirits. Mary was delighted that things had turned out well, and was inviting; she and I exhausted ourselves in activities which may have accounted for the very vague way in which I thought I heard voices raised during the night, voices which stirred me faintly but which, on waking, I could not remember clearly as either dream or reality.

In the early morning Jean and Henry drove off straight after a very matter-of-fact breakfast during which she concentrated on their plans and travel arrangements. We said a practical goodbye out on the drive. Henry hardly spoke. There was a preoccupied air about him which made me faintly worried, an air which did not somehow fit with his previous night's moral resolve. After their car disappeared I went inside for a last coffee before leaving for work and asked Mary how she and Jean had got on.

'Oh, fine,' my wife said. 'Jean and I have always got on well. I think she's a bit concerned about Henry, though.'

'Really?' I tried to sound unconcerned. 'Why?'

Mary shrugged. 'Oh, you know. Middle-aged problems, I think. He's getting a bit tedious about this and that, apparently. Jean's so ambitious about her work that it's a bore for her.'

I smiled quietly. The way in which Englishwomen can describe life's ruling passions as 'this and that' or 'a bit of a bore' accounts for the mistaken view of foreigners that they are cool and dull.

'Did you hear voices during the night?' I asked.

Mary's brow furrowed. 'Funny you should ask that. I was so tired – ' she gave me a meaning glance – 'that I mostly slept like a log, but I did think I heard voices. They didn't have a blazing row or something, did they?'

I shook my head. 'I don't think so. Just a sound I was vaguely aware of. Voices, that is. Probably something else.'

The guest bedroom is deliberately well away from ours so that sounds are insulated by distance. You would have to be speaking quite loudly or shouting for voices to penetrate as far as our room.

In the next few days I was busy and Mary had arrangements for half-term to complete. We barely discussed the Battersbys' visit. It was four days after they left that I got home from work to find Mary waiting for me at the door, her face white and strained. She was in tears.

'Oh Jimmy,' she cried. 'Something terrible has happened to the Battersbys. A smash. On the continent. It's Jean; I got a phone call an hour ago. Dreadful news.' She stared at me in shock. 'One dead, the other untouched. Horrible.'

I took her quickly in my arms. A rending fear made my heart thump erratically. In my mind's eye I recreated Henry at the pub, and Rupert Fletcher's car, and heard once again his bitter complaints murmuring in my ears. I had described to him only too clearly the circumstances of Fletcher's escape.

'What happened?' I demanded. 'Quick, what on earth has happened?'

'It was a mistake at a crossing.' Mary's voice was muffled. 'Driving on the right. You know how easy it can be when you're over there and you have to drive on the wrong side of the road. They came out at a crossroads apparently, looking the wrong way, and a car went into the front side. It was instant death. The whole of that side was stove in but the driver was quite unharmed. Isn't it horrible? Their car must have had a crumple zone just like Rupert Fletcher's. Oh Jimmy, isn't it appalling?'

'Ghastly,' I croaked. 'Absolutely ghastly.'

One should never make marital confessions of Henry's sort. To anyone. Such knowledge as I now possessed was dangerous indeed.

'I mean it sounds terrible to say it, but it really would have been better if both of them had died, wouldn't it? Awful for one to be left with that. I know the children will at least still have one parent but they're virtually off on their own now. It's the one left behind that's so lonely. And all those super trips they made together.'

'Yes. Yes I'm sure.' I released her and took her arm as we went inside to sit down. 'Would you like a drink?'

'Oh yes, Jimmy, please. A strong one.'

I handed her a stiff whisky and took one myself. My mind was still whirling as I voiced my thoughts. 'I wonder how Henry will get back? There are awful formalities when this sort of thing happens on the continent. Police, and so on. It can be a rotten business.'

Mary paused with her glass and gave me a peculiar look. 'Get back? Isn't that a bit macabre, darling? I expect it will be in a coffin, won't it?'

The room spun. My whisky seemed to have hit the back of my brain.

'Coffin?' My voice sounded disembodied. 'What do you mean, coffin?'

Mary stared at me. 'Well he's dead, isn't he? Oh Jimmy!' Her face suddenly cleared. 'I'm so sorry! You didn't realise. I haven't been very coherent, have I? It's poor Henry that's dead, darling. Jean was driving at the time. It was she who called. Terrible for her; you know, she sometimes took over, specially when Henry complained of being tired. That's why it's such an ironic thing. I remember she said they saw Rupert Fletcher's car as they came through the village and I told her all about it while you were at the pub. Almost the same type of accident.' Her expression softened. 'What's the matter? You look awful! Of course, it's a terrible shock. I've had a bit more time to absorb it. You rather liked Henry, didn't you?'

I put my head in my hands. 'You told Jean about Rupert's smash? The way he escaped?'

'Oh yes. She was very interested. Their car must have been made the same way, mustn't it? Gosh, it's lucky.'

'Lucky?' I almost glared at her. 'What's lucky?'

'That Henry was well covered for insurances and pension and so on. From his job. And that Jean wasn't hurt.' She looked up thoughtfully from her whisky. Her eyes on mine were disconcerting. 'Jimmy, does our car have the same thing? I mean, would our car do that?'

I stared at her. My throat had become inexplicably dry. 'Oh yes,' I said, uneasily. 'It certainly would. I've always believed in having a crumple zone.'

Good Investments

CELIA DALE

Eunice Christine Hilda Bradshaw grew up in the crisply stony seaside town of Seaham with her maternal Auntie Florence, her father having been killed on active service in 1944, her mother dying of heart trouble two years later. Eunice was in her late teens by this time, studying clerical skills at the local polytechnic. She and Auntie Florence knew each other well, as the sisters had lived near to each other, and the transference from one terrace villa to another was painless. Auntie Florence was a dressmaker, a stout exclamatory woman who had never married, and she doted on Eunice – so clever, so competent, such a churchgoer, a sweet girl. And it was all true.

Eunice graduated through several jobs, each better than the last; and for the past twenty-seven years she had been head of the department dealing with Bereavement Claims in the Seaham branch of a national charitable organisation.

She was a neat, refined woman now, neither fat nor thin, discreetly made-up (but nothing so vulgar as eye shadow, merely powder, pink lipstick, and on off days perhaps a brush of rouge), with hair parted at the side with a half-fringe and which grew just a little browner with each fortnightly visit to the hairdresser. She ran her department impeccably, with a smile and a word of praise when merited. She ran Auntie Florence's house impeccably also, especially as Auntie grew older and fatter and weaker, leaving more and more of it to Eunice and never ceasing to exclaim what a treasure she was. And she was.

She liked everything to be dainty. Frilled curtains, cushions and aprons; flowered bed linen; potted plants in pretty containers standing on doilies; embroidered traycloths and nightdress cases. She cooked delicious cakes, scones, puddings, even made fudge and fondants. She tried out whimsical recipes from magazines such as Sponge Easter Bunnies, Chocolate Yule Logs, Guy Fawkes Brandy Snaps. A spot of spillage in the kitchen was whisked away in a trice, the oven was almost as pure as the day it was installed, the teacloths rinsed and drying after each use, and herself and Auntie sitting in front of the television eating dainty snacks off trays daintily laid with embroidered cloths and matching flowered crockery.

'What a girl you are!' Auntie would wheeze, tucking in. 'What a treasure!'

'Silly Auntie!' Eunice would murmur indulgently. 'It's my pleasure.'

And it was.

So when Auntie died Eunice felt it keenly. People were very kind; she had, of course, the support of the church among whose congregation she had many friends. Auntie had left the house to her and a few – a very few – thousand pounds in the bank. Eunice was due to retire the following year, when she would be sixty. The pension would not be much but she had some savings in the building society; she would be able to manage.

But she missed Auntie. She missed her wheezing presence, her cries of love and appreciation. She missed having an audience for her excellence; making rock cakes and peppermint creams for the church bazaar was not the same, glad though she was to do it, as making them for immediate, face-to-face applause. She missed having someone to demonstrate her virtues to.

She had caused a rosebush to be planted for Auntie in the crematorium's Garden of Remembrance, and she was pruning it one gusty November Sunday (she visited the Garden every fortnight and preferred to look after the rosebush herself as Auntie would have liked) when she fell into conversation with a gentleman performing the same task a bush or two away. His bush was newer than hers by several months; his wife had passed away only recently, he still wore a black band on his sleeve, and had hardly any idea of how to wield his secateurs.

Eunice showed him; she had a ruthless way of pruning which would, she knew, result in a mass of dainty blooms in summer. Mr Stafford – Stanley Stafford, a retired Water Board official – was full of admiration. The wind was cold, his nose dripped slightly, he suggested a cup of tea.

Eunice had never considered marriage. She knew nothing of men save socially (married or semi-celibate around the church hall) or in business (often overbearing or unreasonable, with cigarette ash everywhere and not too careful about how they emerged from the toilet). As a television viewer and a client of the public library she had perforce had aspects of male behaviour presented to her; but television sets could be switched off, and although it was becoming more and more difficult to be sure no unpleasant antics or language appeared in novels, the librarians were fairly good by now at recommending those that might not offend, and there was always travel and biography – although even there one could no longer be sure nowadays, what with fertility rites and hitherto unpublished diaries.

No, men had never attracted her. They seemed, on the whole, selfish and dirty. But she did miss Auntie. Poor Mr Stafford was so pitiful, with his sad eyes and reddish nose, trying to look after himself in the rented flat he had shared with his late wife, the lease of which was nearly up. And there was she, lonely in Auntie's two-bedroomed house.

As a lodger? That would hardly be nice, people would talk . . .

They were married quietly in the spring. Eunice wore navy blue with touches of white and Mr Stafford wore a rose from his late wife's remembrance bush in his buttonhole. Eunice had made it quite clear from the beginning that there was to be none of 'that', and Mr Stafford had thankfully concurred. He was seventy-four and had never had much taste for it. He moved into Auntie's bedroom and Eunice remained in hers, and they never saw each other unless they were fully dressed. But he revelled in her competence, excellence and daintiness (his late wife had not been much of a housekeeper), in her cheerful small-talk, her tasteful presence alongside him in church or when viewing telly, and in the daintily delicious meals she set before him.

He was not used to them, and when they had been married less than a year he had a coronary thrombosis and died in Intensive Care.

Eunice was shocked. The arrangement had worked so well. Stanley had been no trouble, grateful for all she did, taking his own dirty clothes to the launderette so that she never had to handle them, giving up smoking so that there was no mess or fusty smell. He had praised her, comparing her favourably (but with good taste) with his late wife. He had been nearly as good as Auntie.

But better than Auntie in one way; he had left Eunice £9,000 and his life insurance policy. He had, surprisingly, turned out to be rather a good investment.

She missed him. Perhaps not exactly *him* but the appreciation he, like Auntie, had given her. Besides, now she was retired (she had resigned at marriage but in consideration of her twenty-seven years' service the organisation had not diminished her pension) she had very little to do. She would be willing – on the same terms, of course – to take on another man. And there seemed to be money in it . . .

The Garden of Remembrance was a lovesome thing, God wot, and Eunice continued to visit it as regularly as before, for she now had three rosebushes to care for – Auntie, Stanley and Stanley's late wife (as she considered only nice). She observed the other visitors discreetly, and if a funeral were taking place would find out who was the deceased. If it was a gentleman she took no further action. But if it was a lady she would slip into a pew at the back of the chapel and take discreet part. Afterwards she joined the mourners to view the floral tributes and, some months after Stanley's death, stood in line to press the widower's hand and murmur, 'I was a friend of your wife's.'

'Oh yes – thank you,' he said, dazed, a small, bald man in a well-cut suit, his relatives prosperous looking.

'Perhaps, when your grief has eased, I might call on you? So many happy memories . . .'

'Thank you. So kind.'

She pressed his hand and moved on. She knew who he was from the cards; his address would be in the telephone book.

This time it took longer, about eighteen months; and this time she sold Auntie's house and moved into Kenneth Gratton's handsome semi-detached on the Cliff Road. The arrangement was as before: separate rooms and no intimacies. But Kenneth was not otherwise at all the same as poor Stanley had been. He had been head of a building firm and used to ordering men about and getting his own way. Although he was small and bronchitic he had a will of concrete, drank whisky in the evening, refused to give up his pipe, which made the whole house smell disgusting as well as leaving dottles of burnt tobacco in every dainty ashtray and even on the floor. He expected her to watch *Match of the Day* and, horror of horrors, wrestling. He disliked made-up dishes, dainties of every kind; liked fried onions, pickles and stout.

It was no hardship at all for Eunice to slip a sleeping pill or two into his bedtime whisky and, when he was snoring loudly, place a pillow over his face.

Kenneth did not leave her his house (he left that to his son who lived in Newcastle and took no interest in his father's affairs) but he left her a reasonable sum – not as much as she had expected but she realised that Kenneth had been an error of judgement in many ways, something of a disappointment altogether. But there was always tomorrow, and pressing yet another widower's hand the following autumn she felt her instincts could be relied on this time.

Gilbert Phelps was pale, frail and asthmatic, almost unbecomingly eager for someone to continue taking care of him. He ate little and worried about his health and was, in fact, a very poor companion, although he possessed some sound investments and a house in the best part of Seaham which she sold at a good profit as soon as probate was granted; it had been a happy release for them both.

Now, on the whole, she thought it would be wise to move from Seaham and start afresh elsewhere. She moved further along the coast, into a genteel private hotel, found the local Garden of Remembrance and a neglected rose-tree, and in not too long a time became Mrs Reginald C. ocker, with a nice first-floor flat overlooking the promenade and a husband who was eighty-four years old.

No one was surprised when he apparently died in his sleep.

As Mrs Christine Crocker, Eunice married the following year a retired solicitor called Wilfred Jessop, who left her some more useful stocks and shares and property in Cornwall. This she sold, and with the proceeds bought herself a luxury bungalow (but big enough for two) in Redcliff-on-Sea where, as Christine Jessop, she became the wife of Bernard Barnes, a company director and diabetic, whom she nursed daintily till his peaceful passing during the night not very long afterwards.

Redcliff-on-Sea had a large population of senior citizens, and before long, as Hilda Barnes, she married an ex-Army man, Major Desmond Heath. She found him crying under the pergola of the Garden of Remembrance, shamefaced into a large handkerchief, and, as with the first, harmless Stanley, gave him comfort and accepted a cup of tea.

The Major was small and stringy; he had served under Monty at Alamein and liked to tell stories of how sometimes, at first glance, he had been taken for that great warrior, standing sharp and keen in his jeep, battle-browned soldiers cheering his passing.

'Great days, marvellous days!' he would say, take out his handkerchief and blow his nose.

He and his late wife had been living in one of Redcliff's more expensive hotels. 'Never seemed to put down roots anywhere,' he said. 'Army life, rolling stones. Eleanor – 'he gulped a little, as he always did in those early days at the mention of his late wife's name, 'Eleanor was content to be an Army wife – camp follower, I used to tease her. Longed for a home though sometimes, both of us. Home is the soldier, home from the lea, and the hunter home from the hill. We were looking around, but then – left it too late.'

He absolutely agreed with Eunice's provisos. 'Companionship, that's what you and I are about, isn't it, Hilda? Grow old along o' me. And to tell you the truth, that wound I got at Mersa Matruh . . .' He coughed, embarrassed, and Eunice changed the subject.

The Major moved in and they settled down in a way now very familiar to Eunice. As a military man, used to being on the move, he was sparse and neat in his belongings, orderly in his habits. He did not smoke, drank only one gin and tonic before supper, enjoyed gardening and the same television programmes that she did. His late wife had left him comfortably off and, what with one thing and another, Eunice had accumulated an extremely tidy sum over recent years. The Major had a sweet tooth and appreciated her cakes and dainties. He paid her little compliments, which none of the others since Stanley had done; but chivalrous compliments, with no nasty suggestive undertone.

She really was getting to like the Major very much. He was a perfect gentleman. If this was marriage, she could begin to see why so many people recommended it: companionship, appreciation, nothing messy or disagreeable, privacy and respect, nothing that wasn't nice. She really felt she might settle for this one; marriage with the Major, growing old along o' him, no more speculative attendances at unknown funeral services, no more business prospects to consider, for surely the two of them had quite enough between them to live comfortably to the end of their days?

She was very surprised, therefore, to be wakened in the middle of a night some months after their marriage by her bedroom door being opened and footsteps padding across the floor.

'Desmond? Is that you? What on earth . . .?'

But he made no reply. And even if he had she wouldn't have heard it, for the pillow he pressed down on her face blanked out for ever all senses save terror and panic and an outraged incredulity.

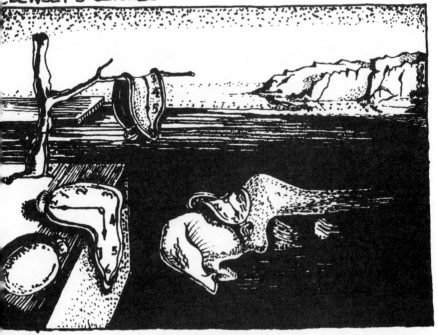

CLEWSEY'S CLICHÉS

COME, COME, MAJOR— DID NOTHING PECULIAR STRIKE YOU ABOUT THE TIME?

Chased Delights; Or, The Missing Minutes

KEITH HELLER

'Who is it, William?' Catherine Blake called to her husband who was standing hunched in the open front door of their apartment.

'Only a starling, madam. Many of them lose their way in the spring.'

She tried to see past him, but all that was visible in the early daylight was a high, wide-brimmed hat that did indeed seem to float above her husband's head like a confused bird.

A rougher, more imperious voice pushed in through the door: 'Talk to me here, Mr Blake, or talk to me elsewhere. It is nothing to me one way or the other.'

Craning over to one side, Catherine caught sight of a long coat, a thick waistcoat with shortish trousers, and a distorted cane wielded by a gloved hand with an index ring on the outside. Part of a face could be seen as well, and that was so full and red in the lips that she wondered for a moment if her husband might not be the focus of attention of some Billingsgate fishmonger.

'Mr Townshend,' William Blake replied calmly, 'I fear you have miscounted your doors, sir. The Old King's Arms Tavern is only a few more along your way. Pray, don't dawdle, or your fine imitation of a gelded swine will be greatly missed.'

It was a trembling spring day in May 1790, and the Blakes were enjoying their final few months in the house at 28 Poland Street in which they had lived for the past five years. Sick of the narrow interior and the loud neighbourhood, they had started meditating a move across Westminster Bridge to Hercules Buildings, Lambeth. If for no other reason, Catherine was anxious to remove her husband as far as possible from that same tavern he had just named. There were too many idling artists, foreigners, and even Druids there to make any wife feel at ease about her man spending most of his evenings inside it.

Now, after a minute of murmured argument, William Blake was turning towards her with a dark anxiety in his eyes.

'I have to go out for a time, my dear. Mr Townshend here has a new song which he wants to whistle to me in private.'

'Will you be long gone?'

'I cannot say. Where is my hat?'

Together, they rummaged through the room, Catherine all the while feeling her heart growing colder within her chest.

'Where will you be going, William?'

The poet glanced at the pompous man at the door, frowned, and said he was not yet sure.

'But I'll send you a message by a boy as soon as I can.'

Catherine followed him to the door, slightly unsteady on the uneven floor.

'I'll prepare our supper as usual, of course,' she said as hopefully as she could.

'As to that,' Blake said, 'I shall probably eat with my good friend Mr Townshend here.'

'You are paying, since you are inviting, aren't you?' He raised his voice to the man waiting just outside.

'I shouldn't worry about that just now, Mr Blake. You have graver concerns before you.'

The artist cocked back his head to take in all of the man's arrogant girth as he replied, 'Well, if I can only catch a fraction of what must fall from those well-worked chaps of yours, I think I shall survive.'

The two men were out the door before Catherine could think of anything else to say, and they faded into the flying colours of Poland Street as quickly as dew off a heated stone.

For most of the day she tried to busy herself in the house, deliberately not looking too much at the door and concentrating on work that she knew would please her husband. Even when she went out for an hour for some errands, she stayed nearby and kept the front door in sight. She was not above peeking through the window of the tavern each time she passed, but she doubted that the men had gone there. William had seemed far too concerned for that.

By the end of the afternoon, Catherine had done as much as she could to distract herself from the uneasiness that was now simmering within her as briskly as her boiled spinach salad. It was not a question of trust. After eight years of being together, she had never known him to lie to her. He was almost thirty-three years of age, and he needed no one to tell him how an adult ought to behave.

Still, last year's revolution in France had started a sudden fire in him that his wife was having difficulty in understanding. He sometimes denounced all restrictions on the individual, and since the unspectacular publication last year of his *Songs of Innocence* and *Book of Thel*, he had been fuming over the slow spread of his reputation. On 28 November he would arrive at Christ's age at his transfiguration, and he was determined that the moment should see the exaltation of his own spirit. His wife frequently wondered what might happen if he did not. She could still recall the despair that had overcome the engraver when his brother died in his arms in this room three years ago, and she did not relish the prospect of any other attack on his sometimes fragile soul.

As evening fell with the salad, Catherine found herself more and more often at the door, squinting out into the darkness that was as spring fresh with spring as wet metal. She shivered at the endless noise of London at night, and listened for an echo of the voice she would recognise even in a mob. But all she heard was the droning that every great city makes as it breathes, broken only by the shouts of those set free after their daytime routines.

Finally, as night began to deepen, she came to a decision, set the salad to one side, and threw a shawl over her shoulders. She pushed recklessly up Poland Street, turned right on to Oxford Street, and walked as rapidly as she could past the glitter of Soho until she came to the wedge of buildings that angled into High Street, St Giles. There, she turned sharply to the right and entered Hog Lane, where the darkness deepened until it clung to her shoulders like her shawl. Yet she kept on moving, through the angry barkings of dogs and noise of drunkards, penetrating the depths of a neighbourhood that even the worst minds had no hope of comprehending.

Fortunately, Catherine Blake had somewhere to go.

In the past ten years or so, Saunders Dance had managed to groom himself into one of the best thief-takers in the city. Ever since the days of Jonathan Wild, some men had tried to augment London's system of watchmen and its fledgeling police force by starting out on their own as private enquirers into justice. Too many of them had followed Wild's lead by arranging a robbery, solving it, then turning in the culprit for reward and fame. By betraying everyone, they had come to be regarded as only a bit above attorneys.

Dance, on the other hand, had never lowered himself to such a level, and as a result was constantly pining after the bright favours enjoyed by his betters. It was whispered that he had come from a successful merchant family and that his decision to pursue the unlikely career of thief-taker lay at the root of all those chronic ailments that no doctor had yet been able to notice. Yet for all his frailty, Dance was as good as he was poor and as wise as any learned lord or churchman. He never despaired, and only sometimes did he allow his friends to sit up late with him to talk him out of losing all hope.

Catherine Blake and Saunders Dance had grown up more or less together in a lane in Battersea, and since then they had kept in monthly contact for springtime strolls or winter conversations in steaming coffee houses. To any ignorant onlooker, they might have been sister and brother. If the woman had never told her husband of her friend, it was only because the artist might have been too passionate to understand fully. It was a common enough subterfuge among London wives, and Catherine consoled herself by remembering all the friends William had whom she had never even been asked to meet.

When Dance finally opened his door to the dark of Hog Lane, he was shocked to find his old friend standing shivering from her frantic walk.

'Mrs Blake! What is it? But step inside at once.'

Seating her before a grey fire in a room that was perfumed with the clinging scents of gum ammoniac, liquorice root, fennel, hyssop, and Peruvian balsam, Dance coughed and sat himself down. The woman looked at his fallen face and at the blankets he had wound about his throat and asked, 'How are you this night, Mr Dance?'

'Oh, better not to ask, Catherine. Better not to ask.'

'Is it so very bad? What is it, do they know?'

Thus encouraged, the thief-taker brightened for a moment, then he grumbled for a while against physicians and apothecaries. 'But if they can't help me,' he concluded, 'I shall have to learn to help myself. Just now, you see my asthma receding before the combination of olibanum and opopanax, and the gleet that has been my constant companion for months is meeting its match in two pills of mastic and turpentine. Only a few more days of agony and I shall climb over this stile. You shall see.'

A juicy cough interrupted him long enough for him to notice his visitor's haunted look.

'But you're white with exhaustion, Catherine. Let me run out for some coffee.'

'No, please, don't vex yourself. But if you should have some gin in the room . . .'

After restoring his guest, Dance said, 'Still, you would not have come at such an hour if something terrible had not happened.'

'Mr Dance, they've taken William away.'

'Away? Who has taken him? Why should anyone want to?'

Catherine shook her head hopelessly. 'All I know is that he left this morning - '

'Pardon me, but of his own will?'

'Yes,' she admitted, 'but I'm sure it was not by choice. A man came for him . . .'

'Who?' the thief-taker asked more energetically.

'Do you know a man named Townshend?'

Dance made a growling sound in his throat, but this time it had nothing to do with phlegm.

'Who does not? To know him is to wish to have been born deaf and blind. If there is anything about the animal that offends the taste more than his womanish clothes it must be his fool's ideas. I myself would rather pass a year under a bread and milk poultice than a day in his company.'

Dance's hostility to Townshend was not primarily due to any dispute concerning fashion. The two often found themselves at odds over business. John Townshend had by some trick worked himself up into a position of honour as the leading member of the Bow Street Runners, though no one knew quite how.

By this time the select officers – usually no more than a dozen in number - who worked out of Bow Street had become the most famous among London's embryonic police forces. In direct line of descent from the Flying Squad founded forty years earlier by the novelist Henry Fielding and a watchman named Man, the Runners performed duties that varied from guarding the King to keeping an eye open during balls to prevent common thievery.

Some of their finest work was in investigation, a field they were forced to invent as they went along, and in a deduction that was based more on human than on physical evidence. Even with all their corruption, the Runners were able to discover the truth somewhat more often than they lied, and their presence in London had gradually made the streets habitable. Townshend was neither the best nor the worst of the Runners, only the vainest and the most extravagant.

Suppressing his aggravation, Dance begged his guest for more detail, and Catherine Blake told him about the morning.

'And you have heard nothing since?' Dance said when she had finished her story.

'Not a breath. But where could they have taken him?'

'Oh, that's solved easily enough. Townshend undoubtedly took your good man to Bow Street, where fewer people than usual detest his laughable appearance. Townshend's, that is.'

'But why?' Catherine sobbed.

Saunders Dance seemed to retreat behind his medicated blankets. 'The fact is,' he began, 'I do happen to know what Townshend has been involved with since this very morning.'

'And that is?'

The thief-taker studied his visitor closely.

'Do you mean to say, Mrs Blake, that you know nothing of what the whole town is talking itself hoarse over?'

'I've been at home almost all day, and when I went out to do some marketing I was too distracted to hear anything.'

'Well,' Dance said carefully, 'there has been a murder, and John Townshend is the man who is closest to it.'

'What murder?' Catherine said.

'An artist, a copier, rather, who lived in Great Queen Street somewhere. A maid found him murdered amongst his own sketches at sunrise this morning just a few minutes before his agent arrived. The poor painter had been tortured to death, it seems.'

'What was his name?'

'Who? The agent? Howard Young. Quite a fox, that man is.'

'No,' the woman said weakly. 'The artist.'

'Caxton, I believe. Yes, that's it. Samuel Caxton.'

At the sound of the name, Catherine Blake almost fell from her chair and was obliged to ask her host for more gin.

'He was a member, with Mr Blake and myself, of the New Jerusalem Church since we joined in April of last year.'

'Ah,' Dance commented a little mockingly, 'the Swedenborgian gathering in the building with the moon-dial on the outside wall down in Great Eastcheap. But I thought your husband had left that man's peculiar wisdom behind him by now.'

'I think he has. At present he is busy with some work about marriage that I conjecture argues against the Church. Recently,' the woman sighed in a long-suffering way, 'he has even talked wildly about the superiorities of the passions of Hell over Heaven.'

As she imparted the blasphemous theory, the thief-taker quickly turned his eyes away, and his face darkened with heat.

'I thought I heard something else, Mrs Blake. Some trouble that lately had people talking about the Church out in the streets.'

'You must mean the expulsions.'

'Yes. What was that all about? Was your husband involved in those as well?'

'Not directly, no,' Catherine replied. 'The six members who were expelled from the Church were nothing to either one of us.'

'But why were they shown the door at all?' asked Dance.

'Oh, it was just some foolishness over a translation of one of the Master's works.'

'Which one?'

'Well,' she answered, taking a long breath, 'the full title is *Chaste Delights of Conjugal Love: after which follow the Pleasures of Insanity and Scortatory Love*. I have not glanced into it myself, you understand,' she hurriedly added, 'but William has read a few pages of the translation aloud to me.'

'And is it so awful that these people had to be banished because of its words or ideas?'

'As I was told, they were exiled from the Church because of some of the conclusions they drew from the writings.'

'And what were they?'

Now Catherine Blake stared into the frail fire and swallowed her natural womanly diffidence.

'I'm sure it has no relation to what has happened today, but they - they maintained that men should be allowed to add whores to their houses, if their wives do not accept the Master's teachings with an open enough heart.

'Apparently,' she murmured drily, 'only males are born with the *amor sexus* that permits them any outrages. Women, of course, must rest content with nothing beyond the occasional disorder of our sleeping minds.

'Not but that even the finest husband in the world will sometimes conceive notions that no wife could endure. As if,' she whispered mainly to herself, 'a harlot should stand beside me in my own kitchen!'

A brief and uncomfortable silence fell between them, until Saunders Dance asked, 'Have these six continued with their translation?'

'They have, in a magazine of their own making. You should know, Mr Dance, that most of what I say comes from talk I have heard among the Church's women and the few pages of our minutes that I had a chance to read before they disappeared.'

The thief-taker sat up. 'What's this? Disappeared? But why?'

'No one knows,' Catherine said. 'But it is a fact that every record of the Church's meetings between May of last year and this past month has been stolen from us. No one can think why any thief should want to take such harmless pages. Who could be so interested in the details of the Church's daily business?'

The thief-taker rose to stir the fire into more heat. 'The reasons for crime among the race of Adam are as various and dark as the endless streets of London itself,' he intoned. 'But tell me, Mrs Blake,' he went on, 'could the murdered artist, Samuel Caxton, have been connected with these missing minutes?'

'I think not,' Catherine said slowly. 'He was not close with the administration of the Church, although he did arrange all the decorations for the building. He was a small, quiet man who only wanted to pass as much time within the walls of the New Jerusalem as he could. I think he was there oftener than the churchmen.'

'Perhaps, then,' suggested Dance, 'he was in league with the six who were expelled for their lecherous proposals.'

Catherine Blake looked up in surprise, now heartened by the effect of the tots of gin.

'Mr Caxton? It's clear that you did not know him. He would not have enough theology to follow their arguments, nor the style to run among their company. I think Mr Caxton exhausted most of his ardour through his eyes during our services in the church.'

'He was a man for the ladies, then? But only from afar?'

The thief-taker's guest nodded, but the rocking of her body led Dance to imagine that this detail lay somewhat closer to home.

'Don't tell me, Mrs Blake, that this Caxton looked too much your way as well? Not, of course, that anyone could fault him – '

'It's true,' Catherine admitted, 'though I am sure he looked on me more as a mother than as a sweetheart. The problem is that William noticed before long and spoke loudly to Caxton in the street one day.

'It seems to me,' she went on, 'that this had more to do with Caxton and his successes as an artist than with me. He had been painting a series of country scenes from all over the Midlands for my Lord Soane during a year or more, and my husband has always felt a low regard for those who paint strictly for pay – and succeed.'

With a long groan, the thief-taker rose to his feet and moved over to the fireplace. He was now plainly worried, much as he tried not to let his friend see it in his face.

'What is it, Mr Dance?' Catherine asked anxiously. 'You cannot think that William really could have had anything to do with the death of Mr Caxton simply because he was jealous of his attentions to me and of his commissions?'

'Are these not reason enough?' he cried, lifting his arms. 'And it hardly matters what I think. What John Townshend and the Runners at Bow Street think is what matters now. Not to mention the opinion of whatever magistrate they are undoubtedly standing before even now with the unhappy Mr Blake secured snugly within their circle.'

Finally acknowledging the fears she had been trying to deny all day, Catherine pressed her palms together before her, raising her eyes to her old friend. 'Is there nothing we can do?' she implored him.

'Oh,' Saunders Dance said, 'there is almost always something that can be done. What we must do now is find out the best way of doing it.'

It was no mere accident that Catherine Blake should meet Howard

Young in the roadway before the Bow Street offices. Having come separately to enquire after the same case, they might yet not have encountered each other if Catherine had not been weeping tears of frustration just as Young walked out of the building.

Gallantly handing her a handkerchief, he looked backwards and said, 'Madam, I quite sympathise with your crying at the sight of one of the ugliest architectural monstrosities in all of London, but we must make our best efforts to bear up. After the burnings of the Gordon Riots ten years ago, it's a marvel that this should stand before us at all.'

Catherine could not help smiling at the shining face of the man before her, at his carefully sculptured clothes and the eager youthfulness of his attitude.

'If it were only that, sir, I could turn my eyes down towards the kennel. But it is one inside the building who tears at my heart so.'

'A loved one?'

'My husband.'

'Nothing too grave, I pray?' Young asked delicately.

'Grave enough, I'm afraid. I have only now learned that they have formally charged him with the one crime that he must be the last in London capable of committing. The way he reveres all life – '

'So it is murder he stands accused of?'

Catherine nodded, staring more closely at the man.

'As it happens,' Young continued, 'I too have had business here with respect to a murder. Would it be presumptuous of me to think that we both have an interest in the same affair?'

The wind in the street was as transparent and keen as every true spring wind is, and Catherine had to wipe a hair out of her eyes as she asked, 'Did you know Mr Caxton well, Mr . . .'

'Howard Young, madam.'

'And I am Catherine Blake, wife to William. Are you counted among the town's many artists, too, Mr Young?'

'Hardly that,' the man laughed. 'But I do make it easier for them to sell what they draw. Most artists are too strange to the everyday world to pay sufficient attention to finding those men of wealth and power who can sponsor them.'

'And you provide that connection between them – for a price.'

The charmer bowed slightly and flashed his sound teeth.

'It is my thought that all artists deserve their due, and I am as much an artist at my craft as is your husband at his.'

'You know William?' Catherine asked in surprise.

'Mainly by rumour. But it is said that his relief printing in last year's *Songs of Innocence* is the most revolutionary etching since the plates he cut for Joseph Ritson's *English Songs* back in '83.'

'He has done some truly remarkable work of late,' Catherine boasted as she began her walk up Bow Street towards Long Acre and the exhausting trek home. Seeing Howard Young fall into step by her side, she asked, 'I suppose you think my husband could profit from your services.'

'But of course! Was it not Dr Johnson himself who said that "no man but a blockhead ever wrote, except for money"? Mr Blake, I am sure, must be of much the same mind.'

'You obviously know nothing of him ,' the woman said with a weary sigh of wifely endurance. 'To him, such worldly engravers are but heavy lumps of cunning and ignorance.

'But our Mr Caxton, now,' she went on as they walked. 'Was he one who welcomed the usefulness of your talents, Mr Young?'

The gentleman preened himself in the striking air. 'I think he was,' he replied. 'When I first met him, he knew no one of any worth, and all his energies were wasted on journeyman work and commissions from merchants who would have done better to hire any common painter of business signs. Once I began to work beside the fellow, he started to gain in the race.'

'It was you, I suppose, who procured for him the commission from Lord Soane for some scenes from the Midlands.'

'It was, indeed,' said Young, surprised by the woman's knowledge of the situation. 'It was one of my finest triumphs, and certainly the best that Caxton could ever hope to do. My Lord Soane contracted for as many country scenes as the artist had the strength to visit and execute from the life, but he agreed to pay only for an entire and authentic series. The commission was a new kind of security for Caxton that he never could have found on his own without the help of the Lord – and myself.'

'What a tragedy his death must mean to you all, then.'

The handsome man pursed his thin lips and made a gesture of concession with his hands in the sunlight.

'Well, as it happens, Caxton had finished the final painting some days before his unhappy death, and all that remained was to gather up the canvases and transport them to his Lordship's house. In fact, that is what I was about when I arrived at his home with the maid and found him dead. It was a tragedy, for I respected the man,' Young sighed, 'even with his extreme scrupulousness that came so close to ruining us both.'

A look of resentment spread over his fine face. He continued, 'At any rate, his apartment is where I am bound even now, to carry those works away and deliver them to their rightful owner.'

'And Bow Street will permit this?' Catherine asked.

Young reached into his pocket and drew out a small metal rod.

'My dear Mrs Blake, they have given me the key. By law, the paintings are Lord Soane's, so I shall only be acting as an agent of the magistrate. There can be nothing there that could be of use to John Townshend in his investigations now.

'Besides,' he went on uncomfortably, 'as it seems they have their man in custody already, there can be no harm in it. And I should like to add, Mrs Blake, that I can only think that your good husband must have suffered some momentary madness to – '

They had come to a stop within the wide expanse of Long Acre. Catherine turned slightly to the left towards her house and Howard Young steered off to the right towards Caxton's.

'Would you mind terribly, Mr Young, if I were to come with you to Mr Caxton's home just now?' she asked.

With only a second's hesitation, the man asked her why.

'Well,' Catherine declared, 'I could tell you that I wanted to visit the area where my husband lived as a youth when he was with his master, James Basire. But the truth is that I hope to find something among Mr Caxton's effects that I might be able to use to save my husband from prison, or worse.'

'Such as what, madam?' he asked suspiciously.

'Who can say? But I must do something. And if you do not wish me to come, then I shall just have to follow behind you like some sad, abandoned dog. With you or without you, Mr Young, I mean to search the rooms in Great Queen Street before this day is done.'

Whether because of the woman's forlorn look or the prospect of a pathetic female tagging along at his heels, Howard Young decided reluctantly that Catherine Blake could accompany him.

'But I should not raise any great hopes, if I were you. The man's apartment holds nothing more than papers and inks and those scenes that I am going there to remove. John Townshend may dress himself as if in a nightmare, but I have never known him to fail in his duties as a Runner. As I understand it, the only papers to be found there were those notes that he has already secured.'

'Which notes are you talking about, sir?' Catherine asked.

'Why, only those from Mr Blake himself! Savage letters, by Mr Townshend's report, that threatened jealous attacks upon Mr Caxton for his hot ogling of you during the services at your New Jerusalem Church. Those are the words, madam,' Young intoned, 'that may very well hang your husband before this unfortunate business is done. They will be published in the town before tomorrow is out.'

The rooms that had belonged to Samuel Caxton betrayed the chaos and the focus that seemed to be the opposing forces within every artist. Catherine had no trouble recognising such debris as these crumpled preliminary sketches, those peculiar smears of colour on the plain wooden floor, and the smells of oil and acid that had long since transformed the entire room into an old rag. As the wife of an engraver and poet, she knew there was no lasting cure for the disorder that somehow made a creative day more bearable.

In addition to such domestic scree, the sitting-room boasted a wall of nooks and pigeonholes that had once been stuffed with a covey of nesting papers. These now lay in a spreading heap across the floor, pages and sheets and the backs of yellowing magazines, most of them smoothed open to reveal whatever stray thoughts the artist had once considered important enough to save. Gazing about her, the woman saw again the grey eyes that had so eagerly stared at her across the main room of the church, and she felt an aching loneliness that made her suddenly slouch in pity and weariness.

'Evidently,' Catherine observed as they waded through waves of soiled clothes, 'whoever killed Samuel hoped to find something among his papers before he left.'

'Is that not always so?' said Young. 'Just this morning, the Runner was telling me that he knew of hardly a case where murder was not followed by thievery.'

'Is there any way of knowing if papers were taken?'

'Who can say? Even the maid knows nothing. When Townshend's men found – well, found your husband's letters to Caxton, the slut seemed as surprised as if they had uncovered a box full of gold.'

'What about his paintings?' Catherine asked, glancing about. 'Did the Runner think any of those had been carried away?'

In answer, Howard Young led the woman into an adjoining room and came to a stop before a crowd of canvases that stood leaning against the wall. Samuel Caxton had apparently been a painter of some ability, though his obvious realism would have offended William Blake with his insistence upon symbol and spirit. Restful scenes from rural England predominated, muted in colours and deficient in drama, and the predictability of the treatment somehow gave the observer a sense of numbing harmony. Yet Mr Caxton had been talented enough, and Catherine silently decided that she had underestimated the pale little man.

'Are these the paintings intended for Lord Soane?' she said, ticking some of them off with her fingers.

'They are,' replied Young. 'As you can see, they are mostly all of a kind, simple studies of the unspoiled countryside.'

'And I notice that they are all dated within the past year.'

'I suppose so. Caxton worked very conscientiously on them. I sometimes wondered how he found time for anything else.'

Still frowning over the stacked paintings, Catherine finally halted at one that showed a bridge vaulting over a small river, with a familiar building rising like a shadow in the background.

'There is something odd about most of these,' she murmured. 'Look. This one, for example. It is a fair likeness of the houses at Clapham, I grant you that. But I don't recall ever having seen such a bridge at that place.'

'Perhaps,' suggested Young, 'it has only lately been added.'

'No, you don't understand. What I mean is, I don't remember such a bridge there because there is no such river. There is some kind of pond, but it's much too broad for any arching walk.

'And look, in the corner here,' Catherine added, pointing at the bottom edge of the frame. 'This date is of only a few months past. And this other one, and this one, and that one – these date from the past year as well, and I would swear that almost all of them portray scenes not as they are now, but as I recollect them from journeys I took when I was a girl. Some I know for a fact show houses and roads that have been vanished for two decades or more.'

Howard Young's only response to the woman's comments was to step slightly away from her and frown darkly.

'Don't you see?' she went on after ordering her thoughts. 'I don't think Mr Caxton painted any of these from the life at all. He must have executed them strictly from memories he had of some period in the past. Surely such a man should not fail to record so many details of a scene accurately, and yet as far as I can tell, most of these appear to be antique.'

'That is quite a serious charge, madam,' the artist's agent exclaimed. 'If such an unlikely case were true, I'm sure my Lord Soane would cancel the contract out of hand. He expects paintings that reproduce the scenes as they are today so that he may show them proudly to other country gentlemen. Any deviation from truth would mark him as a dupe in the eyes of all.

'No, no!' cried Young vigorously. 'I refuse to believe that Mr Caxton would have done anything so foolish. Why should he have endangered his income in such a way, not to mention his reputation in the town? And mine!'

'Perhaps,' Catherine mused aloud, 'because he simply did not have it in him to traipse all over the countryside just to depict scenes he thought he already knew well enough by heart.' Glancing about her, she said, 'He seems to have been quite a houseling, to judge by these rooms. And I know from personal experience that he spent too many days at the New Jerusalem Church during this past year to have found the time to leave London on any long excursions.'

Still moving restlessly in the darkness, Howard Young seemed to be seriously considering the woman's suggestions. After a few moments, however, an objection occurred to him.

'But such an allegation must have more behind it than memory or rumour. How many can recall whether or not a certain man was in a certain place over a lengthy space of time? Lord Soane will require something more concrete, madam, if he is to withdraw from an important arrangement such as ours.'

As they talked, the two continued to roam through the studio filled with canvases and into a smaller room that contained only a few discarded failures. In the centre stood a short wooden pillar with a thick platform at the top. Resting there, an iron moon-dial stared blindly up at the windowless ceiling, as if somehow it could chart the hours of the night sky by hope alone.

Suddenly, Catherine came to a halt. 'Of course!' she proclaimed. 'That must be why – '

'Why what?' asked Howard Young as she hesitated.

'Why someone would want to steal every page of the Church's minutes for an entire year. It must have been Caxton himself. He knew that the minutes would be the only written proof of all the days he had attended and failed to perform his commission for my Lord Soane. Once they were missing, anyone could suspect all they wanted, but no one could charge him positively with anything.'

'But this is absurd,' Young spluttered. 'Even if Caxton stole these minutes of yours, why should he be killed?'

'For those very same minutes. It's clear that the person who murdered him was searching for something among his papers.'

'To reveal them to the world?'

'Or to keep them hidden.'

The dark room seemed to whisper around them, but it was only the scuttling of mice against the walls.

'The killer must have found them and carried them away with him, then,' Young concluded.

'Or he failed to find them at all. It may be he did not know poor Caxton as well as he should have, or know of his fondness for the kind of art that he provided for the church in Great Eastcheap.'

Catherine Blake's gaze fell naturally upon the moon-dial.

'There is a brother of this on the wall of our church . . .'

Reaching out, she wrenched the base of the dial before Young could make a move, and it came away with the rustling of paper.

'The minutes!' the agent shouted.

Catherine gathered them into her arms and began backing away out of the small room.

'Where are you going with those?' Howard Young asked.

'To Bow Street, of course. These may help my husband.'

She had almost reached the light of the sitting-room when the man stepped between her and the door. His face was black.

'I think not, madam. I'll thank you to hand me those pages.' There was a new edge in his voice that sounded odd coming from such a refined mouth, and the hands that took the minutes were claws.

'But why did you have to kill him? Only for these?'

'You don't understand, Mrs Blake. Caxton was a coward and a dolt. After troubling himself so to remove the minutes, he began feeling an effeminate remorse that decided him to return them to the Church.'

'And, of course, your contract with Lord Soane would have no hope of being fulfilled.'

'Ruining himself would have been his own affair, but I could not allow him to bury me with him.'

'So you came here to make him tell you where the papers were so that you could destroy them once and for all,' Catherine said.

A sudden emptiness burned at the back of the man's eyes.

'Who could have guessed that he would choose to perish rather than tell? And that his throat should have been so weak?

'And,' the woman went on, 'after having ransacked the rooms in vain, you must have left only a few minutes before the maid's appearance in the street outside. Then you reappeared to confirm her discovery of the body.

'I wondered,' she added, 'why you told me when we were in Long Acre that you had come here with her to find Caxton when a friend of mine said that Caxton's agent had come only after the maid. I suppose you must have imagined those few missing minutes when you stood waiting for her to make the discovery alone might be of some danger for you should the magistrate think to ask you where you were at the time.'

'It seems, madam,' Young whispered as he advanced towards her to force her back into the darker room, 'that you have known far too much of my business all along. That, I promise you, shall now be remedied.'

With the rolled-up pages held before him like a truncheon, Young came nearer until the woman could feel his cold breath on her face. He had just raised his hands towards her throat when the mice at the wall seemed to make their way through the litter on the floor and out towards the standing moon-dial.

'You have played your part admirably, Mrs Blake,' Saunders Dance said, as he emerged from a corner shadow, 'from those false tears you sold him in Bow Street until now. I never thought that he would talk to you or let you come along, not to mention give himself away once the papers had been found.'

The thief-taker took charge of the minutes and the killer.

'But,' he complained, his hard hand closing on the other man's arm, 'why did you leave nothing for me to do? What sick man can take any pleasure merely in throwing out the trash?'

William Blake looked across the table at his quiet wife.

'I hope, madam, that the events of the last few days have in no way frightened you. This Howard Young who murdered poor Caxton had evidently been impoverishing himself by chasing more delights than was good for him. Happily, you never had to meet him.'

'I was concerned for you, William, of course.'

The engraver pushed himself back from his plate and let his stomach expand comfortably.

'You really need not have concerned yourself, wife. I am coming on to be an eminent man in this town, so much so that even John Townshend has not the power to damn me to a magistrate for no sound reason. Why, all I had to do was – '

Coming to stand beside her husband, Catherine Blake leant and kissed him thankfully on the top of his head.

'All you had to do, William, was show them how beautifully a man can write when he is fighting to keep his wife by his side.'

🎔 *The Christmas Present*

BOB LOCK

Dear Santa,

The present I want is quite simple, but you see I just can't ask my wife. She knows of my vice, and it's not very nice . . . So please bring me a lovely new KNIFE . . . One with edges as sharp as a razor, and tapering down to a point . . . So that when I feel rash I can cut, stab and slash – and even hack through to the joint.

I had one – Oh, yes – *and* I used it. Now it seems like a terrible dream. I dropped my dear knife as I ran for my life, when that little girl started to scream . . .

So dear Santa please bring me a new one, then I'll know it is SAINSBURY time. With my knife at the ready, in a grip that's rock steady, I'll return to THE SCENE OF MY CRIME. Once again I'LL RIP OPEN the CORN FLAKES . . . the PUFFED WHEAT, the SHREDDIES and more. With eyes just like icicles I'll stab through the RICICLES . . . and LAUGH AS THEY STREAM ON THE FLOOR!!!

Please remember my present, Dear Santa, though my letter's a bit of a chiller. Despite this sad verse, there are crimes so much worse than being . . . A CEREAL KILLER.

JACK R

Something Happened at the Time

MADELAINE DUKE

We relished our new life, free from pressures and obligations. Jack had retired from medical practice, I had given up journalism and settled down to writing my dreamed-of novel. Our move from London to a Spanish village between mountains and sea worked as well as we had hoped. Selva is an attractive place, old enough for the orange trees and palms to have matured, new enough to have a large swimming pool where everyone meets.

There is a good mix of generations and nationalities, young Spanish and Gibraltarian families, retired Scandinavian and British couples.

Jack and I had no problem switching from hard work to playing golf, swimming and running an easy, uncluttered house. We had no problems until we met a man we had not come across before, a tall Englishman in his middle sixties.

Coming out of the village telephone kiosk he asked, 'What's the code for Gibraltar?'

'I think it's 9567,' said Jack.

'That's what I dialled,' he told us, 'but nothing works in this benighted country.'

'Have you tried the operator?' asked Jack.

'I don't speak Spanish.'

'You are new here?' Jack was going to be helpful.

'My wife and I have been living in Selva five years.' He looked at his watch. 'It's lunchtime. I might have another try later. It's not that I want to book a flight to England. All that expense if it's for nothing. On the other hand . . . I have been feeling below par. You're a doctor I believe . . .'

'Retired.' Jack looked at the man. He was grossly overweight and too pale for someone who lived in a sunny climate.

'I'd like to consult you. My name is Don . . . Don Price. We live over there,' he pointed to the corner house of a narrow lane, 'top apartment. Call in any time after lunch.'

'I can't give you a medical,' Jack told him, 'I have no equipment here. And I can't advise you whether or not to fly to England. Sorry.'

Don turned his back on us. 'Well, call in anyway.'

'It was a form of blackmail.' I watched Jack put his stethoscope into a plastic bag.

'I know, Helen. But the man's worried. One can't just ignore him . . . an Englishman in a foreign country.'

'Which has perfectly good medical services.'

'Well, I don't intend to get involved.'

Brave words, but within a very short time we both got involved. Don asked us to dinner. Jack thought it would be best to treat him as an acquaintance rather than a patient and we accepted, neither of us with enthusiasm. The invitation was at seven o'clock for seven-thirty, dress informal. As no one in Selva ever wore anything remotely formal we were a little surprised when Don received us in pinstriped charcoal grey, Mary in beaded cocktail black.

We were offered drinks on one side of the shabby living-room; the other was taken up by a table elaborately set with silver, candles and a dozen crystal glasses. The divide of the two contrasting lifestyles had a depressing effect on me, not helped by the firmly closed doors. One of them, Mary told us, had led to a balcony but Don had eliminated it in favour of an enlarged kitchen.

As we progressed through an uncompromisingly English meal of tomato soup, roast chicken and trifle, Mary told us that they'd come to Spain from Zimbabwe. She called it Rhodesia. Don had been the manager of a mining company, a big boss accustomed to a luxurious life of game hunting, fishing, golf and servants.

Don waited for the cheese platter before changing the subject to his health. He had been born with a slight abnormality of his heart but it had never bothered him. The trouble now was his stomach, his digestion.

'You shouldn't eat so much,' said Jack.

'I've always had a good appetite. But maybe I eat the wrong food. More salads perhaps . . .'

'There's only one wrong food for you.'

'What's that?'

'Too much. As I mentioned before, you need to lose weight. At least twenty kilos.'

'Don's been on a diet once,' said Mary. 'We used to count the calories of every meal. I know all about it.'

'Then you know more than I do.' Jack's patience was running out. 'Forget calories. Just cut his meals by half. Why not start now? Half a pound of cheese after a good dinner is a bit excessive.'

'You could be right.' Don did not sound convinced.

I found his arrogance irritating. Jack did, no doubt, but he responded to the touch of my foot under the table and dropped the subject. Mary, her hostess smile in place, promised to do her best about Don's diet. It sounded as if she was doing Jack a favour.

I did not know how trapped I had felt in the Prices' apartment until we were out of it and I smelt the scent of orange blossom and nightshade.

Anita came out of the swimming pool and spread her towel on the grass. 'Good dinner?' she asked me.

'What dinner?'

'With Mary and Don of course.'

'How do you know about it?'

Anita laughed. 'Carmen told me. Nothing's secret in Selva. Carmen probably smelt a difference in Mary's cooking.'

'And watched from her balcony?'

'I expect so. Don and Mary are not in the habit of inviting people. It is so new . . .' Our Swedish neighbour, unusually for her, seemed to search for words. 'They made isolation. Years ago Don used to come to us for drinks. Mary came just two three times to borrow English books from Olaf. She said she'd invite us to their place but she never did. And then they stopped coming. Helen, I think they're strange.'

'People *are* strange until one gets to know them.'

'I don't think I want to know the Prices.'

Neither did I, but there was no way of avoiding them in a community as small as ours, especially as Don and Mary had made no effort to learn Spanish. The Gibraltarians knew English but they too spoke Spanish even among themselves. Besides Mary disapproved of the way they congregated at barbecues outside their houses, allowed the children to play in squares and patios until late at night and hung their washing on the balconies. To her they were as primitive as the blacks in Zimbabwe. She had managed to live in Africa for thirty years without any contact with Africans other than the servants. She could also do without her Gibraltarian neighbours.

After the dinner Don took to dropping in on us, usually after his late breakfast. Jack kept him out of my study, telling him that I spent the mornings working on my novel. In time, when it was too late, I wondered whether my presence would have stopped Don from revealing intimacies that we should have been spared.

There was Don's habit of taking exercise. He was proud of walking three miles a day. With the choice of seashore and countryside close to Selva he picked his two-roomed apartment for walking back and forth, keeping count of each turn by taking a match from a box. Jack, good physician that he is, felt he had to do something to get Don out of his self-imposed prison. He suggested golf.

'He obviously liked the idea,' Jack told me, 'but there's a snag. He can't afford it. Don retired with a good pension but it's paid in African money which is down 50 per cent. It means they've got to live on half the pension. I've been thinking . . .'

'Of nominating him for membership of your golf club.'

'It's a possibility.'

'And you would be paying his annual subscription?'

'I suppose so. What do you think Helen? The question is, would he accept?'

'I guess he would. He'd play for free and it would cost us five hundred a year.'

'I know, but it wouldn't break us. It'll be awkward . . .'

'Suggesting it to him?'

'Well, yes. The man has his pride.'

Don did accept. He bought a second-hand set of clubs and changed from walking his apartment to playing golf with Jack.

Within a year he'd lost his excess weight and looked fit. But there were episodes when Mary came to our house in near panic. Don hadn't slept all night. Don was feeling faint.

Jack discovered that he was dosing himself with a variety of pills, years old, from Africa. He ate aspirins and drugs against indigestion. Jack tried to stop him but almost certainly failed. Don considered himself an expert at just about everything, including medicine. Don knew it all. When Jack realised that nothing less than doctors in white coats in a surgery or a hospital would get sense into Don's head he suggested a Spanish physician or a check-up in England. Don and Mary decided on England; Manchester, where Mary had cousins.

Jack suspected that the congenital abnormality of Don's heart might have got worse. So it turned out. The Manchester consultant answered Jack's letter, saying he hoped to have persuaded Don against dosing himself with unsuitable pills. He did not think that heart surgery was necessary at the moment but it could become essential in the future.

On their return I asked Mary whether she had considered living in England again.

'We couldn't,' she told me. 'It's too cold after our years in Africa. And it's too expensive. The heating bills alone . . . There was South Africa. Don would have liked to live there. He has relations and friends in Durban. But a black country! I wouldn't contemplate it. I can put up with Spain.'

Arrogant. Inflexible. No, I didn't like Mary. But I had to tolerate her just as Jack put up with Don on the golf course.

Jack did not enjoy the almost daily company. Don refused to take part in competitions or any other club activity. He would not speak to other members, standing aside when they were talking to Jack. But over the next couple of years Don unfolded enough of his story to keep Jack's compassion. There had been a son, an only child. On holiday from his university in Cape Town he told his parents that he'd be spending a weekend with the son of a plantation owner some twenty miles from Don's mine.

It was at the time when Zimbabwe was in the grip of civil war, when armed men were rampaging and killing. While Peter Price stayed with his friend a band of blacks raided the plantation and butchered every white, including Peter.

'You didn't know, did you?' Jack asked me.

'No. Mary's talked about her family in England, her early life. But she never mentioned a son.'

'Strange. It must have happened all of ten years ago. Does she speak to you about Zimbabwe?'

'Yes . . . about her house and the parties they gave. I suppose she still can't bear to speak of her son to strangers.'

Jack shook his head. 'You're not exactly a stranger, Helen. My impression is that she looks upon you as a friend.'

'There are a lot of things she's bottled up.'

'So has Don.'

'But he's told you about Peter. Do you understand why?'

'I think so. Mary believes he should have stopped Peter going to that plantation.'

'How? Peter wasn't a child. He must have had a mind of his own.'

'It seems Don and his son weren't very close. Don was aware that the owners of the plantation were unpopular with Africans. Mary thinks that he should have foreseen the danger to Peter.'

'Does Don believe that?'

'He doesn't know what to believe. Perhaps he told me about it because he needs *somebody* to say that he can't be blamed for his son's death. Not that Mary brings it up. I asked him. He said Mary hasn't mentioned Peter for years.'

We saw no way of withdrawing from the Prices. They did not mix with anyone in Selva apart from us. They made no attempt to learn Spanish and they went nowhere except to a supermarket and an English bookshop some five miles away.

Jack continued to play golf with Don. We sometimes invited him and Mary for a meal at the club and they invited us to dinner in their claustrophobic apartment. If only they hadn't closed in the balcony in favour of a larger kitchen, if only their table hadn't pretended to gracious living, those occasions might have been less depressing.

One evening Don talked of his wealthy brother. George had recently retired from an international executive post. He owned houses in several countries, flew his own plane and went to the major race meetings all over the world. The only thing Mary said about George was that Don's brother didn't care for anything except money.

We had known the Prices for four years when Don confided to Jack that his pension from Africa had gone down again, to 20 per cent of its original value.

'He's desperate,' Jack told me.

'Does his brother know?'

'He won't tell his brother; it would upset Mary.'

'What is she trying to do?' I was feeling exasperated. 'Keep on pretending that she is the wife and hostess of a big white boss?'

'Helen, it's not like you to be so unsympathetic . . . Look, I've thought of a way out.'

'For them or for us?'

Jack ignored that. 'We could offer to buy their apartment. Let them stay there for life . . .'

'Rent-free, of course. They'd invest the money we give them for the apartment, get an extra income . . . and reduce ours.'

'We can afford it.'

'Jack, we are not wealthy.'

'But we are well off thanks to your good management.'

'Perhaps we are, perhaps not . . . depending on a highly unstable world. Another point; if ever the Prices vacated their place we wouldn't find it easy to sell. It's about the most unattractive home in Selva.'

'No good thinking about that now. Look, Don has a heart condition. Worrying doesn't help it. You must see . . .'

'Yes, either you're trying to play the big benefactor or you're a bloody saint.'

'Will you think about it Helen?'

'Oh, I'll think about it.'

I did more of course. I saw a FOR SALE board on an apartment balcony in Selva with a beautiful view of the gardens. The position of the place was such that it would easily attract potential buyers. And it would be a great improvement on the Prices' home. I did not tell Jack about it until I'd met the agent, seen the apartment, and found the price affordable.

Jack approved of my idea, but with a proviso. We'd give the Prices the choice of their own apartment or the new one. If they wanted to move they were free to sell their place or let it if they could not find a buyer. In Selva it was easy to find tenants. Either arrangement would give them an extra income. Under either arrangement there would be no profit for us.

Jack was concerned that Don and Mary would be too proud to accept our proposal. He needn't have worried. I felt almost grateful when they opted for the new place. I would have hated to become the owner of their ugly home.

The sale went through quickly. None of us wanted Selva to discover who the new owners were and we managed to give the impression that the Prices had bought a more attractive home and put the old one on the market.

'We're mad,' I told Jack.

'I know,' he agreed cheerfully, 'but aren't you glad we've done it?'

'I'm not so sure.'

When the winter rains came water leaked into the new apartment. Don was supposed to have done a survey – being an expert, of course – but he had failed to spot a fault in the roof. Had he seen it the previous owner might have accepted a lower price. Instead we had the cost of the repair.

Then there were traumas with a succession of tenants in the old flat. They came and went. They damaged the furniture or burned saucepans. They were untidy or did not clean the place according to Mary's standards, but at least they paid the rent. If Mary didn't tell me about her tribulations the stories were passed on by Anita or Carmen, Paco or Fernando.

Yet, on the whole, we had a trouble-free year until Jack became aware that Don's heart condition was getting worse.

From the beginning Jack had made it clear to Don that he had no facilities for making tests and no access to hospital beds. Yet it took weeks of persuasion before Don agreed to see a local Spanish doctor. He was entitled to free treatment in Spain. Whether he had a right to the British health service after living abroad for some thirty years without contributing to it was doubtful.

Jack accompanied Don to Dr Garcia's surgery, ostensibly as an interpreter. On his return home he was visibly relieved. 'Garcia's done everything a competent GP would do in Britain,' he told me. 'The necessary tests and an arrangement for Don to see a specialist in a couple of weeks. In Malaga.'

'Are you going to drive him there?' I asked.

'No. Garcia said the specialist speaks English. He's worked in the States. Besides, Mary's taken over. She wants to go by bus.'

'So your services have been dispensed with.'

'Yes, at least for the moment.'

Not for long. On their return from Malaga they came straight to our house.

'We made the right decision,' announced Don, 'using the Spanish health service.'

I listened with mixed feelings, glad that Jack had apparently succeeded in channelling Don into a system he required, rueful that Don took the credit.

'Dr Murillo spoke quite good English,' said Mary, 'and he was so sympathetic. I think he really understood our position. Not like the usual run of medical men.'

I tried to read her fat hamster-face but its expression was as genteel as usual, set in that polite near-smile. Nothing in the blue eyes either. Nothing to tell me whether she had meant to insult Jack or taken his years of care for granted. *The usual run of medical men.*

'We think highly of Dr Murillo,' said Don. 'He told me it's a good thing I kept my weight down and took up golf again. In fact he thinks I've handled myself pretty well . . . considering. But now something's got to be done about the old heart. He wants me to have an operation . . . within six months. Bit sooner than I expected.'

'He recommended an operation,' Jack corrected quietly. 'The consultant you saw in Manchester believed you'd need surgery eventually.'

'I suppose so. The question is . . . what do I do now?'

'That has to be your decision,' Jack told him.

'Dr Murillo admitted that there's a risk.'

'There's a risk in all major operations. That's one reason why you have to make up your own mind. If Dr Murillo – '

'Don's very tired,' Mary cut in, 'he must have a rest. We can discuss this another day. There's no hurry.' And that was the end of their visit.

Jack said, 'I'll have to explain to Mary that Don can't just walk into a hospital and demand an instant operation.'

*

Don took to lying down most days and changed from golf to walking the apartment again. Mary gave us a daily bulletin on how he felt. Several weeks had passed when Don told us that he was waiting for the arrival of a friend of ours from England, a doctor who had spent a golfing holiday with us the previous year. He announced his intention of consulting Dr Blair.

And so he did, much to our embarrassment and Tony Blair's. Our cornered friend put up with the intrusion on his holiday and explained patiently that he could not advise Don whether or not to have the operation. But he mentioned that Spanish heart surgeons had a good reputation in medical circles abroad.

Mary, on her own with us, complained about the difficulties of making *arrangements*. Money came into it. Under the Spanish health service, the operation and hospital would cost nothing but her stay at a Malaga hotel and transport would be expensive. And she would be among strangers who didn't even speak her language. Jack asked her if Don's brother knew the situation and whether he would help.

'I mentioned to him some time ago that Don wasn't . . . too well.' Mary was picking her words. 'He thought of visiting us.'

'That would be good.'

'Well . . . I wrote to George that it would be better if he left it for a while. He talks rather a lot and it would tire Don.'

'Does George know that Don has been advised to have a major operation?'

'He may have guessed.'

'But he doesn't know,' Jack persevered.

'Well . . . we haven't decided yet . . . Actually I was wondering . . . I was wondering about taking Don back to Manchester.'

'What does Don think of that?'

'I haven't yet mentioned it to him. It's just a thought. It would be so convenient . . . staying in my cousins' granny flat. And the bus services are good . . .'

'Mary, I don't think you understand. In England Don couldn't have an operation on demand, for free, especially when he comes from abroad.

But even if he is accepted it could be weeks before he is seen by a specialist and as much as a year before a bed is available for him. If you're even considering England you should write and ask the doctor in Manchester how long Don might have to wait for the operation.'

'I'll think about it.' Mary left us in no doubt that her mind was mind up.

There was nothing more Jack could do for the man. When I saw Mary in the village I went to see Don. He was on his own. He looked pale and listless but he cleared a chair for me.

'The place is in an uproar. Mary's sorting things out.' He sat down among piles of papers and clothes. 'I suppose it's got to be done before we go to England.'

'You've decided to go?'

'Well - ' he turned his hands palm up – 'it'll make it easier for Mary. She'll have the support of her family.'

'Is that what you want?'

'What I want doesn't really come into it.'

'It must, surely.'

'Helen, I know that Jack would like to see me in the Malaga hospital . . . the sooner the better. But I can't forget my obligation to Mary.'

'Obligation? Isn't it a matter of priorities?'

'You're saying that I should put myself first because I'm living on borrowed time.'

'Does Mary understand that?'

'I think she does. But it's not a matter of logic or priorities. It all goes back to when we lived in Africa. Something happened at the time . . .'

'The death of your son?'

'Yes. But I'd rather you and Jack didn't mention it to her. Anyway, for all the doctors know I might survive even if I do have to wait for the operation longer than Dr Murillo estimates.'

At the swimming pool Anita and Carmen were talking about the Prices.

They knew that Don was a sick man. The story had come from Carmen's sister who worked in the Malaga hospital.

'They're going to England,' Carmen told us. 'Do you know when, Helen?'

'No.'

'Next week,' said Anita. 'Don told Olaf.'

So Don had talked to a neighbour. I was glad of it.

'He doesn't really want to go,' said Anita.

'What makes you think so?' I asked.

'It's Olaf's impression.'

'So why is he going?' Carmen was angry. 'Isn't a Spanish hospital good enough for him?'

Anita smiled. 'Here we go. Spanish pride.'

'No, good sense. My sister says the operation is urgent. In England they'll make tests all over again. There'll be delays and . . .'

Anita glanced at me. 'Carmen, leave it alone. We don't know enough about it.'

'Don't we? The only thing I don't know is what Mary's trying to do. Does she want to kill her husband?'

I was at home on my own when Mary dropped in to tell me that she had tickets for a flight to England in three days' time. She had made all *arrangements*.

I asked her whether she'd written to the doctor in Manchester.

'No. I didn't think it was necessary.'

'It's what Jack advised.'

'Well, yes. But we're playing it by ear. My cousin's going to meet us at the airport, so the luggage won't be a problem. This time we'll have to take more. I expect we'll be in UK for several months, so we'll be needing winter clothes.'

'You must be good at packing,' I suddenly knew what I wanted her to talk about, 'with your experience of travelling between Africa and England . . . especially with children.'

For a moment the usual half-smile gave way to a shut-down look. 'Children?'

'I thought you had a family.'

'I had a son. He was killed in a car accident . . . We won't take overcoats. Too bulky. If necessary we'll borrow coats from my cousins. Would you take whatever's left in the fridge? It won't be much.'

What had I hoped to achieve? That talking of her son at last would break through those locked emotions? A new insight which would change the woman's plan? Not a chance.

Once the Prices were in England Mary sent us regular bulletins. Don had a good day, or not so good. She was keeping him quiet. Jack wrote back saying that it was exercise Don needed. She replied that she was seeing to it that he got plenty of rest. At one stage we heard from Tony Blair. He had phoned the Prices to tell them that he was in Manchester and would like to call on them. Mary, sounding less than pleased, said that he would find parking too difficult. Tony gave up but, not surprisingly, he was puzzled.

While Don waited for the operation the weeks passed into months and Manchester turned wet and wintry. And then the bulletins stopped.

Concerned as he was, Jack was against our getting in touch with the Prices. 'They're not obliged to report to us. They're entitled to their privacy.'

'Privacy!' I was exasperated. 'Pity they didn't stick to it when Don was after your medical care and money.'

'You're feeling bitter, Helen.' Jack looked surprised.

'Just angry. The Prices asked for your advice when it suited them and ignored you when it didn't. You made it perfectly clear to them that they should write to Don's Manchester doctor . . . that they should find out how long Don might have to wait for the operation. And they didn't.'

'You can't stop people going their own way.'

'No, but they might at least let you know what's happening.'

'They will eventually.'

Eventually the lack of news became a strain on us. Our friends in Selva were waiting too, asking how Don was getting on, surprised that we had heard nothing, wondering what had happened – if anything – between the Prices and us.

After three months of it I called Manchester. The voice that answered the phone appeared to be Mary's but the woman did not know who I was. I explained.

'How nice of you to call.' She sounded as genteel as Mary. 'I think Don mentioned you. I'm Doreen, Mary's cousin.'

'May I speak to Don or Mary?'

'Oh dear . . . I suppose I should have let you know. But everything came together. It was absolutely frightful. I thought we'd never get rid of the police and – '

'The police?'

'Well, I suppose they had to investigate. It was all so sudden. I did explain to them how much Mary felt the cold, I mean after living in Africa and Spain. Of course we have central heating but – '

'Please,' I stopped her. 'We have no idea what's happened.'

'Oh, of course. I forgot you're in Spain. I suppose you haven't seen the papers. It was in the *Guardian* but not on the front page. I thought it should have been . . . I mean, as a warning to other people. Mind you, I do blame myself. I should have got rid of that electric fire ages ago. But I do hate throwing things away, don't you?'

I just had to let her rattle on.

'The fire . . . that's what killed Mary. Fancy taking it into the bathroom with her. Electrocuted herself, said the police . . . though it took them days to come to the same conclusion as Don. Poor Don . . . he had an awful time making them see it his way. I mean, *he knew*. He's an expert.'

'How is Don?'

'It was a terrible shock for him . . . naturally. But he's done well, considering. He phoned the hospital and told them about Mary. They took him in the day before the funeral. Only just in time too. His surgeon said he'd have preferred to operate much sooner but Mary was dead against it. She said she didn't want Don to be rushed into it.'

❦ *Night Flight*

JAMES MELVILLE

They eyed each other warily at the start. Then the man rose courteously enough from the aisle seat to make way for the woman, and offered to put her light woollen coat in the overhead locker for her: but in a polite, un-pushy way. She would as obviously need the coat on arrival at Heathrow in March as she certainly hadn't in Singapore, he thought as she handed it to him with a brief, grateful smile and settled into the window-seat.

Travelling alone on an intercontinental flight was inevitably a chancy business. One could so easily be stuck with a neighbour who turned out to be unstoppably chatty, or a fidget, or objectionable in some other way. He hoped very much that the vacant middle seat would remain so, and having a vague idea that airline check-in staff had instructions to avoid seating lone men and women next to one another, he thought he might be lucky. An empty seat might by some inscrutable process of thought be considered to preserve the proprieties. A kind of cordon sanitaire. The economy-class cabin was by no means full when all the passengers had boarded, and the vacant seat remained unclaimed. The man was gratified to realise that he was destined to spend many hours in proximity to a well dressed, good-looking woman in, he judged, her mid-thirties. Some ten years younger than himself. Her left hand, he noted with a furtive glance, was innocent of a wedding ring. He felt reasonably confident that his own appearance was that of an educated' comfortably off professional man. Non-threatening, in the current jargon, which was how he liked to be thought. As a confirmed observer of others he was satisfied to be unobtrusive himself. It was amazing what you could get away with if you didn't make yourself conspicuous.

'They're closing the doors,' he remarked to her. 'Looks as if we shall get away pretty much on time *and* have room to spread ourselves. Good old Singapore Airlines.'

'Yes. They deserve their reputation.' The woman's response was no more than civil, and she pointedly reached for the airline magazine in the seat pocket in front of her, leafing through it during the routine announcements over the public address system.

Rebuffed. Oh well, never mind, he thought, and began to speculate about the cool but attractive lady travelling alone. Her voice was pleasantly modulated and low in pitch, and he thought she might well be a singer. Not a professional musician, but perhaps a member of the alto section of one of the better amateur choirs such as the Royal Choral Society. She would look well in an elegant white blouse and long black skirt, and would inevitably be one of the photogenic ladies the cameras would zoom in on from time to time during a television broadcast from the Royal Albert Hall of, well, the *St Matthew Passion*, say.

With a slight jolt the aircraft began to move, backwards, and the man watched the safety precaution video demonstrating the use of the life-jacket and pointing out the position of the emergency exists. Few of the other passengers paid the slightest attention, and out of the corner of his eye he noticed that the woman in the window-seat was apparently immersed in an article about the bargains to be found in Kathmandu.

The plane took off only ten minutes late, and the man looked through the copy of the *Straits Times* he had accepted when the willowy, batik-clad flight attendant offered it to him. Then the drinks trolley came round, and the leave-me-alone prickliness was no longer evident when his travelling companion stuffed her magazine back into the seat pocket and turned to him with a lazy smile, manifestly disposed to chat.

'I'm about ready for a drink, aren't you?'

Careful now. Keep it banal at this stage. 'Yes, I am. They always say you shouldn't, but I find that a drink before a meal and a glass or two of wine with it puts one in the right mood to sleep as well as it's possible to do during a long night flight. I say, would you like my peanuts? I don't care for them.'

'Why, thank you.'

Time for a tiny advance. 'My name's Timothy Benedict, by the way.'

'I'm . . . Sarah Middleton. Hello.'

He quite understood her slight hesitation before giving her name. A woman alone must always feel some reluctance to give any sort of hostage to fortune. They were handed their drinks: hers a gin and tonic, his a Manhattan.

'Your health,' he said, raising his glass to her. 'Funny thing, but I seldom drink Manhattans except on planes, when for some reason I almost always fancy one.' That was anodyne enough, he thought. She'll expect me to talk about double-glazing in a minute.

'Have you been staying in Singapore? Or are you in transit from somewhere else?'

'No, I mean no, I'm not in transit. I've been in Singapore for the past two weeks or so. You?'

'I've been visiting an old schoolfriend there. Her husband's with the Chartered Bank. Were you there on business?'

She's ready to be intrigued. 'Well, sort of. I've been gathering background material for a book.'

'Oh, you're a *writer*! How fascinating.'

It was the sort of response he had learned to expect in social situations when he mentioned writing a book. People who hadn't personally done it almost always jumped to the conclusion that anyone who did was necessarily a full-time professional novelist, famous and rich. They seemed surprised to the point of disbelief when he pointed out that most of the books that are published aren't novels, that only a handful of them earn their creators more than pin-money, and that the overwhelming majority of writers depend primarily on other sources of income. He could truthfully have given several alternative, partial answers to a straight question about his occupation, but wasn't inclined to reveal much about himself in a casual conversation. It would be more diverting simply to fire her imagination while seeing how much he could find out about the woman at his side.

'Hardly,' he said, and she looked disappointed.

'Oh. You mean you haven't had one published yet?'

'I've had several published, actually.'

'Gosh. Are you famous? I mean, do you write under your own name?' His mouth twitched with amusement as he observed the expression on her face. He was sure she was desperately trying and failing to recall seeing a Timothy Benedict up there with Jeffrey Archer, Jilly Cooper and the other airport bookstall authors.

'I don't write under my own name, and I'm not in the least bit famous.' It was like playing a fish, he thought, seeing her eyes glisten with interest as she moistened her lips with the tip of her tongue.

'I don't believe you. What sort of books do you write, then?'

'Detective stories, actually. Murder mysteries.'

'*Really*? How fascinating!' She put her hand to her mouth and he saw her nibble her finger in excitement. Her teeth were even and very white, and her lips full. He found the effect distinctly erotic, and thought she was probably a sensual person. Amazing eyes, too, light brown flecked with gold: almost tigerish. She was, clearly, sexually experienced. Divorced, possibly, and amenable to a safe adventure. How marvellous if their journey together were to be like that never-to-be-forgotten flight to New Zealand years before, when he had begun a conversation with a shy young newly-wed on her way back from her mother's funeral in England to rejoin her husband! She had been heavy going at first, but during the endless hours aboard a half-empty jumbo jet had gradually revealed herself to be both shameless and inventive.

Timothy wrenched his mind away from such fantasies and concentrated on enjoying the present as he and the agreeable Sarah Middleton went on chatting throughout the meal, she pleasingly animated and he quietly enjoying her incessant stream of questions. He established that, though she preferred biography, she had read a good deal of crime fiction and admired Patricia Highsmith and Ruth Rendell. He complimented her on her taste, and when asked who were his own favourite writers, mentioned two whose names would probably be familiar to her. They were; and she had, it emerged, even read two or three of his own books, professing to have enjoyed them.

By the time their trays were taken away they were swapping not very controversial opinions like old friends. When she got up and made her way to the washroom he took advantage of her absence to raise the arm-rests between their seats. On her return he noticed with a flicker of pleasure that she had put on fresh scent.

'I thought it would be more comfortable with the arm-rests out of the way,' he said, not making a big thing out of it. She nodded her agreement, and asked him if he planned to watch the film.

'I don't think so, no. I'll try to snooze later on. You know, I feel as if we've known each other for ages rather than, what, an hour and a half or so.'

She nodded. 'True. Well, after all, it's a very concentrated way of getting acquainted, isn't it? The friends I've been staying with got married after knowing each other just a few weeks. Rather quick, but not all that unusual. When I think about it, though, I doubt if they'd been on their own in each other's company for more than a total of, oh, perhaps twenty hours before deciding. But that was over ten years ago and they seem happy enough.'

He smiled enigmatically but made no direct comment, and she coloured slightly, perhaps sensing, he thought, that he was wondering if she was looking for a man and by any chance saw him as a prospect. That might account for the scent. At all events, as the cabin lights were lowered and the film began she deftly turned the conversation back to crime fiction, asking some informed questions. Then she wanted to know how he thought up his plots.

'Oh, that's rarely a problem. Any and every situation can be applied to serve as a background and starting point. Lots of thrillers have been set at least partially in airports and aeroplanes, to take an obvious example. You've got one of the classic ingredients: a closed community, most of whom are strangers to each other. And look around you. Every person on this flight, passengers and crew alike, is a frail human individual with hopes, fears and secrets. Several, no doubt, would be more pleased than sorry to learn that somebody of their acquaintance had died. And who knows, someone might be contemplating murder.'

'What a ghastly idea!'

'Not really. I dare say murder has been done on board an airliner. In real life, I mean, not in a film.' With a suggestive smile he added, 'Everything else has, I'm sure.'

She shuddered attractively, and – she had kicked off her shoes – he saw her toes wiggling. He thought again as he had done when she bit her finger that she was probably easily aroused. She certainly aroused him, and the fact that all the other passengers in their neighbourhood were wearing headphones and intent on the film gave him the pleasant feeling that for the present they were alone in a private, dream world of their own in which anything could happen.

'That's a really creepy idea,' she said. 'But . . . well, I mean, murder on a plane? Nobody could get away with it.'

'Oh, I don't know. I've given a lot of thought to murder, and I should have thought it would actually be rather easy. I know a woman who used to be a flight attendant, and I was surprised when she told me how many passengers die in mid-air, as it were. From natural causes usually, of course, but some commit suicide. And some, it's quite possible, are murdered.'

'You're scaring me, Timothy,' the woman said, to his great satisfaction. The conversation *was* stimulating her, he was sure, and she had used his name for the first time. This was a development he could and would follow up.

'You'd need a subtle murder *method*, of course. So that it would be taken for granted that the death was the result of a heart attack. They generally are, my friend told me. And the timing would have to be thought about. A night flight like this would be ideal.'

Before continuing, Timothy looked for a second or two at the screen, on which Goldie Hawn's mouth was opening and closing. Then he focused again on Sarah, who was staring at him with those curious eyes of hers. 'After the film's over, most people will huddle under blankets and settle down to sleep, and the cabin staff won't disturb them. So a murder victim could be dead for hours before anybody discovered him. Or her,' he added in a deliberately sinister undertone, which produced another very satisfactory shudder from Sarah Middleton, who even reached across and clutched at Timothy's hand.

'You have a gruesome imagination,' she said huskily. 'I'm beginning to wonder if you've tried your hand at it yourself!'

He chuckled at that and squeezed her hand in response before releasing it with regret. 'Oh, no,' he said then, cosily. 'I've never murdered anybody to my knowledge. Might have frightened a few readers to death, I suppose, but it's very improbable. Any more strenuous technique would be beyond me. Besides, I've forgotten the fatal judo holds that would be needed. Never knew them, to tell the truth. Tell you what, Sarah,' he went on in a carefully neutral voice, 'do put your feet up on the spare seat if you'd be more comfortable.'

It was a fairly transparent ploy, but he was hoping that alcohol, food and the titillating conversation had put her into a sufficiently devil-may-care frame of mind for her at least to snuggle up to him later on; which would be very nice. And it might just lead to a kind of replay of that delightful squeezing, fumbling and rubbing that the young woman from New Zealand had proved herself to be eager both to administer to him and to receive at his hands. Sarah Middleton wasn't cool at all; she was a ripe, hot-blooded woman who if she did let herself go would do so with abandon, Timothy felt sure. There were many hours of darkness ahead, and they could give each other considerable if fleeting pleasure, heightened by the consciousness that they were virtual strangers. On the ships-that-pass-in-the-night principle.

It worked. An hour or so later the cabin was in near-darkness, overlapping blankets covered them and Sarah's head was resting on his shoulder, her legs tucked up beside her. Achieving this degree of familiarity had been a very gradual process, by no means all the stages having been initiated by him. Sarah's breathing was calm and regular, but he felt sure she was only pretending to be asleep. If she was enjoying the physical contact as much as he was, it might suit her to feign ignorance in welcoming a greater intimacy that, if obviously conscious, she would no doubt feel obliged to repulse.

Slightly shifting his position, Timothy placed a hand directly on her left breast as though by accident and kept it there motionless for a few seconds.

Sarah made no attempt to move it away, but Timothy knew for certain from the pounding of her heart that she was awake, excited and probably aware of his own racing heartbeat. Their childish conspiracy both amused and intrigued him, and he began to caress her breast, brushing his fingertips lightly over the erect nipple and wondering how much further he would need to go before Sarah acknowledged what was going on. He craned his neck and kissed her hair gently; then felt her hand slide on to his thigh. It was sweetly thrilling, like being an adolescent again, and when they began to exchange proper kisses, still in silence, her lips and tongue were warmly eloquent.

It was Sarah who spoke, or rather whispered, first. Into his ear, after teasing the lobe with her tongue and catching it fleetingly in her teeth. Her warm, moist breath was exquisitely exciting. 'Did you ever play doctors and nurses when you were small?'

'Of course I did, and I enjoyed it too, even though I was a bit scared. It wasn't half as delicious as this, though.' Then Timothy in turn attended to Sarah's ear, plunging his own tongue deep into its perfumed recesses. Her whole body squirmed and she exhaled violently before abruptly sitting up and looking intently into his face with a small, secret smile. Then she kissed him hard on the lips, before breaking the spell in a distinctly unromantic way. 'I'm sorry Timothy, but I simply have to go to the loo,' she murmured.

'So do I,' Timothy confessed. 'But do come back soon.'

They both made their way past the shrouded forms of other passengers to the washrooms at the back, all of which were unoccupied. Timothy took the opportunity to clean his teeth, wash his face and apply a little cologne, and it was several minutes before he was finished. On the way back, elated by the tantalising prospect of what was yet to come, he exchanged smiles with the duty flight attendant sitting with a copy of *Vogue* in one of the crew seats beside the rear door.

Sarah was already back in her seat, the blankets drawn up to her chin. Those amazing jungle eyes widened in welcome and she greeted him with a voracious smile, running her tongue round her open lips. Then she pouted playfully. 'You've been simply ages,' she said. 'If that stewardess hadn't been watching I'd have waited and dragged you into one of the washrooms. Made you a member of the Five Mile High Club.' She smiled again, enigmatically this time. 'Put your head under the blanket.'

When he did so Timothy discovered to his delight that she had removed her bra and unbuttoned her blouse. He lost all sense of time as he nuzzled her breasts, teasing her nipples with his teeth and tongue, and almost forgot to breathe. Coming up for air, he saw that Sarah's cheeks were flushed and her eyes glittering. 'Naughty!' she said. 'That hurt a bit . . . but I liked it. Because you really turn me on, Timothy, and then I actually enjoy a little pain. Do you?' Without waiting for his reply she kissed him, hungrily, and bit his lower lip quite painfully. Timothy wasn't sure whether or not he liked the sensation, but he was so flattered and elated by her enthusiasm that he gave himself up to it.

During a pause for breath she nestled in his arms and he thought how cat-like she looked in her sensual languor. 'Before you came back I took a stroll round the cabin and saw what you mean about a murder victim not being discovered for hours,' she whispered. 'Some of the passengers do look like corpses, don't they?'

'Yes, they do. But let's not talk now . . . just go on doing that . . .' Sarah's arms had snaked up and she was caressing his cheeks and earlobes.

'I'm so glad we met, Timothy. I've learned so much from you.' Then she in turn burrowed under the blanket and with gentle but insistent fingers unzipped his trousers. Hardly believing what was happening, Timothy felt the hot wetness of her mouth engulfing him and he gasped for breath as his heart began to lurch and hammer in his chest. It was an unbelievably thrilling sensation: as if he were sinking helpless through black and red waves of lust and Sarah were greedily sucking out his very soul . . .

When, much later, dawn light outlined the window shutters and the cabin crew were bustling about serving breakfast, Sarah Middleton was sitting quietly in her window-seat, the folding shelf already lowered in front of her.

'Thank you,' she said to the flight attendant, reaching across for her tray. Then she glanced at the blanket-covered heap in the aisle seat. 'He's dead to the world, it seems,' she added with a smile.

Give Us a Clue

Some problems of detection

JOAN LOCK

Picture the scene of the crime: an elderly man is lying across a bed, his throat cut. Not surprisingly, there is blood splattered widely across the walls, floor and furniture. On the bedpost there is a bloody handprint, fingerprints, too, on the stained weapon which lies glinting on the quilt, and more on the frame of the window where the murderer made his hurried exit. From these, it appears that he is minus one thumb.

More blood – this time more likely to be that of the murderer – around some broken window glass. In the soft soil of the flowerbed, under the window, there are some nice deep footprints and a candle stump. Ten minutes before the discovery of the body, a bloodstained man, wearing a blue cap, black jacket and grey trousers, was seen running from the grounds.

Easy peasy to solve this one – surely? If an 'all stations' broadcast doesn't get him, a photofit, blood grouping, DNA profiling, fingerprints and *Crime Watch* should do the trick.

Well, no, actually. One thing I omitted to mention – the year is 1840. That's your DNA, fingerprints and blood grouping straight out of the window. It is not even possible to differentiate between animal and human blood or hairs. As for informing other policemen that the bloodstained, one-thumbed suspect might be heading their way – bit difficult that. No radio, telephone or even telegraph yet in use, you see. True, there is quite a good postal service and the Metropolitan Police Route Paper system is fairly effective – considering. In an emergency, route papers can be passed to surrounding divisions - spreading outwards as when a stone is thrown in a pond – so that within six hours most of the force has the news. The problem is, of course, that in such circumstances news rapidly becomes outdated.

Why am I telling you all this? Well, when this story is retold 150 years on, as a true crime tale, chances are there will be no hint of these problems. The reader is unlikely to be told that before giving chase, the policeman will have to try to find a cab or, if he is very lucky, one of the new omnibuses – hoping that the Commissioner will agree that the expense was justified. Or, that he won't be able to preserve the scene with a photograph, because the new science is not far enough advanced for that. The past *is* another country and they did things very differently there. I do wish we got more sense of that.

Early Victorian detectives did have one or two advantages over their modern brothers. While they may not have been able to obtain descriptions of their quarry circulated quickly, these could be more useful than they would be today. Initially, people were divided into rich or poor by their apparel, whereas nowadays even your actual lord wears jeans. They were further subdivided by their working clothes. 'Has the appearance of a servant', 'Dresses like a mechanic' were terms often used, and farm labourers wore smocks.

Furthermore, in 'the hungry forties', many suspects were so poor that they could not afford a change of clothes – even if they were bloodstained – so an important part of the description would often remain constant. The servants in one house were so concerned that their cook's brother resembled the description of a suspected murderer that they clubbed together to enable him to buy some more trousers or a different hat. Had he merely gone out without a hat he would have looked even more conspicuous.

Hats played a prominent part in many murder investigations, either by being left at the scene or picked up by mistake. So, too, did the candle factor.

Early Victorians were unable to move about indoors at night without tapers, candles or oil lamps and the whereabouts of these objects at the scene of a crime might tell the detectives where suspects had been, as opposed to where they said they had been. Not surprisingly, some villains got wise to this. A servant who had stolen some of his master's plate might well dump a candlestick just inside the street door to give the impression it was an outside job.

The poor quality of indoor lighting also affected the quality of witness identification. In one early Victorian murder case, the maid was unable to describe the 'gentleman' brought home by her mistress on the fateful night because she did not take a candle to the door when they arrived home. In a later case, much play was made of the likely veracity of identification as the room had been lit by gas.

The fact that our initial suspect had one thumb could be both a blessing and a curse in those days. Unalterable distinguishing marks have always been a gift to the detective. Many more people had them then – health and safety at work having a rather low priority, while the correction of birth defects such as club foot were still undeveloped skills. In a true case featuring a one-thumbed suspect, so many possible culprits were unearthed that it resulted in a mass of messages flying about the country, asking which thumb was deficient and to what extent.

Some scientific techniques were in use. Even the Bow Street Runners had made plaster casts of footprints at scenes of crimes. Post-mortems were thorough and the surgeons usually had a stab at pinpointing the weapon used. PMs were also of huge interest to the public who were regularly regaled with details of the condition of victims' muscles and viscera – Latin names and all.

Other differences were: the preponderance of large households - extended family, servants, lodgers – many of whom were dependent on the goodwill of the master so that if he himself were the suspect . . . No registration and little control of aliens made it nearly impossible to trace the movements of the multitude of revolutionaries in our midst; all police reports having to be laboriously handwritten. I could go on.

No one would read crime stories weighed down with extraneous detail and, of course, it is vital to maintain narrative pace. But I am sure just a little more information about the nitty gritty would add to the interest while doing more justice to those concerned.

So, please – give us a clue.

Second Best Man

DAVID WILLIAMS

I suppose I resented Harry Smith from the very start, deep down and without admitting it to myself. It's why I was ready to kill him in the end. Before that, there was always reason to keep the special friendship going – or what everyone saw as a special friendship, and that included me, best part of the time.

At school Harry was deeply unpopular. Short, fat and pale, he was supposed to be anaemic, wore thick glasses and was excused all games. None of that stopped him being bullied. Well it wouldn't, not in our part of south London – not in a run-down comprehensive school where a bunch of dedicated yobbos only stopped making life a misery for the weaker boys while they did even nastier things to the girls. Except I protected Harry. It was for a price; not money, but he always had more of that than I had, and it came in useful.

It was brains Harry had, brains and cunning – enough to get us both through the term tests, and the exams at the end. Harry turned exam cheating into an art, not that he needed to cheat on his own account. He just worked out all the answers fast, and found original ways of passing them to me. It was thanks to Harry I got five GCE passes, and thanks to me Harry never got his nose broken, or worse. It was a fair exchange.

I was always a well-built lad, and handy with my fists. It made up for not being so brainy. My dad had been a professional boxer. He taught me the rudiments of the manly art early on – before he left my mum to join a circus act. That was the last we ever saw of my dad: I was twelve at the time.

When I got older, I developed what they call rugged good looks. It was Harry who said I ought to have been called Byron not Bryan, after Lord Byron the poet who'd had all the birds begging for it: we were doing *Childe Harold* and *Don Juan* for English class at the time. Harry started calling me Byron after that, and it stuck. Even my mum called me Byron. I didn't mind; I was quite pleased really. I was pulling more than a fair share of birds myself by then, young Debby Moxton for one.

I left school before Harry. He went on to London University; well he would, of course. Me, I went from job to job. I tried to get into acting. My mum used to say I had everything it took for that, except there wasn't the money for drama school and you don't get far without. It was those GCE certificates that saved me from ending up in labouring, I suppose. They got me the interviews, and – no point being modest about it – my winning personality and looks got me the jobs. Only none of the jobs lasted; I don't know why, really. Mostly I was in selling – a rep for dog food, lavatory cleaners, encyclopaedias, this and that. Of course, I deserved better, a lot better.

It was Harry Smith, the bountiful, who gave me my first good job.

Harry's old dad had always been in building supplies, in a small way. It surprised everybody when Harry joined him – took over the business really; that was after getting a degree in economics. Only there was method in Harry's madness. There was a big building boom on, with everyone short of materials. Harry specialised. He just bought and sold partitioning, all kinds of partitioning – wood, chipboard, hardboard, plastic, metal, you name it, for every kind of building – houses, offices, schools, factories. He bought big, too, going all over the world in the end to get what he wanted. At the start he cashed in on his dad's goodwill, and his credit rating – and his dedication. That was clever. People had always trusted his dad, and the old man worked for Harry like a stoat. After two or three years, Harry had all the banks queuing up to lend him money – first in thousands, then hundreds of thousands, then millions. Marvellous how that lot'll back you when you're successful; not a sodding one would lend me enough to see me through acting school.

I didn't know about Harry's success at the start; we'd lost touch for quite a while. That was partly because I'd given up living at home for a bit – until I found things too expensive and moved back. Harry and I met up again at a dance for old pupils in the school hall one Christmas. When I saw him, I wondered what the hell he was doing there: he'd hated the school and he didn't dance. Physically he hadn't altered that much, he was still small, fat and ugly, only the clothes he was wearing were smarter than anyone else's, and he seemed to breathe confidence. Debby Moxton was there too, with another girl we'd known called Beryl.

Debby had definitely been the best looker in the school in our day, and probably any other day, come to that. Three years younger than Harry and me, at twenty-two, which she was at this point, she was an absolute knock-out - a tall, natural blonde, with an English rose complexion and a smashing figure. I reckoned she'd still have been gone on me if I'd made anything of myself. We'd knocked around together for a while after I left school. Unlike the other girls though, she'd never given it away, if you see what I mean. Bit of petting and a kiss good-night was all you ever got from Debby. She made it pretty plain she was saving the real favours for a husband, and whoever married her had better prove in advance he could keep her in the manner intended. Till then she was happy enough working as a director's secretary in some big Croydon company.

So the four of us ended up spending that evening together. It seemed almost that Harry had intended we'd do that from the start, though how he knew we were all going to be there I never found out.

It was while the girls were in the ladies' room that I told Harry about my career progress, or lack of it.

'You ought to come into my business, Byron, boy,' he said, straight off. 'Plenty of room. We're expanding all the time.'

'No, I couldn't do that. Couldn't take advantage,' I said, hoping he'd insist, and wishing I'd got on to him before this.

'Yes, you could,' he answered, on cue. 'Anyway, I owe you.'

In a way he was right. If I hadn't protected him at school he could easily have turned out an insecure adult with a persecution complex, prevented from reaching his true potential. I read somewhere about that happening to people who'd been bullied a lot.

'So what would I do?' I remember asking next, but in a positive way, not to encourage Harry to have second thoughts. 'I don't know too much about partitioning.' Except I knew even less about portable air-conditioning units, which, as I'd told Harry, was what I was supposed to be flogging at the time.

'Anyone who can sell air conditioning can sell partitioning,' he said. 'It's all part of the building trade. *And* you've got the presence for selling, Byron. Always have had. And the looks.' He'd always envied my appearance.

I didn't bother admitting I hadn't actually sold any of the air-conditioning units yet – and that I hadn't exactly reached star salesman status with the dog food, the lavatory cleaners or the encyclopaedias either. Anyway, I think Harry had really guessed all that, and he wasn't asking for references in any case. So it was agreed I should start with Smith Partitions Limited two weeks from the following Monday. Harry told the girls when they came back from the ladies': it all happened as fast as that. The girls were impressed too. Well, with Harry they were – especially Debby.

At the end of the dance, Harry drove us all home in the new Jaguar he'd got parked outside in the school yard. Caused quite a sensation that car did, and it was meant to. This was Harry showing off in front of his old mates and enemies – mostly enemies – and you couldn't blame him either. He dropped Beryl and me at her place which was just round the corner from my mother's, then drove on with Debby who was looking gorgeous and regal with it in the front passenger seat.

Debby and Harry were married three months later. I was pretty sore about that. I didn't show it, of course. There was no point, especially since Harry had kind of asked for my approval in advance. He said he knew I'd have Debby's best interests at heart since he remembered we'd been close some years back, and did I think she'd make a good wife for a rising industrialist who could afford to give her everything she'd want out of life? So what could I say, except wish him good luck? It happened to be the day after he'd promoted me by making me responsible for selling to the solid 'house accounts' - building firms who'd never have dreamed of buying partitioning from anyone else but Harry. All I had to do was make courtesy calls, buy the customers lunch sometimes, and collect the bloody orders. To have told him what I really felt about his marrying Debby would only have upset the apple cart, and risked my job probably with nothing achieved. I mean she wasn't going to marry me, was she?

So short-arsed, four-eyes, anaemic Harry Smith landed south London's most desirable dollybird – and he got a virgin into the bargain.

I was best man at the wedding. Beryl was chief bridesmaid. When it came to appearances, Beryl was never exactly a show-stopper, not in the same class as Debby, not by a thousand miles. She looked pretty good that day though, which was when I took up with her seriously. We got hitched ourselves not long after. I figured she'd stay close to Debby, so it was a way for me to keep the business relations cemented, if you follow me? Not very high-minded of me perhaps, but practical.

At first we saw a lot of Harry and Debby socially. When Harry moved the business out beyond Reading, in Berkshire, he bought a home there too, and we did the same – not on a golf course like his, and it wasn't a mansion like his either. Harry set up a factory as well as a warehouse in the new location because by then he was into more than just buying and selling partitions. He'd decided he was going to manufacture the stuff himself, and not just partitions either. In no time the company was making complete, integrated portable buildings for temporary and permanent use, and undercutting everybody else in sight. It was a gold mine.

All this moved Harry into the really big time. Of course, before long the people close to him had to be in the same league as he was, and for one reason and another that didn't include me. I'd already been shifted off 'house accounts' into office management. It seemed you had to be a qualified architect with an MBA to handle the big accounts at that stage, even the tame ones. I was paid a bit more, but it was a downward move since I had less real responsibility. If I saw Harry at all at work it was only in the corridor. I noticed he looked worn, and I swear sometimes he didn't seem to remember me; anyway, he was hardly ever in the office, or in the country for that matter, especially after we won a Duke of Edinburgh Award for Export. There was no holding him then. People said he had his sights on a knighthood, and every time a newspaper ran a list of the country's highest earners, Harry would be there in the top hundred.

I'd lost touch with Debby and Harry socially by that time too, though that was mostly because Beryl and I had got divorced. We hadn't been compatible from the start. I was only worried that if Debby sided with Beryl over our break-up, it might lead to me losing my job, but it didn't. I came to the conclusion that Debby and Harry had probably moved so far above our level, neither of them knew about the divorce, or if they did, neither could have cared less. At least, that's what I thought until that Friday night in November four years ago when I had to take something from the factory to their house.

Don't misunderstand, I hadn't been reduced to delivering parcels for the company on a regular basis – not quite, anyway. A silver tea-set, a wedding present Harry had ordered for someone, had been sent to the office by mistake. Harry had been abroad, and his chauffeur was already at Heathrow meeting him. His secretary was in a flap because the wedding was next day and the Smiths were supposed to be taking the present with them. It was already gone six and the secretary was late for a date with her boyfriend. She knew my house wasn't far from Harry's, so she'd rushed into my office almost in tears to ask could I possibly?

Debby answered the door herself. I hadn't seen her for nearly three years, not to speak to anyway. At thirty-four she still looked smashing; figure a bit fuller, which you'd expect after she'd had two kids, both boys incidentally, and both, I gathered later, already away at boarding-school. Only I wondered why she was wearing the dark glasses.

She seemed glad to see me, kissed me warmly on the cheek, and invited me in. She wasn't much interested in the story of the silver tea-set, and dropped the box it was in on one of the hall chairs.

I'd been to the house before, often, but not for a long time. They'd made some improvements. For a start there were a lot more expensive-looking antiques and pictures about the place.

She linked her arm in mine. 'What'll you drink? Whisky still, is it? Water but no ice?' she asked, steering me into their drawing-room.

I said, 'I don't think I'd better stay that long. Harry'll be home any minute won't he?'

'Harry won't be home till Monday, and only then if he remembers where he lives. I just got a fax from the Paris office. He has to stay over. Pressure of work, poor dear. Tough titty having to spend the weekend in Paris by yourself, I don't think,' she went on in a really acid tone as she poured my drink from a trolley across the room.

'What about the wedding tomorrow?'

'Screw the wedding. If he's not here to take me I'm not going. They're his friends, not mine. Business friends. We don't have any of the other sort, not any more.' She came over with my drink.

'Aren't you having one?' I asked.

'Of course I am. It's over here. I'm a . . . I'm slightly ahead of you. I'm sorry about your divorce.' So she did know about that. 'I meant to ring you. Haven't talked to Beryl either. She always had personality problems, of course. You two should never have got married in the first place. Applies to a lot of us. Let's sit here.' So I needn't have worried about the divorce costing me my job. She motioned me to the sofa in front of the blazing log fire in the huge open hearth. The fire was a gas jet and the logs were imitation, but it was all pretty cosy.

'Something wrong with your eyes, Debby?' I said when we were sitting quite close together.

'Yes. One of them got blackened by my adoring husband on Wednesday.' She took off the glasses. Her right eye was almost closed and the flesh around it puffed and bruised.

'Accident?'

'Yes. He was aiming for my ribs, but he was drunk, and missed. Made up for it though with the next punch. Want to see?' Without waiting for an answer, she put her glass down, sat up straight, and in one showy movement pulled the cashmere sweater she was wearing over her head. 'How about that? I thought he'd broken a rib. Feel the lump.' She'd hollowed her back and leaned closer to me. Then she took my hand and ran it gently over the blue-black area above her midriff.

It was a massive bruise all right, but I was paying more attention to the rest of what she'd exposed. All she'd been wearing under the sweater was one of those lacy half-bras. It was white, making a nice contrast with her smooth, tanned skin, and didn't leave much to the imagination. Her breasts looked as firm and perfect as they had when she was a girl, well, they did to me at least.

'Worn well otherwise, haven't I, Byron,' she said quietly, following my eyes as well as my thoughts. Then, without shifting her gaze from mine, she undid the bra and shook it off to prove the point further, before putting her arms around my neck. 'Why don't you stay for dinner? It's all prepared. Pity to waste it. No hurry, of course, it'll keep.' Then she kissed me, on the lips this time, slowly and very sensuously while she began undoing the buttons on my shirt.

'Are you alone in the house?' I asked.

'No, silly, you're here. Handsome, adorable, sexy Byron,' she giggled, thrusting her arm down under my shirt, fingers exploring.

'I meant . . .'

'I know what you meant. But even the fabulous Smiths don't have live-in servants. So you can stay the whole night if you want. But let's not wait till then,' she added.

And we didn't. After all, I'd been waiting over twenty years for Debby.

It was when we were upstairs in bed much later that she began pouring her heart out to me, lying close in my arms. By that time we'd eaten, and the stimulating effect of what she'd drunk had worn off – and I guessed she'd drunk quite a bit before I'd got to the house. Now she wasn't kittenish any more; a bit maudlin really, but very affectionate still.

She gave me more depressing details of her life with Harry, about the way he beat her up, his drinking, his frequent absences, his infidelities, his lack of interest in the children, and his always putting her down in public, something that hurt her as much as the physical cruelty, only in a different way.

'So why don't you leave him?' I asked.

'And leave all this too?'

She had a point there. She'd certainly come a long way from Mafeking Street, Lambeth. Even so, breaking with Harry didn't mean she had to go back to that kind of lifestyle.

'In a divorce you'd get half his estate, probably,' I explained. 'He's stinking rich.'

'I wouldn't get half. Or anything like. You know what a clever sod he is. I'm scared he'd fix it so I'd hardly have enough to live on. *And* he'd get custody of the boys. I couldn't bear that.'

'But you're wrong there. The wife always – '

'Not this wife,' she interrupted. 'If we divorced, I'd be the guilty party. He's . . . he's got grounds. I know he's unfaithful to me, but, the difference is, I can't prove it.'

'So what sort of grounds does he have?' It was a funny question to be asking when we were lying beside each other in her matrimonial king-sized bed.

She didn't say anything for a bit, just fingered the sheet, then she looked up and shrugged. 'What the hell, I can tell you. My darling, oldest friend.' She kissed me behind the ear before going on. 'Four years ago, I had a brief affair. Well, Harry was neglecting me. He'd insisted on both the boys going away to school. I felt unwanted, unnecessary, and so lonely. I . . . I needed someone.'

'I wish you'd needed me,' I said.

'You were still married,' she answered. I suppose it was a good enough reason. Beryl had once been her best friend, after all. 'Anyway, the man I was involved with was a young assistant pro, here at the golf club. Harry got suspicious and had us both followed. That's how he got the evidence. Nothing's come out in public, but Harry made me sign a confession. And I had to promise never to see Rickie again. That was his name. Rickie. He was so beautiful,' she added dreamily, then completed quickly, 'like you, Byron.' She squeezed my arm, but I remember thinking she'd been a bit late. 'Harry still arranged to have Rickie fired. And fixed it so he'd never get another job in golf. Not anywhere. God, he's a mean bastard.'

'I still don't think one affair should stop you getting a good divorce settlement, or custody of the boys,' I offered, although I wasn't exactly speaking from experience. Beryl and I never had any kids.

'Except there's something else. Something . . . something that turns off divorce judges more than casual affairs.' She sighed and clung closer to me, the fingers of one hand playing with the hairs on my chest. Her head was on my shoulder, but her eyes were now avoiding mine. 'You haven't seen me for so long, of course,' she went on. 'Three years ago I was a mess. After I'd had to break with Rickie, I . . . I started taking drugs.'

'Hard drugs or soft drugs?'

'Both. Well, one sort led to the other. That usually happens, doesn't it?' I didn't answer. I've never been into drugs. 'I . . . I was a fool, I know,' she added, 'but what with the beatings and the loneliness . . .'

'You don't have to talk about it,' I said quietly.

'But I want to. To you. There's no one else I can unburden on. The drug bit's over now. I took the cure. In a clinic. In California. Harry told everyone I had a blood disease, but you can bet he's got the sodding details in writing somewhere. That's why I'm scared I wouldn't get custody.' She breathed out noisily. 'I hate Harry. And I hate my life. I often think of doing myself in. I'm so unhappy, and it's all so unfair.' She started to cry quietly.

It was my turn to sigh – because I was aggravated. 'But there's got to be some way out for you?'

She leant right across me. I thought she was getting amorous again, until her hand reached out to unlock the drawer of the small table on my side of the bed. When she moved back she was holding a handgun. It was a smallish, heavy black revolver with a short barrel.

'Suicide's not the way,' I said quickly, taking the gun from her with care. 'You're still beautiful, with plenty to live for.' I meant what I said, too, and was already vaguely trying to fit myself into an ongoing scenario.

'I've never thought of using the gun on myself.' She paused. 'Sometimes I think of using it on Harry, though.'

That shook me, because I could tell from the tone she was serious. 'Murder Harry?' I said. 'But that wouldn't solve your problems for you.'

'It'd solve them if a burglar did it,' she answered coolly. 'Harry had a pair of guns brought over from the States because we've had three break-ins this year. He swears he'll shoot the next thief if he gets the chance. The other gun's at the London flat. We've been burgled there too.'

'Isn't there an alarm system here?'

'Yes, but the thieves always get round it. They're so sophisticated these days. If Harry went after the next one, if there was a fight, and if it was Harry who got shot, I could be a witness to what happened, that it was he who had the gun, not the burglar. We could do it, Byron,' she whispered at the end, breathing the words quickly close to my ear.

'It wouldn't be as simple as that,' I said.

'It would, you know,' she answered. 'And then I'd be very rich, and we could get married later, and live happily ever after. Isn't that what you always wanted, darling Byron?'

There were any number of times later when I could have backed down, but I didn't. Like she said, it really was very simple – and the reward was so big.

It was one in the morning, on the Thursday, three weeks later, when I left the car in a copse, close to the house. I remember being glad it was cloudy and dark, with the ground bone dry. Wearing gloves and a balaclava, I went in through the unlocked kitchen door. The gun was in one of the drawers where Debby had put it that afternoon. I went softly up the stairs to their bedroom. There was no alarm: she had switched it off earlier, after they had gone to bed, pretending she'd forgotten to do something downstairs.

When I got to the bedroom door I began taking long breaths to steady my nerves, going over the final part of the plan.

When I opened the door, Debby was to switch on the lights over the bed. I was to go straight to Harry and shoot him in the head while he was still searching for the gun in the drawer. Then I'd leave straight away, dropping the gun on the landing, and breaking the panel of glass next to the lock on the kitchen door as I left, but from the outside. Debby would wait fifteen minutes, the time it would take me to drive home on back roads. Then, feigning hysterics, she was to call the police. Meantime she'd have turned the alarm system on again, forced open the jewellery drawers of her dressing-table, and arranged things to look as if there'd been a fight on the bed between Harry, who'd gone for his gun, and the burglar who'd woken him. There was less than no chance anyone would hear the shot and fix the time of it. The house was set in the centre of ten acres of garden and paddock. The bedroom windows would be shut, in any case they overlooked a golf fairway, and miles of common land beyond that.

That first comment of Debby's had been pretty accurate. There was really nothing to it if we kept our heads. And the more I'd thought of pulling the trigger on Harry, the more acceptable the idea had become.

Getting practical experience of the gun had helped a bit. Debby had brought it to the house one morning when he was away, and I'd taken it to practise with in the local wood where people were always shooting rabbits. I'd cleaned it afterwards, and refilled the chambers with the extra shells she'd brought. She'd collected it again later that day.

It was while I was firing the gun that I got to thinking Harry was right about what he used to say he'd owed me – except the menial job I'd had in his company over the last years didn't show lasting gratitude, or anything like it, not when you realised he'd become a multimillionaire. As for what he'd done to Debby, well that put the lid on it. But I have to admit that what egged me on the most was I'd be ending up with Debby after all – and with Harry's fortune to go with her. There was sweet justice in that.

I was pretty calm when I finally opened the bedroom door. I wasn't three paces into the room before the lights went on as arranged. I kept going, the gun already held out in front of me in my right hand, left hand supporting the right wrist. My gaze was fixed on Harry, but in the corner of my eye I saw Debby slip out of the bed on to the floor out of the way: good girl.

By now a bleary Harry should have been fumbling with the drawer key – but he wasn't. He was sitting up in bed putting on his glasses and grinning. Grinning! He could see the gun. Did he have a death wish or something?

When I was two paces from Harry I stopped, straightened my arms, and levelled the barrel at his forehead. At that range I couldn't miss – but for a split second looking into his eyes made me hesitate. I might not have gone through with it, except Debby saw what was happening to me.

'Do it! Do it!' she screamed.

I pulled the trigger, my ears instinctively preparing for the explosion. There was a click but no bang.

I pulled the trigger again, and the same thing happened. I pulled the safety catch on, then off again, and pulled the trigger again, and again, and again – and all I could hear was the sound of Harry's mounting laughter. I was panicky and confused. I looked down at the gun. It had to be jammed.

It was then I decided to club Harry to death. I looked up and was about to spring at him when there was an explosion, and a flash. Harry was holding a smoking gun in his hand. He'd been holding it under the bedclothes. The shot he'd just fired could have killed me, no question.

'Keep still, Byron,' he said, eyeing me. 'And Debby, my love, come round and stand next to Byron where I can see you. And do it now or I'll shoot him in a tender place, and that'd be inconvenient for both of you.' He chuckled as she did as she was told.

'I'm afraid you've got the gun with no firing pin, Byron,' he went on. 'I use it just to frighten people. It doesn't frighten me, of course. I switched guns after Debby lent you the other one to practise with. Taking it to your house was a mistake, of course. Just made it easier for the people I had following her. You'd have been better meeting in a supermarket or on a park bench, even. Don't you watch crime movies? Oh, and Byron, please take that ridiculous sock off your head. Slowly though, no tricks.'

I took off the balaclava.

'That's much better,' Harry said. 'Now we can see your famously handsome face again. I knew it was you, of course, Byron. I have a perfect recording of you both putting the plot together that night I was delayed in Paris. Only, as I remember, it was Debby who did all the plotting. Never really an original thinker were you, Byron? Not a thinker at all, come to that. You always relied on others for the brainwork, didn't you? Still do, of course.'

'How did you find out?' I asked.

'That you were planning to murder me? In cold blood?' Without taking his eyes off me, he tapped the bedside table drawer with his hand. 'Undoing this lock starts a miniature tape recorder at the back of the drawer. Simple but ingenious, don't you think? I never told Debby about it for . . . for various reasons. It's recording now, as a matter of fact. I like to have a complete record of things. By the way, the tape I referred to just now is lodged under seal with my solicitor – to be played in the event I should die in suspicious circumstances.'

That was enough for me. 'Harry,' I said, 'shoot me, or hand me over to the police. Either way, get on with it.'

Harry looked shocked. 'Shoot you? Shoot Byron, my old buddy? My childhood companion and protector. My best man? How could you think I'd do anything so barbarous? It'd be like beating up my wife. Giving her a black eye. Punching her in the ribs.' Suddenly his voice rose as his gaze turned to Debby. 'Tell him you lied about that, you little slut, you druggie, you bloody whore. Tell him how you got those injuries. Tell him now!' he shouted angrily.

Debby had been silent up to then. Then she sank on to the end of the bed and started weeping. 'I'm sorry, Harry, I didn't mean . . .'

'Tell him now,' he repeated with a roar.

She swallowed, wiping her eyes with her hand. 'It . . . it was an accident. I fell down the stairs.'

'You fell down the stairs when you were stoned out of your mind. One night when you had your teenage lovers here. Two of them. That's the truth, isn't it?' he roared again.

'Yes, Harry,' she answered with a whimper.

Harry nodded and looked back at me. 'Curious that after being a professional virgin up to our marriage, she's been making up for lost time ever since. Though not with me, I'm afraid.' He pulled a face. 'Now then, as for turning you over to the police, Byron, I don't think that'd do a lot of good, do you?' he asked, as if it was a perfectly normal question to which he needed an unbiased answer.

'What are you going to do then?' I asked.

'I'm going to let you go home now,' he answered, in the same serious tone as before. 'But you'll be taking my wife with you. She's leaving me, Byron. Leaving me for ever. Eloping with you, you might say. In fact, that's exactly what we will say. All of us. It's been bothering me for a long time how to get Debby out of my life. To turn her over to someone who'd care for her. Her and her problems, with drink and drugs and men. Big problems they are, too. Have been for me and my sons for a long time. We're all fed up with her, I'm afraid.'

'That's not true!' Debby screamed.

'Oh, but it *is* true, my love,' he answered quietly. 'You know, Byron, my sons begged me to send them away to school because they couldn't stand living with their mother any more, especially when I'm away. Did you ever hear of such a thing? I try to be here as much as possible, especially in the school holidays, as much as the business allows at least. That's often difficult but I'm making arrangements for it not to be in the future. And contrary to what you've been told, I don't have girlfriends, oh, and I don't drink either. Well, you know I never did.' He waited for Debby to protest, but she didn't. 'No, it'll be much better if Debby goes with you. Then I can divorce her. I would have done it earlier, but the men she's been associating with wouldn't have stayed with her for ten minutes, not unless I'd paid them. And if she'd had money of her own, they'd have robbed her blind. And I care about her, and her future, you see? That's why I'm ready to trust her to you. Trust you to stay with her. To look after her. Especially since you have no alternative. Either of you. And I'll make it worth your while.'

'I wouldn't need paying to – ' I began, rashly probably.

'No, but money will come in handy,' Harry interrupted. 'It's a big responsibility you're assuming, Byron. But in a sense you're right. This could be a case of true love where mine has failed. After all, you've been lovers since childhood.' He smiled gravely. 'I've often thought if Debby had ever really cared for me, and if I'd been able to spend more time with her, I might have been able to straighten her out. But she never did love me, you know? She was just after a good life. It's you she's always loved, Byron.'

'You can't do this to me, Harry,' Debby blurted out at last, and sounding desperate. 'I did love you. I love you still. I'm not going with him.'

'Oh, but you are, my sweet,' he replied. 'You've had your chances before, but they've all ended in broken promises to me, haven't they? If, as you said on the tape, if you were ready to marry Byron after he'd murdered me, surely you're ready to do it now? Surely you're relieved he hasn't had to shoot me after all? Don't all our years together mean you're glad my life's been spared at least?'

There was silence for a bit, except Debby started weeping again.

'If the two of you refuse to do as I say, then I'm afraid I'll have to turn the matter over to the police. Tapes and all,' said Harry solemnly. 'It'll mean a long prison term for both of you, of course. Some would say that's no more than you deserve. Anyway, it's up to you.' He was looking at me hard as he spoke.

'Assuming we leave tonight, what's the deal, Harry?' I asked. 'The whole deal?'

'That's more like it,' he said. He got out of bed, and pulled on a dressing-gown. He still had the gun in his hand but we both knew he didn't need it any more, that he'd won: the tape at his lawyers saw to that, and he knew me well enough to accept I wouldn't make some dangerous and bloody pointless heroic gesture.

'You always were a practical chap, Byron. Where your own best interests were involved,' he said, moving to the chair in front of Debby's dressing-table, turning it round and sitting in it where he could contemplate us both, his chin buried in his neck like a Buddha. 'The deal is that you leave together now. Debby can pack a case for immediate needs, the rest of her stuff can be sent on. She'll leave me a note saying you've gone away together. That she never wants to see me or our children again. That'll be grounds enough for an uncontested divorce with no nonsense about huge compensation for an unfaithful, unworthy wife and mother.'

Debby drew in her breath sharply, but didn't utter otherwise.

'I shan't be able to go back to the company,' I said.

'I agree, that would be difficult for all concerned,' he answered with a half-smile.

'So what are we going to live on? We'll starve,' cried Debby, and meaning it.

'You'll live well enough. In Perth.'

'Perth, Scotland?' I asked warily.

'Perth, Western Australia,' he answered, as I was afraid he was going to. 'There's been a vacancy on the general management staff of our distribution company there for some time. You're appointed, Byron, with a ten-year contract. The salary's better than you're getting here. Great country, Australia. You'll leave before Christmas, all travelling expenses found. There'll be a generous annual bonus too, from me to you, Byron, so long as you two stay together. You can't do better than that now, can you? Not in the circumstances. So take it or leave it, both of you.'

He had to be right, of course. In the circumstances. Even Debby agreed in the end. She didn't relish the prospect of prison any more than I did.

Harry always was right, of course. Clever Harry. We've made a good life here, too. When we got married, Harry sent us out that silver tea-set as a present.

CLEWSEY'S CLICHÉS

HOW DID YOU KNOW THE VICTIM WAS A PAWNBROKER?

Trumpets for Max Jericho

ROBERT BRACK

When Max Jericho fell out of bed that morning, it was already half-past ten. He lay with his head on the worn sheepskin rug, which, once white, was now grey and strewn with cigarette ash and old butts. His left arm hurt. He had fallen directly on to his elbow. Slowly he opened his eyes and his vision fell on the space below his bed. There was a considerable amount of dust there. A bright, broad strip of sunlight streamed diagonally across its surface. Max took a short breath and then blew. For a second a whirlwind raged through the dust. His nose began to tickle mercilessly. He had to sneeze. The dust storm raged again. Then he had to cough. Slowly, he turned himself round and was greeted by thousands of sunbeams pouring insistently through the dirty window. There was no longer any hope of escape: Max Jericho, unemployed, forty-two and single, prepared to face the day in his own inimitable way.

He groaned and got up. He was a little unsteady on his feet and his head was pounding. Carefully he sat down on the edge of the bed and closed his eyes one last time. When he opened them he had to blink to adjust to the bright sunlight. Then he began to find his bearings. An armchair and a standard lamp, both ripe for the rubbish dump, stood out from the total chaos which dominated the room. His clothes had disappeared somewhere between boxes and old newspapers. Except for underpants and vest, he was naked.

At last he struggled to his feet and steered himself clumsily towards the bathroom door. After a few paces his bare foot banged against a cold, hard object. He glanced down. 'Aha,' he murmured.

It was a whisky bottle, its golden brown contents now lapping temptingly back and forth in the sunlight. It was still half full. He nodded happily and placed it carefully on the floor next to the bed. Then he shuffled his way into the bathroom.

He turned on the tap and looked in the mirror. He hadn't shaved for days. His hair stuck to his head in a confused knot. He took a comb to it with little success. His large nose had a reddish sheen whilst his angular cheeks were more violet in colour. His small eyes looked tiredly out from beneath heavy lids. Everything was as usual, only his ears seemed to have grown overnight. Max opened his mouth as wide as he could, revolved his eyes and tried to look scary. It didn't work. He gave up, reached for the soap, and began to wash himself.

When he had finished he looked for his clothes, dressed and took a pre-prandial mouthful of whisky from the bottle. After he'd retrieved his wallet from beneath the pillow, he hurriedly left his one-room apartment. Two streets down there was one of those stand-up cafés where he planned to have breakfast.

'Two coffees and two doughnuts, please,' said Max Jericho to the woman at the counter, who, although he was a regular, had never once bothered to look at him. Max paid with a hundred-mark note – he'd recently won some money at lotto. He really had, although nobody wanted to believe him. To prove it he always carried a few thousand-mark notes around with him. Things were going well at the moment.

The café was almost empty. A businessman was reading the *Abendblatt* and a young girl was taking embarrassed sips from a cup. Max swallowed the doughnuts and washed them down with coffee. The door opened and Peter and Paul entered.

Peter and Paul were in fact one person called Peter-Paul Harbach, but his friends all called him Peter and Paul. He stood next to Max and gave a friendly nod.

'Morning, Max. Another win at lotto?' he sniggered. 'You can buy me a coffee.'

Max nodded, 'Yo!' and pushed a one-mark piece over to him. He looked down at the small figure of Peter and Paul. If he'd been thin you'd hardly have noticed him. Everything about him, however, was round – face, bald head, belly. Despite the fact that things were going badly for him, he was usually in a good mood.

Peter and Paul fetched a cup of coffee. When he came back he took a newspaper out of his jacket pocket. 'Look at this,' he said. 'Man runs amok! Small town massacre. Isn't that great?' He sniggered again.

'Let's have a look.' Max took the paper out of his hands. 'Three dead, ten wounded,' he murmured. 'Not bad.'

'Blood,' said Peter and Paul, with a radiant smile.

'Hmm, hmm.' Max studied the ten-line article for a few minutes. Then he crumpled up the newspaper: 'It's about time we had something to drink.'

Peter and Paul began to nod enthusiastically. 'Sure thing.'

They left the café and paid a visit to the grocery section of a small department store. A bottle of cognac for Peter and Paul and a bottle of whisky for Max, and they were on their way to the park. The place was teeming with children, mothers and old age pensioners. Max and his friend retired to a bench in a secluded corner. Peter and Paul pulled out a horror novel. Max took a mouthful of whisky and looked at him doubtfully.

'You're a bit of a bright spark,Peter and Paul,' he said. 'Always got something to read with you, very educated.'

'Went to college once,' said Peter and Paul. 'Twenty years ago I was actually a student.' He nodded sagely and took a mouthful of cognac.

'A student?' Max looked at him doubtfully. 'Really? What did you study?'

'Ah, well, philosophy for one term.'

'And why did you stop?'

'I've forgotten.'

'So you're not really that bright after all.'

'Nope, not me.'

'Now *that* we can drink to.'

'Cheers.'

While Peter and Paul continued to leaf through his horror story, Max read the newspaper. Gradually it grew warmer and the level in the bottles dropped steadily. At some point, after his blood pressure had risen considerably, Max threw the paper on the ground and yawned loudly, 'Oh boy, oh boyoboy.'

'What's up with you?' Peter and Paul glanced half-asleep over the top of his book. *His* blood pressure appeared to be dropping.

'I've just come to a decision. Today I'm going to run amok,' explained Max.

'What?' Peter and Paul looked at him uncomprehendingly.

'Amok,' said Max and picked up the paper again. 'Here.' He pointed to the bold capitals of the word: 'Amok. A-M-O-K. That's what I'm going to do.'

'Well then,' said Peter and Paul, and buried his head in his horror story again.

Max looked at him disappointedly. 'You're no damned fun at all.' He grasped the bottle. 'I'm off now. You can do what you want.' He crumpled up the newspaper, stuck the whisky bottle under his arm and got up and left. Peter and Paul didn't look up. At that particular moment he was busy with a monster.

By the time Max arrived in front of the gun shop he was soaked with sweat. He stuffed the bottle into the pocket of his jacket, checked that the thousand-mark notes were still in his wallet, and walked in. Behind the counter stood a thin man in a grey coat. He had a long face and red eyes, and looked as if he'd just been crying. Max cleared his throat and looked around. There were rifles and guns everywhere, on the walls, on tables, in cupboards. Even the thin man held a gun in his hand.

'Yes, well,' said Max, planting himself in front of the man, 'I want something big . . . it has to be a rifle . . .'

The thin man put down the gun and smiled at him. 'You've come to just the right place. Could you give me a better idea of what you're looking for?'

'Well,' Max made a vague movement with his hand, 'you know, to shoot with . . . a rifle . . . not too small.' He spread his arms to indicate that the barrel could be at least two metres long.

The salesman began to grow suspicious: 'Do you have a gun licence, sir?'

'Well of course I have. Hey, no problem, no problem at all.'

The thin man coughed and nodded thoughtfully. 'I expect you'll be wanting a hunting rifle, now that the season's starting. Take a look at this.' He turned and took a heavy rifle out of the cupboard. Max took it awkwardly from him and weighed it uncertainly with both hands. Then he turned round, raised it to his shoulder, and peered through the telescopic sights. Through the glass window in the door he could see across the street. A young girl, long legs emerging from a short skirt, was standing there. She moved away and an old woman came hobbling into his sights.

'Is it loaded?' asked Max.

'Of course not.'

'Bang!' said Max, 'Bang!'

The old woman hobbled away. Max lowered the rifle. 'It's pretty heavy.'

'We also stock lighter models. This one, for example.' The salesman handed him a shorter rifle in a paler shade of wood. Max liked this a lot better. He waved it around in the air and the salesman had to duck to avoid being hit. Max tried using it as a walking stick and grunted contentedly. Then he placed the weapon back on the counter. 'I'll take it. How much does it cost?'

'It's 1,146 marks, plus VAT. However, I'm afraid I must first ask you to show me your gun licence.'

Max sighed, 'I haven't got one.'

Hastily the salesman removed the rifle from the counter and Max had to look on longingly as it was placed back in the cupboard.

'If you haven't got a gun licence, the only thing I could possibly sell you is an air rifle.'

'Air . . . ' mumbled Max uncertainly.

'How about this one here?' The man pointed to a gun that looked no less imposing than the others.

Max thought it over for a second and then sighed resignedly, 'Hand it over.'

'It's 598 marks including VAT.'

Max slapped a thousand-mark note on to the counter.

'Keep the change!' he shouted imperiously. 'Just give me some ammunition.'

The salesman placed a box on the counter and handed him the weapon. Max tore it from his hands, shoved the box into his jacket pocket, and turned to leave.

'Would you like a rifle bag, perhaps?'

'Forget it!' growled Max and stormed out of the door.

At the next corner he stopped for a moment to admire his new acquisition. The sunlight gleamed on the polished barrel. Max felt inspired. He got out the whisky bottle and took a big mouthful. Then he tucked the rifle under his right arm, the bottle under his left, and ran across the road to the S-Bahn station.

He took a seat in a first-class compartment and began rather awkwardly to load the rifle, every now and then taking a sip from the bottle. If a conductor comes along, no problem, he thought; I'll just blow him away.

Apart from himself there were only two other passengers in the compartment: a sleeping tramp and a woman in a knitted hat who stared at Max with a mixture of fear and hate through a pair of thick glasses. Max paid no attention. He was making for the town hall.

When he left the train he noticed that the bottle was empty. He threw it back into the compartment, almost hitting the woman. He laughed as loudly and as meanly as he could and moved off towards the exit with big, swaggering steps. Outside he purposefully cut a course for the town hall square. Soon he was going to run amok.

When he arrived at the town hall, his legs were beginning to hurt, and he sat down on a bench to rest. He laid the rifle across his lap. A few metres away a mass of pigeons was bustling around and picking at bread crumbs which a pensioner had shaken on to the ground from a plastic bag. The pensioner moved off, throwing the bag into a rubbish bin.

A devilish grin spread over Max's face. The crooked corners of his mouth took on an almost lecherous expression: Amok! he thought. Then he took the rifle in his hands, removed the safety catch, and raised it to his shoulder. He remembered what Peter and Paul had once told him about notch and bead. He looked at the pigeons through the sights. He singled one out and aimed for its eye. Amok! he thought again. Then he fired. There was a small explosion, more of a plop, and the pigeon keeled over. Max laughed triumphantly. The other pigeons paid no attention. Max aimed at another. Plop! It fell over. Max kept the rifle in firing position and grunted happily. He felt as if he were at war. In quick succession he shot down seven more pigeons. He was really an extraordinarily good shot.

A woman in dungarees and Dr Scholl sandals ran up to him shouting, 'What on earth do you think you're doing?'

'Whatsa matter?' asked Max, his tongue thick.

The woman's voice rose in pitch: 'Those poor creatures!'

'Don't deserve any better,' said Max, 'and anyway, I'm only practising.'

'They're harmless, peaceful birds, you brute!'

'Bugger peace,' grunted Max and took aim again.

The woman turned away and began to shout at uninterested passers-by: 'Can't you see what he's doing? The man's an animal molester, a murderer!' Nobody listened.

Max now took aim at her: 'Fly, my pretty pigeon.'

The woman began to yell for help. At the same moment a siren started to wail behind Max. The woman stopped for a moment.

'Aha, the pigs,' muttered Max, lowered his rifle and looked around enquiringly.

In front of a large building a red lamp was flashing on and off. It was from here that the noise of the siren was coming. A number of people were running down broad stone steps which led to the entrance doors. On the other side of the street a group of onlookers had begun to form. Above the entrance of the imposing building, in powerful, glittering gold letters, stood: TRANSATLANTIC INTERNATIONAL BANK.

'A bank robbery,' concluded Max. 'Oh boy, count me in!'

He jumped up and ran towards the building, swinging his rifle wildly about in the air. Passers-by looked at him in astonishment, some of them pulling back in fright.

'I'm on my way!' shouted Max.

He reached the stone steps. From inside the noise of several salvos of automatic fire could be heard. A black BMW came to a halt with a screech of tyres. Max stormed up the steps.

'Hey!' he shouted, 'Hey!'

As he arrived at the entrance to the bank, the doors were pushed open and two figures in black masks, carrying machine guns and large sacks in their hands, came storming out. They demolished the glass in the doors with a generous burst of fire.

'Hey, guys!' called Max. 'I'm with you, count me in.'

He raised his rifle.

The gangsters froze and looked at each other through their masks in confusion.

'Who is this nutcase?'

'No idea. Clobber him!'

One of the gangsters struck him in the face with the barrel of his machine gun. Max tumbled back and banged against a broad pillar. Both hands still grasping his rifle, he slowly collapsed and remained lying against the pillar.

The gangsters leapt into their getaway car and sped off with a screech of tyres. The loud wail of police sirens came nearer.

When Max opened his eyes, the whole area was full of flashing blue lights. Police officers, panic-stricken customers and pale-faced bank clerks were running backwards and forwards. Max struggled to his feet.

With the rifle in his hand he went over to one of the uniformed officers and tapped him on the shoulder. 'OK, I give myself up.'

The officer turned to him in surprise, which rapidly developed into anger. 'Get out of here. Now!'

He grabbed Max by the arm and pushed him down the steps. Max staggered to the nearest corner, leant against the wall of a house and shook his head, muttering to himself, 'What kind of policeman do you call that . . . God, if they only realised . . . the number of deaths I've got on my conscience . . .'

At that moment a Salvation Army band came around the corner, an accordion, guitar and two trumpets. Max Jericho straightened himself, shouldered his rifle, swung to the right and marched along with them.

The trumpets gleamed in the sunlight. Two old women in uniform were singing a battle song in shaky voices. Max joined in. Then a tremulous little man tugged at Max's sleeve and said, 'Some people think that you can't talk to God any longer today. But we have proof that the old man is still alive.'

Max nodded enthusiastically. 'Count me in!' he said.

Translated from the German
by William Adamson

Cold and Deep

FRANCES FYFIELD

The ice had formed over eighteen hours. Sarah could sense it on the outside of the train travelling north from King's Cross to the Midlands. Fortunately, it was too cold to snow. Snow would only trap her for longer, and she was trapped enough already. What a fool, what a silly idiot she was to agree to help her sister when it wasn't as if she even liked children.

In a split second, on stepping from the train, Sarah examined her reasons for being where she was and found them lacking. It was simply that she was so successful at being single, she had nowhere else to go. Mary had asked, and Christmas was a nightmare anywhere.

There would be quite a crowd. Sarah struggled to remember how many. Mary, of course, with her husband Jonathan, plus two daughters aged six and eight, plus a baby. Then there was Richard, Jonathan's brother, and his utterly devoted fiancée, the lovely Fiona, who had been on site three days in advance to organise provisions and prepare the house.

Richard would follow her slavishly like the Magi in thrall to the star in the East, the way he always did. While the rest, Mary said in admiration, bowed to her practical wisdom and followed her orders.

In comparison to this elegant paragon, the prospect of the elderly father was almost appealing in Sarah's estimation. He and she could celebrate their single status, with herself in the role of a hard-bitten aunty, and he as a hard-drinking Grandad. They could survive the season with the aid of a litre of gin. Since grandfather was recovering from a stroke, Sarah doubted the accuracy of this dream, but it was the best she could do.

The station of the small industrial town – foreign territory to a refugee from the fleshpots of central London – was ugly, chilly, and not a place to linger. Sarah remembered her instructions to call the invincible Fiona, but somehow balked at the idea when she saw the queue for the phone. Get a taxi, she thought, with the lazy London habits her successful career allowed her to afford. Ask the driver to stop at the end of the road, walk to clear her head from the fuggy warmth of the train, anything to postpone the claustrophobic wretchedness of it all.

At least there would be a dog for company. A bitch, with puppies, Sarah recalled, and in the remembering, she was violently sick while standing at the rank. On that account, it took a while longer to get a taxi.

In a slow-moving car, approaching the same town from Manchester, weary bickering had trailed into dreary pauses. 'I don't know why we have to do this,' Mary was saying for the last time. Jonathan was beyond yelling and banging the wheel by now; all that had come earlier. He could scarcely speak. His head was full of the incessant calculation of how long his redundancy money would last, sums which buzzed and hummed like a persistent insect. The New Year beckoned like an old nightmare. Mary was trying to be noble, attempting to hide a kindred form of depression which left her constantly tired, often petulant.

'You know for why: because it's good for us. The girls get to run around. Dad can't come to us since he had his stroke, which is just as well for the sort of Christmas we'd be able to give him. And,' he added cunningly, 'with Fiona there, you don't have to do anything, except sleep. Surely Sarah will help?'

Oh clever, very clever, Mary thought. The prospect of sleep was unbearably appealing. Jonathan looked at Mary's face in the rear view mirror, and saw a pinched, exhausted look beyond his expectations or his curing. He envied the insouciance of his younger brother and the careless decade which came between them. He envied not only Richard's life, but his car and delicious, competent, caring Fiona.

'We got Sasha! With puppies, this time!' Beth shrieked, sick of the silence. 'And I can go swimming in the lake!'

Mary winced. 'I don't think so, darling.'

'Can I tell you something, Daddy. Can I, can I, can I?' Beth continued. Mary's eyes closed. She was remembering the only holiday they could afford that past summer: a week with Richard and Fiona at Grandad's, just before his stroke. Fiona had been wonderful: so wonderful she had made Mary feel perfectly useless. Sylvie was always getting scratches, but somehow all the children's noisiest toys, such as Sylvie's recorder and Beth's drum, had disappeared.

Mary still wondered why it was that the children stayed so clean and mysteriously quiet around Fiona. It had been such a relief, herself so grateful, she had failed to question, and she was too anxious for peace to question now.

'What do you want to tell me, love?' Jonathan asked Beth. The child drew breath.

'I don't like Fiona, she wears horrible rings. Not after the summer holidays, I don't like her. Not much.'

Mary's eyes opened and her voice rose in desperation.

'Don't be silly. Fiona's lovely. Everyone loves her.'

'Sasha doesn't. Grandad doesn't. I doesn't.'

Mary lost control. 'Rubbish! You must be mad! Without Fiona, we don't eat or sleep for two whole days. So shut up . . . Just shut up!'

Silence fell until another small voice rose from the back.

'How very long till we get there, Daddy? How long? How long?'

'Soon. If you're good, you can play with Grandad's dog.'

A yellow bitch, mostly labrador, called Sasha and still Richard's pet.

'We'll have to be very patient,' Fiona was saying to him on his car phone. 'But at least we've got the best bedroom and the best bed,' she breathed seductively. Richard smiled like an idiot. He liked the sound of bed.

'Was Dad pleased to see you?'

'Oh yes, but not as much as the home helpers and the night nurse when I took over. I thought they were going to kiss me. But he doesn't really like me. You know that . . .'

Her voice was velvety, like the soft pouches beneath the labrador's jaw where Richard tickled until she rolled on her back, presenting her pink and yellow belly in ecstasy. Clutching the beloved car phone, his business as well as his delight, in lane three of the motorway, Richard checked the mirror at the same time and saw himself grinning. There was another BMW on his tail. He made it wait.

'You know your father doesn't like me,' Fiona was saying sensibly, 'but I thought I'd better warn you, he's much worse. Swears like a trooper, when he can talk at all. Says awful things about people, me included; you, even. Much worse than last month. He may not say much this evening because he's very tired, but he might blow bubbles.' She kept thinking of bubbles.

'What kind of bubbles?' Richard asked stupidly, but the car lurched and the line began to crackle. No snow, his phone dead without apology, the BMW behind suddenly in front as he drifted left and he hadn't had a chance to ask about his darling golden bitch Sasha, and her late, aberrant pregnancy.

As he witnessed his father's judgement diminish, Richard saw himself losing one rudder to replace it with another. He shook his head and spurred the car into life. Fiona was simply a miracle.

The pudding was almost cooked. There was a brace of geese stuffed and wrapped in the larder. What an ugly house this is, Fiona thought. No country mansion, but pre-war Gothic, stuck on the edge of an awful conurbation once made rich by the industries of coal. The villa was the last in the road; a privileged position, with a field sloping down the bank to a pond in a gully – a stagnant stretch of water which Jonathan and his romantic brother still described as 'the lake'.

This puddle might have looked larger to kids, Fiona admitted condescendingly, but it was still only a pond. Small, but deep and cold, or so she had discovered as she warmed her hands in the sink after a second brisk walk to the crumbly edge, just to get out and see how the ice was progressing. It had been forming slowly ever since she arrived, more solid by the hour.

There was a keening sound from the dog's basket; a vague noise of distant thumping from the living room reached by a horrible lino passage. Sasha regarded Fiona with eyes of helpless misery. The bitch lay one side with her milk-swollen tits exposed, the blanket beneath her freshly clean as a replacement for the torn and bloody newspaper of yesterday.

Fiona strode across and forced a pill between the unresisting pink jaws. The effort left her own fingers damp with saliva. She looked at them with disgust. 'There,' she said. 'Vet's orders, you revolting beast. You mothers are such a trial.' She kicked the dog lightly with a small, well-shod foot. 'Come on, show a leg, you stupid brute. Come on.'

The almost labrador obeyed with ponderous reluctance, her unclipped claws clicking on the lino, which gave way to a tartan carpet. There was nothing here she would want to keep, Fiona thought, everything frightful. But it could make a beautiful and valuable dwelling.

We'll commute, Fiona planned. Have stone flags for the garden; gravel for the driveway. Plenty of ground. The pond could become a swimming pool. I could call Richard from there on his best mobile phone and ask him to bring down the champagne.

Sarah approached on foot, passing closed-up dwellings with eyeless windows set back from the road, the odd glimmering of light emphasising her own exclusion, until she reached the last house. The rutted drive was large enough for three cars in a row, containing only one, which must be Fiona's.

That single smart and feminine motor told Sarah she was the first of other guests and made her reluctant to knock; left her standing in a state of uncertainty by the front door next to an enormous terracotta plant pot, pretentiously out of place and housing a small shrub on a bed of fresh compost. The shrub branches were festooned with tiny baubles, tinkling softly as she breathed, the whole decoration slightly repellent in its tasteful newness.

Still reluctant, inhibited by this sign of festivity, Sarah moved to her right and looked into a window. There were leaded panes through which she could see multicoloured fairy bulbs on a Christmas tree, hear muffled sounds, blurred like the lights, by the distortions of the glass.

An old man was sitting in an armchair, so far upright he might easily have risen with the aid of the stick which someone else had placed out of reach, leaning against the door sixteen feet away. He seemed to be yelling for his prop, screaming with rage and beating his wrists on the arms of his seat. There was a tall, fair-haired young woman about the business of shushing him, followed by a faded yellow dog with a pink underbelly.

Sarah stared and rubbed her eyes. She thought she saw a plastic bib ripped from the crêped neck, revealing a clean, white shirt; a hearing aid rammed in, the stick retrieved and placed where it belonged; a brush dragged through the thick, grey hair, yanking back a full, round face into a scream. He looked like a baby. Sarah felt sick all over again. The bright blue eyes in his face turned to the window as if for redemption, saw headlights behind her and began to focus.

Sarah scuttled towards the door. Her back was illuminated as she rang the bell, a dinky, irritating chime which defied the last illusion of ancestral splendour and also cut across the modern good taste of the expensive pot. One car pulled up behind her, another, more slowly behind that. Fiona flung open the door, framed in the light like an angel, laughing her hallos, uttering warm and lovely platitudes. 'Come in, come in, how clever of you all to arrive at once, come and see Daddy . . .'

Father smiled at Richard. He was desperate to talk, it seemed, but Fiona was busy organising which room was whose, wash your hands and come and eat. Besides, father looked healthy, clearly so well cared for he must be content.

Then there was home-made soup; sandwiches, biscuits and Coke for the kids. Lots of red wine for the adults. Perfect for a family on Christmas Eve.

It was Beth, as usual, who created the discord by pointing at Sasha with a trembling finger. 'Where are her puppies?' she shouted impatiently, forgetting her manners and the lecture in the car.

Grandad arched in his chair, looked as if he was about to shout, but hissed instead. 'She didn't want . . .' he began. 'She didn't want . . .'

'Oh dear,' said Fiona, laying a hand on his arm, looking at Beth with sympathy. 'I think it was a false alarm.' She turned to Richard. 'Hysterical pregnancy; Sasha's had them before, the vet told me. So I'm sorry, darlings, no puppies this time. The poor thing thought she was: her poor old body thought she was, but she wasn't. She just got fat.'

Beth began to weep. Slow, solid tears of frustration.

I wish I was like that, Sarah thought wryly. I wish that my condition was the result of hysteria instead of careless fornication. I like my single, trouble-free life, my prospects of promotion to partnership over the heads of other accountants. I need nothing. I do not like spending Christmas marking time until I can find the right kind of discreet clinic for an abortion, so I can go on as before, and the awful misery I feel can only be because I always detested Christmas, anyway.

The dog raised a paw, suddenly acquiescent with a child warm against her throbbing flank. Dad thumped his stick. He shouted for scissors to deal with his sandwiches; ate with voracity the pieces which Fiona had cut so kindly and without comment or condescension, staring at her calm and beautiful face.

Yes, you are wonderful, Sarah thought. Richard's a lucky man. Mary's eyes were closed again. 'He has such trouble with his speech,' Fiona explained, leaning away from her prospective father-in-law, 'since his stroke.'

The children and Sarah were in one heap by now, as if Sarah had somehow acquired them all. How peculiar it was that little girls and boys should take to her so, Mary thought. They lollop towards her like puppies.

So it was Sarah who took them to bed soon after Grandad had been shepherded away by Fiona without protest, as if to give a good example.

The ugly house was strangely silent apart from the plumbing: the children spoke in whispers. They should be more excited, Sarah reflected. Suddenly protective of their dreams and against her better judgement, which applauded the convenience of their subdued behaviour, she found herself trying to stimulate some of the old and naughty fever.

'What's Santa bringing you? Will he be able to get everything down the chimney?'

'He was bringing me a puppy,' said Beth savagely.

'No he wasn't, stupid,' said Sylvie. Beth eyed Sarah in challenge. Sarah was silent and the glance slid away as honesty prevailed.

'I wanted to see a puppy. That's all. Grandad said on the phone, it was dog's last chance. He could speak all right then. Only Fiona says Sasha didn't have nothing. No puppies. Nothing.'

'Dogs have lots of chances. So do people.'

'No, they don't. I don't think they do. Grandad said they don't. You've got to grab chances, he said.'

'Shush, now. Everyone's tired. Shush . . .'

As she tiptoed away down the corridor, full of relief, she saw a light beneath a door, prepared to creep past that too, until she heard the sound of sobbing. Grandad's room. She scarcely knew the man; she should leave him alone, she wanted a drink. But still she pushed the door and went in, cursing herself.

The old man lay on his side, foetally curled, his hand stretched out to a bedside light and a book which seemed too far from his fingers for easy reach. He turned his face to the door as she entered, and all at once she recognised that look of pellucid sanity in his blue eyes which she had seen before, distorted by the glass in the windows.

'Do something,' he hissed. 'She'll eat him up. Do something.'

Sarah was embarrassed, arranged his blankets, smiled in the conciliatory way she imagined Fiona would smile, and put the lamp and the ever-elusive stick within reach, listening all the time to the laughter from downstairs which beckoned her to where she really belonged.

'Shall I turn off the light?'

He stuck two fingers in the air, a gesture obscenely at odds with his laundered fragility. Awkward old cuss, Sarah thought, retreating in good order.

Downstairs, there was no relief either. They were family; together they could only speak of their young and the old, and this was the season for both.

'Your dad can't cope,' Fiona was saying gently, lying like a lioness at rest across Richard's knees. 'He's determined he can, but he can't.'

Richard bristled. 'I could get him a mobile phone,' he said, pointlessly, to universal silence. 'We could get someone in to look after poor Sasha . . . how could he let her get into that state and not notice it was wrong?'

'But he should never go into a home, should he, darling?' Fiona murmured reassuringly. 'We could always keep lovely Sasha for a while. You'd like that, wouldn't you?' Richard nodded.

'So I just think we step up the support for now,' Fiona continued. 'I mean, actually, we could live here, once we're married . . .'

'Yes,' said Jonathan, relieved at the mere suggestion of solutions half as tidy. 'Yes.' Since the birth of his children and the even more momentous loss of his means to support them, he too had felt old. Sarah nodded and smiled: her contribution was not required. She was the only one distant enough to watch. So she did.

No snow on Christmas morning. A milky mist melted against the windows. By some miracle, it was as late as seven o'clock when the first piece of chocolate was presented by Beth; eight when Sarah rose and padded towards the Christmas tree like a pilgrim unsure of her religion. The old man was sitting there in his chair, haphazardly dressed.

'Did it all by myself. Easy, when I can reach the stick. What the hell does Richard think I normally do? I'm not mad you know,' he announced with surprising clarity. 'Only as mad as a man with sons who are deaf and blind after all I taught them. Listen to me; you didn't listen to me, did you? They don't either.'

'When?'

He seemed to slump, then rallied into a murmur. 'I love Richard best. Is that so awful?'

'No. We all love someone best. It's allowed.'

'Which is why it's important for him to know that she is trying to . . .' the voice declined to a mumble. Grandad's face contorted. 'That woman . . . she's trying to kill . . . No, she's trying to . . . trying to . . . kiss me! Oh yes, she likes to kiss!' he shouted while his other hand waved in a mockery of greeting.

Sarah turned. Fiona was in the doorway. 'Silly old Daddy,' she said fondly. 'You do go on.' Her face was perfect, without a trace of tiredness. 'Sarah, could you be an angel and help peel a few spuds before all hell starts? Then we can relax.'

Sarah followed her out, looked back once. Grandad was slightly purple in the face.

'He's better in the morning,' Fiona confided in a whisper. 'But he does talk nonsense.'

'Some of the time?'

Fiona responded sadly. 'No, I daren't tell Richard. All of the time.'

No one listens to the old, Sarah was thinking as they all opened their presents.

While Mary and Jonathan meekly exchanged books and records with a peck on the cheek before turning full attention to the pleasure of their children, Sarah lingered over the unwrapping of her token gifts to make them last, said thank you politely, delivered hers, then helped a listless Grandad open up a sweater, a shirt, and a tie, while the children tore into parcels like wild beasts. Even they had finished with the smallest and greatest of these long before Richard and Fiona ceased presenting to each other gift after perfectly wrapped gift.

'Oh, darling you shouldn't! A silk shirt! Sweetheart!'

There was a hunky suede jacket, a night-dress, jewellery for both, shoes, then more and more until the whole room was ablaze with their luxury.

Mary had begun to look a little stiff to remind Richard he seemed to have forgotten his nieces. From a forest of pretty paper, it took some time for him to remember where he was.

'Oh, I got this for the kids . . .'

Beth perked up, then her face assumed a stony expression of no expectation as Fiona handed her the parcel. Inside was a mobile phone.

'Oh,' said Jonathan, doubtfully.

'There's another one for Sylvie,' said Richard happily.

'I get a discount. They can try them in the garden.'

'Crap,' said Grandad suddenly and distinctly. 'Crap.'

'Lunch in an hour,' Fiona announced brightly, gathering up paper. 'Is it worth going out?'

'We'll go,' said Sarah, desperate for air, feeling frantic with heat from the fire. 'Won't we? Come on Sylvie, we'll take a phone and phone Grandad. He'll like that.'

'Crap,' said Grandad.

'If you must,' said Fiona. 'Do be careful with it, they're expensive, the very best. I should stay in the garden if I were you. No, don't take the dog. She's been out already.'

Outside the mist and the mood cleared. Beth shrieked her way down the long, unkempt garden, holding the mobile phone as a kind of balance, yelling 'Yuck' as she skirted the tentacles of the dripping bush, bellowing out of sight.

Sarah's arms clutched her bosom as she ran through a gap in the hedge, yelling after them, 'Wait for me, wait for me!' There was no real cause for concern. The children were in awe of the lake they approached. Gingerly testing the steep, friable edges with the insensitive toes of wellington boots, both quieter than before, sulking with their feet because they could go no farther and dare not try the ice.

Sarah desperately wanted to revive for them the simple excitement which seemed to die indoors: felt the same desire in herself as the last evening, to make them noisily, joyously responsive.

'Let's break the ice,' she yelled. 'Come on, get stones. We can crack it!'

Sylvie threw a branch she had lugged to the edge; Beth threw lumps of earth. Then Sarah found a large stone, which was an effort even to lift. Beth helped. Between them, they dropped it rather than threw, watched it roll heavily down the side, bounce the last yard and make a hole in the edge of the ice. The water heaved and burped. Bubbles rose.

'Yeah, yeah!' Beth howled.

'I hate Fiona!' Sylvie shrieked. 'She slaps me with her rings on! She steals stuff! She takes everything!'

She picked up the abandoned phone and threw it towards the hole.

'Stop it,' Sarah shouted, but too late. Sylvie's aim was bad. The phone slid two, three feet distant from the hole. She began to cry.

Oh no, please don't, Sarah thought, I wanted to see you both happy: we were doing so well.

'Silly,' she said sternly. 'Don't be silly. We'll get it back.'

It was stated, but by some common instinct, they all knew that the wrath of Fiona would be terrible. Sarah scrambled down the bank and stood at the edge of the water, making an act of it, pretending it was fun. On the very edge, she was safe, until she looked at her feet.

A piece of sacking was protruding above the surface and with it the pink snout of a corpse. A pink and yellow body, bloated, pathetic, followed by another. Dead puppies. A whole litter of drowned puppies, the almost labrador's last chance.

Squatting over her freezing feet, Sarah shielded the sacking and talked brightly to the children over her shoulder to disguise the waves of fury which made her tremble.

'Listen,' she said. 'Listen, I've got an idea. Aunty Fiona can't get mad at me, right? I'm a guest and a grown up and I don't care anyway. Right?' They nodded, like two wise owls. 'So you go back to the house, now, tell her I was carrying the phone and I dropped it on the ice.

'Say we don't want to tell Uncle Jonathan, in case he gets upset. Get Aunty Fiona in the kitchen, make it sound secret, right? And ask her to come here with a broom or something, so I can get the phone back. Then stay inside. It's too cold out here.'

Beth grabbed Sylvie by the arm and they both fled, rehearsing lines. Sarah waited. She fished one of the dead puppies out of the water, repelled by the touch, but compelled to wipe the water away from its blind eyes and feel of the softness under the chin. Then she dragged out the sack containing the rest.

The other six were still curled together. There was a pain in her abdomen and a fluttering in her chest. The stone had been too heavy, she felt sick, but she knew she would not wait long. Soon, down the slope, she heard the breathless panting of Fiona, booted, spurred, carrying a yard brush.

'The phone,' Fiona said. 'How could you? Richard lives for phones. We'll have a lousy Christmas if you upset him, how could you?'

She'll eat him up, was all Sarah thought, seeing in her mind's eye the sanity of the old man which they all ignored, concentrating on his weakness. She'll eat them all up; she likes to kiss. Possessions, other people's inheritance, other people's chances, she likes to kiss.

Sarah was halfway up the bank, scrambling with one hand, the other holding the sodden sack behind her back. Fiona saw it and stopped.

'How many did the poor bitch have? What a nuisance for you.' Sarah tried to sound patient and understanding. Fiona pretended she had not heard, then relented, seduced into a sense of conspiracy by the concern in the other's voice, ignoring the prospect of the blinding, ice-cold rage beneath.

'Well, yes it was, a bit. The day I arrived. Can you imagine! He can't cope, you know. Richard would have wanted to keep them, take them home. Can you imagine how awful . . . mess on our carpets, the smell, everything . . . I mean you've got a nice flat, you see what I mean?'

'Yes, I do understand. Anyway, the phone's the most important thing at the moment, isn't it? I mean, it's valuable.'

'Of course it is.'

'Why don't you try to get it?' Sarah said, oozing sympathy. 'I'm afraid my feet have gone numb.'

'Fine, fine.'

Oh, she was such a coper. Sarah squatted, winded with a pain far worse than the sickness outside the station the night before, clutching her chest where the gripe was sharpest, the sackful of sodden babies by her side. She was half-weeping, praying madly for the invisible foetus inside her.

Oh no, oh no; whatever the punishment to me, please do not die. I want you to live. That is what I want; whatever the purgatory, don't die on me. Every dog deserves its day, every bitch deserves a baby. Heaven help me.

Dazed, she watched Fiona stand up to her knees in icy water and fish for the phone, which lay like some ghastly talisman on the frozen surface. The slim body of the fiancée leant forward to sweep the brush over the ice, grunting. Then Sarah watched as Fiona slipped on the smooth clay surface; then Fiona was sliding under the ice up to the waist, her feet flailing for a hold.

Half the bank caved in behind her with a plop. The incline down was now very steep. The ice broke against her back. She slid further, bawling for help and for more than a moment, Sarah was tempted.

But it was a passing temptation. She hurt too much; she had too much to protect to fling herself down a slippery incline towards deep, cold water; she could not run for help anyway.

So she simply wondered about how to harness her small store of energy to bury the puppies in case the children should see them. Stayed where she was, full of the overpowering desire to preserve her own child and aware of the dimmest possible notion that it was better for a woman like Fiona to go like this.

Better in the long run for everyone. Knowing while she thought it, how a woman like herself was the slightest bit mad, but also knowing she couldn't, wouldn't, ever quite regret it.

It was not as if she even wanted to move; she wanted her own child to lie peaceful, but never as still as the cold puppies. Would it be better, she asked herself, if Richard saw these little corpses? She wondered briefly, dizzily, decided emphatically not, neither he nor his nieces.

As the new set of bubbles stopped rising to the surface, Sarah got up. She went round to the front of the house to the enormous planter on which she had stumbled the night before, lifted the tinkling shrub carefully, placed the sack with respect then went back to the bottom of the lawn behind and walked to the kitchen door.

'Where's Fiona?' Richard demanded.

'What? Isn't she here? I left her trying to fish a phone out of the lake. Went for a walk down the avenue. Isn't it remarkable how every house looks the same but manages to be so different? Are they 1930s or sooner? I never know. What's wrong? She said she'd give it five minutes. Isn't she back? Does she like the cold or something?'

He flung himself out of the house. Sarah washed her hands, went into the living room, where Grandad sat with the dog's head on his knee. Jonathan was on the floor, next to his suddenly animated, affectionate wife, with her arm round his shoulder as they laid out a game for the children, all four heads together. The baby was grinning in a carry cot, also studiously ignoring Sarah's glance. The atmosphere was suddenly lighter and brighter as though a stone had been removed and daylight introduced into a cave.

Sarah knelt by the old man's knee and watched while the dog lay down and transferred a trusting head into her own lap. Grandad watched too, with his crêpey hand trembling, Sarah's fingers interlaced with his.

'Trust me,' she murmured.

'You'll have a nice pup,' he said, loudly and clearly.

'One day.'

Sarah did not know if he spoke to her or the dog. Or even if it mattered.

The quotation is:

> There are few objects more compelling to the attention than a dead body in the centre of a small room. Nevertheless when Henry first entered the office his immediate impression was not of Helen herself: it was simply an impression of overwhelming confusion.

Patricia Moyes, *Murder à la Mode*

The clues are:

A	PEWTER	N	MEMPHIS
B	AFGHANISTAN	O	USHER
C	THE FIRTH OF FORTH	P	REJECTION
D	RHINOCEROS	Q	DAWN
E	INFLAME	R	ELEMENTARY
F	CORRESPOND	S	RETCHED
G	INCONTINENT	T	ANTIHISTAMINE
H	ADVERSE	U	LEVEL
I	MOONSTONE	V	AWESOME
J	OWLISH	W	MEWL
K	YES MINISTER	X	OFFSHOOT
L	EPISTEMOLOGY	Y	DELFT
M	SAHIB	Z	ENFEEBLE

Solution to the Cryptic Crime Acrostic

The Crime Writers' Association

The CWA was formed by the author John Creasey in 1953 with the objective of raising the awareness and status of crime fiction.

Founder members included Julian Symons and Elizabeth Ferrars, who are still producing new work. The CWA numbers just over 400 members, among them some of the best-known names in crime writing.

The CWA annual awards of the Gold and Silver Daggers for the best crime novel and runner-up are the longest standing literary awards in Great Britain. They are open to any crime novelist internationally and carry great prestige. The Diamond Dagger is also awarded annually to an established author of a body of work of consistently high merit.

In addition to these Daggers, other CWA awards include those for the best non-fiction work, the best first crime novel, the best humorous work (the Last Laugh Award) and, more recently, the best short story.

Since the short story has, over the years, drawn outstanding work from some of crime writing's finest practitioners, it is fitting that this new award has been established and that the CWA should continue to encourage the form with its annual anthology.

JOHN MALCOLM
CWA Chairman 1994-95

✧ *Biographical Notes*

The contributors to *3rd Culprit* were invited to describe themselves and their recent work in about forty words.

In the real world **William Adamson** teaches English literature for a living and makes the occasional foray into the more shadowy sphere of translation. He is also involved in the running of the Raymond Chandler Society.

Robert Brack, born in 1959, lives in Hamburg working as a journalist. Since 1988 he has published seven novels, including a *Polish Crime Trilogy* and three novels featuring the sensation-seeking journalist Tolonen. For *Das Mädchen mit der Taschenlampe* he received the Raymond Chandler Society's Marlowe award in 1993.

Sarah Caudwell read classics at Aberdeen and law at Oxford, and practised for some years at the Chancery Bar. Her novels feature a group of young barristers practising in Lincoln's Inn: the latest, *The Sirens Sang of Murder*, won an Anthony Award at Bouchercon.

Clewsey's drawings have appeared in the CWA's monthly newsletter, *Red Herrings*.

Born in London, **Liza Cody** is the author of six Anna Lee mysteries, recently televised. Her latest novels, *Bucket Nut* and *Monkey Wrench* (Chatto & Windus/Arrow), wrestle with Eva Wylie.

Mat Coward is chiefly a magazine humour columnist, but becoming increasingly distracted by crime fiction, which he reviews for the *Morning Star* and *Mystery Scene*. He has sold crime and SF stories to several UK and US anthologies and magazines.

Celia Dale's latest novel, *Sheep's Clothing*, her collection of short stories, *A Personal Call*, and an earlier novel, *A Helping Hand*, are available in Penguin. Many of her short stories have been broadcast by the BBC. She lives in London.

Madelaine Duke has written forty books from biography and historical novels to crime and (as Alex Duncan) humour. She was chairman of the CWA and the first winner of the short story competition sponsored by *The Times*.

Frances Fyfield is a practising solicitor with the Crown Prosecution Service. She is the author of six bestselling crime novels, and two psychological thrillers written under the name Frances Hegarty. Her latest novel, *Perfectly Pure and Good*, is published by Bantam Press.

Now settled in California, **Keith Heller** has published three eighteenth-century London crime novels and has recently completed a mainstream novel set in 1945. *Queen Mob*, the first in a series of mysteries with Catherine and William Blake, is in progress.

Maxim Jakubowski used to work in publishing and now owns London's notorious haven for criminals, the 'Murder One' bookshop. He has won the Anthony and Karel awards and fathered over thirty books. Some say his stories are somewhat autobiographical, but he only confesses to crimes of the heart.

Bill James writes a crime series featuring detectives Harpur and Iles. The 11th, *In Good Hands*, comes from Macmillan this summer. Pan recently published an Omnibus of the first three called *Harpur and Iles*.

H R F Keating's first title *Death and the Visiting Fireman* came to him in the bath in 1959. Inspector Ghote arrived as he sat in his red armchair in 1963. Mr Idd manifested himself as he was walking through London in 1985.

Susan Kelly's latest novel – *The Seventh Victim* – was published by Hodder & Stoughton in January 1994. Her 'Hope' series of detective novels, featuring DCI Nick Trevellyan and feisty businesswoman Alison Hope, has appeared in Britain and America.

Michael Z Lewin's latest Albert Samson book is *Called by a Panther*, a call Samson regrets answering. A new Indianapolis book, *Underdog*, introduces the eponymous Jan Moro.

Ex-policewoman **Joan Lock** writes non-fiction crime books. Her latest, *Dreadful Deeds and Awful Murders: Scotland Yard's First Detectives 1829-1878* and *Scotland Yard Casebook: The Making of the CID 1865-1935*, are police history told through colourful cases and characters.

Bob Lock was a policeman in London's West End and magistrates court for thirty years. CWA members find his knowledge useful while his wife, Joan Lock, employs his photographic skills when illustrating her books. His 'poem' was a snap decision.

Peter Lovesey was beguiled into joining the team of *Culprit* editors this year. As a master of plotting with twenty-five years' experience, he now suspects his co-editors of a deeply sinister motive and is devising a brilliant escape plan.

John Malcolm was born in Manchester and spent part of his boyhood in Uruguay before returning to England. He has written eleven crime novels and several short stories since 1984. He is currently Chairman of the Crime Writers' Association.

Val McDermid is Scots by birth, a Northerner by adoption. Manchester-based private eye Kate Brannigan features in *Dead Beat, Kick Back*, and, most recently, *Crack Down*, while *Report for Murder, Common Murder, Final Edition* and *Union Jack* showcase journalist sleuth Lindsay Gordon.

James Melville's first novel, *The Wages of Sin*, was published in 1979, and his most recent is *The Body Wore Brocade* (Warner-Futura, 1993). He has reviewed crime fiction and thrillers for the *Hampstead & Highgate Express* for more than ten years.

Stephen Murray's latest book is *Death and Transfiguration*. He is the author of six previous crime novels and a biography, and lives in Wales.

Sara Paretsky's newest novel is *Tunnel Vision*. Her sequence of novels featuring Chicago detective V. I. Warshawski, began with *Indemnity Only*, and *Toxic Shock* won the CWA's Silver Dagger award. She was a founder member of Sisters in Crime. She lives in Chicago.

Ian Rankin is the author of seven 'Inspector Rebus' books, described by critics as 'Tartan Noir' (an unfair oxymoron, you'll agree). He has also published two thrillers under his son's name, 'to stop him from Martining my Kingsley'.

Ruth Rendell is the creator of Wexford who has appeared in 15 novels, seven short stories, and on television. She has been awarded the Diamond Dagger of the Crime Writers' Association, four Gold Daggers and a Silver. Her latest collection of stories is *The Copper Peacock*.

William G Tapply is the author of twelve mystery novels, most recently *The Snake Eater* (Otto Penzler Books, 1993) and four non-fiction books. A full-time writer and writing teacher, Tapply has published hundreds of stories, essays and articles.

Donald E Westlake has published many novels, several with a comic tinge he's been taking antibiotics for. His screenplay 'The Grifters', from the Jim Thompson novel, was nominated for an Academy Award. He has won three MWA Edgars (including one for *Too Many Crooks*) and the Mystery Writers of America Grand Master award. Three of his first four books will be published in an omnibus edition in Britain by A&B in 1994.

David Williams switched from advertising to writing at 49. Seventeen of his whodunnits have featured banker Mark Treasure (two were short listed for the Gold Dagger). His 1994 *Last Seen Breathing* marked the debut of Cardiff sleuth DCI Merlin Parry.

✒ *Acknowledgements*

Previously unpublished works in this collection are: 'Her Indoors' by Catherine Aird; 'The Hampstead Vegetable Heist' by Mat Coward; 'Something Happened at the Time' by Madelaine Duke; 'Chased Delights; Or, The Missing Minutes' by Keith Heller; 'Six in the Morning' by Maxim Jakubowski; 'Fancy' by Bill James; 'Mr Idd' by H R F Keating; 'The Butcher of St Pierre' by Susan Kelly; 'The Hand That Feeds Me' by Michael Z Lewin; 'The Crumple Zone' by John Malcolm; 'The Writing on the Wall' by Val McDermid; 'Night Flight' by James Melville; 'The Train' by Stephen Murray; 'The Great Tetsuji' by Sara Paretsky; 'Someone Got to Eddie' by Ian Rankin; 'Social Work' by William G Tapply; 'Second Best Man' by David Williams.

Acknowledgements are due for those works which have been previously published, as follows:
'Trumpets for Max Jericho' by Robert Brack was published in *Nautilus Literarischer Taschenkalender 1991* (Edition Nautilus, Hamburg 1990); 'Good Investments' by Celia Dale first was published in the *Mystery Guild Anthology* (1980); 'Cold and Deep' by Frances Fyfield was published in the *Guardian* (1992); 'The Birdman of Bow Street' by Joan Lock was published in the *Police Review* (1984); 'Give Us a Clue' by Joan Lock appeared in the *New Law Journal* (1993); 'A Needle for the Devil' by Ruth Rendell was published in *Ellery Queen's Mystery Magazine* (1980); 'Too Many Crooks' by Donald E Westlake was published in *Playboy* (1989). 'The Christmas Present' by Bob Lock and Clewsey cartoons first appeared in *Red Herrings*, the newsletter of the CWA.